Souls under the Altar:
Relevance Theory and the
Discourse Structure of Revelation

United Bible Societies
Monograph Series

1. Sociolinguistics and Communication

2. The Cultural Factor in Bible Translation

3. Issues in Bible Translation

4. Bridging the Gap: African Traditional Religion and Bible Translation

5. Meaningful Translation: Its Implication for the Reader

6. The Apocrypha in Ecumenical Perspective

7. Discourse Perspectives on Hebrew Poetry in the Scriptures

8. Anthropological Approaches to the Interpretation of the Bible

9. Souls Under the Altar: Relevance Theory and the Discourse Structure of Revelation

10. Structure and Orality in 1 Peter: A Guide for Translators

UBS Monograph Series, No. 9

Souls under the Altar:
Relevance Theory and the
Discourse Structure of Revelation

Stephen Pattemore

UNITED BIBLE SOCIETIES
New York

Books in the series of **UBS Monographs** may be ordered from a national Bible Society or from either of the following centers:

UBS Europe Distribution Centre
Danish Bible Society
Frederiksborggade 50
DK 1360 Copenhagen K
Denmark

United Bible Societies
1865 Broadway
New York, NY 10023
U.S.A.

L. C. Cataloging-in-Publication Data

Pattemore, Stephen.
    Souls under the Altar: Relevance Theory and the Discourse Structure of Revelation / Stephen Pattemore.
        p. cm. – (UBS monograph series ; 9)
    Includes bibliographical references and index.
    ISBN 0-8267-0459-X
    1. Bible. 2. Bible–Translating. I. Title. II. Series.

BS663 .H67 2003
220.8'59–dc21

                                                                2002153253
                                                                CIP

ABS-12/06-100-300-YP 2

Contents

Preface ix

Abbreviations Used in This Volume xi

1 Introduction: Relevance Theory and Discourse Analysis 1
  1.1 Introduction: Why another structure for Revelation? 1
  1.2 Discourse analysis: Some definitions... 3
  1.3 Discourse analysis in the study of the New Testament:
     A review of reviews.. 6
  1.4 Relevance Theory: A brief introduction 16
     1.4.1 Background 16
     1.4.2 The principles of relevance... 19
     1.4.3 Developments and implications for discourse analysis 21
  1.5 Relevance Theory and literary texts.. 24
  1.6 Relevance and translation.. 29
  1.7 Relevance and Scripture.. 38
  1.8 Discourse analysis and Relevance Theory:
     The problem of context.. 45
     1.8.1 Brown and Yule – the identification of context (1983)......... 46
     1.8.2 De Beaugrande and Dressler – the limitation
       of context (1981).. 50
  1.9 Relevance Theory in discourse analysis 52

2 The Structure of the Apocalypse: A Selective Review 59
  2.1 Introduction: The relevance of discourse analysis 59
  2.2 Previous structural studies 61
  2.3 Hellholm's textlinguistic approach 64
  2.4 Müller's microstructural analysis... 73
  2.5 Other contributions to the discourse structure of the
     Apocalypse 81

3 Discourse Structure of the Apocalypse
   Part 1: Large-scale structures 89
   3.1 The integrity of the Apocalypse as a single discourse unit 89
   3.2 The two primary divisions of the text 93
   3.3 Untangling the endings of the major text levels 95
   3.4 Discourse Structure Diagram 1 100
   3.5 Broad structure of the central visionary sequence (1:12–22.9) ... 103
   3.6 Features of the first major vision report (1:12–3:22) 107
   3.7 Discourse Structure Diagram 2 109

4 Discourse Structure of the Apocalypse
   Part 2: The second major vision 113
   4.1 Broad structure of the second major vision report (4:1–22:9) 113
        4.1.1 Integrity and major subdivisions 113
        4.1.2 Revelation 11:19 as a hinge verse 118
        4.1.3 Broad outline of 12:1–22:9 121
        4.1.4 Overlaps and interlockings 121
        4.1.5 Discourse Structure Diagram 3 123
   4.2 Detailed structure of the first sequence (4:1–11:19) 124
        4.2.1 Heaven and worship 124
        4.2.2 Vision and audition in 4:1–8:1 125
        4.2.3 Revelation 8:1 – closure or open-endedness? 127
        4.2.4 Revelation 7 – interlude or hinge? 128
        4.2.5 Discourse Structure Diagram 4 130
        4.2.6 Detail of the text sequence 7:9–11:19 133
        4.2.7 Discourse Structure Diagram 5 138
   4.3 Role of the people of God in 4:1–11:19 141

5 Discourse Structure of the Apocalypse
   Part 3: The final vision sequence of the second major vision 143
   5.1 Integrity of 12:1–22:9 143
   5.2 Visions seen in heaven (12:1–14:20) 145
        5.2.1 Structural features 145
        5.2.2 Discourse Structure Diagram 6 151
        5.2.3 The people of God in 12:1–14:20 156
   5.3 Visions involving the plague angels (15:1–22:9):
        Structural integrity 157
   5.4 Seven plague angels pour out their bowls (15:1–16:21) 159
        5.4.1 Structural features 159
        5.4.2 Discourse Structure Diagram 7 161

CONTENTS

5.4.3 The people of God in 15:1–16:21 164
5.5 A tale of two cities (17:1–22:9) 165
5.6 First vision sequence with angel-guided journey (17:1–19:10) ... 166
 5.6.1 Structural features 166
 5.6.2 Discourse Structure Diagram 8 169
 5.6.3 The people of God in 17:1–19:10 173
5.7 Visions of the opened heaven (19:11–21:8) 173
 5.7.1 Structural features 173
 5.7.2 Discourse Structure Diagram 9 179
 5.7.3 The people of God in 19:11–21:8 182
5.8 Second vision sequence with angel-guided journey (21:9–22:9).. 183
 5.8.1 Structural features 183
 5.8.2 Discourse Structure Diagram 10 185
 5.8.3 The people of God in 21:9–22:9 187

6 Conclusions 189
6.1 The impact of Relevance Theory on the elucidation of
 discourse structure 189
6.2 The discourse structure of the Apocalypse 191
6.3 Implications for translation.. 193
6.4 The people of God in the structure of the Apocalypse 194

Appendixes
A Abbreviated Discourse Outline of Revelation 197
B Narrative Influence of Daniel 7 on Revelation.......................... 205

Selected Bibliography 209

Glossary 229

Indexes
General Index... 233
Scripture References... 239
Greek Words.. 241

Preface

This study has been shaped by both academic and practical factors. It represents a significant part of my Otago University Ph.D. dissertation and therefore seeks to engage with the academic literature on the book of Revelation. But the topic itself was suggested by considerations of the theological implications of translating Revelation into the Urak Lawoi' language of South Thailand. And the two have continued to interact since during the course of my study I have been involved not only in bringing the Urak Lawoi' New Testament to publication, but also in providing consultant help to the Tokelau Bible translation team in New Zealand, and more recently to many similar projects in Papua New Guinea. Being firmly in the context of Bible translation has given a pragmatic edge to my study. While I have focused principally on understanding the text within its original context, the goal always has been not only to add to academic literature on the book of Revelation, but also to provide a secure basis for contextualizing its message in the vastly different languages and thought worlds of contemporary societies. The results presented in this volume are still largely in the academic domain, but it is hoped that they will contribute to that secure foundation for the ongoing task of translating the Scriptures.

The family of United Bible Societies (UBS) has played a most important part at all stages of the process. Dr. David Clark, for many years the UBS Translation Consultant to the Urak Lawoi' New Testament project, taught me much through the period of our cooperation on the New Testament, involved me in the wider family of UBS as an Honorary Translation Advisor, introduced me to both discourse analysis and Relevance Theory, and provided the encouragement and practical impetus toward further study. He has also lent his considerable skills as a student of discourse structure to critique my analysis of Revelation. I am also grateful to the many translation officers of UBS, particularly those in the Asia Pacific Region, for their fellowship and encouragement and for the opportunity to sound out ideas. Particular thanks are due to Rev. Dr. Graham

Ogden, and to his successor as Regional Translation Coordinator, Rev. Dr. Daud Soesilo, for their guidance and encouragement along the way. This study has only been possible due to a generous scholarship from UBS and my sincere thanks go to UBS, including the colleagues already mentioned above. Special thanks to Dr. Basil Rebera, formerly UBS Translation Services Coordinator and now my supervising consultant; to his successor, Dr. Philip Noss, who has recommended this document for publication; and to Rev. Donald Slager, who has been a highly efficient and painstaking editor and whose care for detail has ensured the quality of the production.

The New Testament Greek quotations are from the UBS Greek New Testament, 4th corrected edition. The English Scriptural quotes are from New Revised Standard Version unless otherwise stated.

A limited bibliography is included for the benefit of those interested in further study. The glossary explains technical terms used in Relevance Theory. The translator may find it useful to read through the glossary in order to become aware of the specialized way in which these terms are used in this volume. A set of indexes is also included. First, there is a general index of authors, words and subjects discussed in the Handbook. This is followed by specific indexes on Scripture references and Greek words.

The editor of the UBS Monograph Series continues to seek comments from translators and others who use these books, so that future volumes may benefit and may better serve the needs of the readers.

Abbreviations Used in This Volume

Periodicals, Series, Reference Works, Bible Texts, Versions, and Other Works Cited (For details see the Bibliography)

AB	Anchor Bible
AUSDDS	Andrews University Seminary Doctoral Dissertation Series
AUSS	*Andrews University Seminary Studies*
BETL	Bibliotheca ephemeridum theologicarum lovaniensium
Bib	*Biblica*
BR	*Biblical Research*
BT	*The Bible Translator*
BZAW	Beihefte zur Zeitschrift für die alttestamentliche Wissenschaft
BZNW	Beihefte zur Zeitsfchrift für die neutestamentliche Wissenschaft
CBQ	*Catholic Biblical Quarterly*
ConBNT	Coniectanea biblica: New Testament Series
ELS	English Language Series
ETL	*Ephemerides theologicae lovanienses*
EvQ	*Evangelical Quarterly*
ExpTim	*Expository Times*
GNS	Good News Studies
GNTE	Guides to New Testament Exegesis
HDR	Harvard Dissertations in Religion
HNT	Handbuch zum Neuen Testament
HTR	*Harvard Theological Review*
ICC	International Critical Commentary
Int	*Interpretation*
JBL	*Journal of Biblical Literature*
JETS	*Journal of the Evangelical Theological Society*
JLing	*Journal of Linguistics*
JLSMa	Janua Linguarum Series Maior

JLSMi	Janua Linguarum Series Minor
JNSL	*Journal of Northwest Semitic Languages*
JOTT	*Journal of Translation and Textlinguistics*
JPrag	*Journal of Pragmatics*
JSNT	*Journal for the Study of the New Testament*
JSNTSup	Journal for the Study of the New Testament: Supplement Series
JSOTSup	Journal for the Study of the Old Testament: Supplement Series
Lang	*Language*
NCB	New Century Bible
Neot	*Neotestamentica*
NIGTC	New International Greek Testament Commentary
NOT	*Notes on Translation*
NovT	*Novum Testamentum*
NovTSup	Novum Testamentum Supplements
NRTh	*La nouvelle revue théologique*
NTM	New Testament Message
NTS	*New Testament Studies*
NTTS	New Testament Tools and Studies
OG	Old Greek version of Daniel
OPTAT	*Occasional Papers in Translation and Textlinguistics*
OTL	Old Testament Library
PBNS	Pragmatics and Beyond, New Series
RB	*Revue biblique*
RivBSup	Supplementi alla Rivista biblica
SBLSP	*Society of Biblical Literature Seminar Papers*
ST	*Studia theologica*
STDJ	*Studies on the Texts of the Desert of Judah*
Th	Theodotion version of Daniel
UBS[4]	*The Greek New Testament*, United Bible Societies, 4th edition
UCLWPL	*University College London Working Papers in Linguistics*
WBC	Word Biblical Commentary

Books of the Bible and Apocrypha

Exo	Exodus	Hos	Hosea
Deut	Deuteronomy	Hab	Habakkuk
1 Kgs	1 Kings	Zech	Zechariah
1 Chr	1 Chronicles	Matt	Matthew
Psa	Psalms	Rom	Romans
Isa	Isaiah	1 Cor	1 Corinthians
Jer	Jeremiah	Heb	Hebrews
Ezek	Ezekiel	Rev	Revelation
Dan	Daniel	2 Macc	2 Maccabees

General abbreviations

A.D.	*Anno Domini* (in the year of our Lord)	N.J.	New Jersey
		NT	New Testament
cf.	compare	N.Y.	New York
Del.	Delaware	p(p).	page(s)
diss.	dissertation	OT	Old Testament
ed(s).	editor(s)	Pa.	Pennsylvania
edn.	edition	repr.	reprint
e.g.	for example	rev.	revised
et al.	and others	RT	Relevance Theory
etc.	and the rest	SIL	Summer Institute of Linguistics
f(f).	and the following one(s)		
		SSA	Semantic Structure Analysis
Ill.	Illinois		
Ind.	Indiana	trans.	translated
Mass.	Massachussetts	UBS	United Bible Societies
Mich.	Michigan		
Minn.	Minnesota	vol(s).	volume(s)
Mont.	Montana		

Chapter 1

Introduction: Relevance Theory and Discourse Analysis

1.1 Introduction: Why another structure for Revelation?

The structure of John's Apocalypse, perhaps because it protrudes tantalizingly to the surface of the text, has been analyzed so frequently and with such varying results that another attempt requires a degree of justification. This present study arose for two reasons. First was my need, during my doctoral research into the role of the people of God in the Apocalypse, for a robust analysis of the structure of the book which would not only lead me to the passages where the people of God were focused, but also fit these passages into the framework of the book as a whole.[1] The second reason, the one that more specifically justifies this study, was a dissatisfaction with the methodology behind previous attempts at analyzing the structure.

The structure of the Apocalypse is tantalizing because although there are many obvious indications that there is a structure (indications such as the numbered series of sevens, or the repeated introductory phrases), when examined more closely, the regularities tend to become more ragged around the edges, and a host of difficulties emerge concerning the large-scale structure surface. Commentators generally offer some kind of analysis, but mostly these are guided either by the overt structuring

---

[1] Stephen W. Pattemore, "The People of God in the Apocalypse: A Relevance-Theoretic Study" (Ph.D. thesis, University of Otago, 2000). This present study contains the discourse analysis that formed part of the thesis. The longer, exegetical part is to be published in the Society for New Testament Studies Monograph Series.

formulas only, or by some rather theological presuppositions about the ordering of events in the last days. Only a few have relied on the techniques of linguistic discourse analysis, attempting to discover the semantic and syntactic patterning that lies both on and below the surface of the text.[2] Yet even these are to some degree or other unsatisfying because they underplay the pragmatic dimensions of the text as it communicates within its late first century A.D. context.

Relevance Theory is an approach to understanding the way in which human beings communicate which has certain significant strengths. It accounts for the large amount of information which is not represented on the surface of the text, that is, information which is inferred from hearing or reading the text in a particular context. And thus it pays close attention to context—what sort of context influences our understanding of a communication, how much context is necessary, and how we discriminate between competing contexts within which to understand a text. Relevance Theory has implications for the structure as well as the information content of a text, and when this dimension is taken into account, it significantly strengthens our confidence in the resulting structural analysis. Relevance Theory does not replace or render unnecessary the other techniques by which discourse analysts have examined the structure of a text. Rather, it provides a sharper criterion for their use.

Thus the analysis to be presented here has both a general and a specific purpose. My aim is to uncover the discourse structure of the book of Revelation with particular regard to the role of the various images of the people of God throughout the book, and to do so using the insights into the organization of texts provided by Relevance Theory.

In the remainder of this first chapter, we will examine in greater detail the methodology used in my discourse analysis of the Apocalypse. Determining the discourse structure of a text is not an end in itself, but a means to identifying, interpreting, and translating the meaning communicated by the text. First, therefore, in sections 1.2 and 1.3 we will discuss the place of discourse analysis in the wider field of biblical studies by summarizing a number of review articles that helpfully cover the territory. Section 1.4 will then briefly introduce Relevance Theory in general, as a tool for understanding the process of human communication, and section 1.5 will discuss how this applies to literary texts. The following two sections, 1.6 and 1.7, will consider some objections to the

---

[2] For a review of some of these, see chapter 2 below, pp. 59-88.

2

application of Relevance Theory to biblical text in particular and show that these are unjustified. In section 1.8 we will take a closer look at the problems that the idea of "context" raises for traditional discourse analysts before proposing in section 1.9 how Relevance Theory helps overcome these.

In chapter 2 we will review a number of earlier attempts to analyze the structure of the book of Revelation by methods that rely more or less on linguistic analysis of the text. These all have important contributions to make, though none is in the end without its difficulties.

Chapters 3–5 then present the arguments that undergird a discourse analysis of the Apocalypse which is sensitive to considerations of relevance. The approach is "top down"—examining larger units of text as a whole before concentrating on smaller units. The resulting structure is displayed section by section and the role that the people of God play in each section is highlighted.

Chapter 6 attempts to draw some conclusions from the exercise. Novelty is not the most important value in the results of this analysis. Relevance Theory has certainly uncovered aspects of the structure of Revelation which have not previously been noted. However, more often we find ourselves confirming one or another earlier suggestion. But these are now placed on a firmer footing by attention given to the pragmatics of real communication.

Appendix A provides a convenient outline summary of the structure of the book. Appendix B is a display showing the relationship of Dan 7 to the structure of Revelation. There is also a glossary of key terms used in Relevance Theory.

1.2 Discourse analysis: Some definitions

The development of the science of Linguistics over the past 150 years has made significant contributions to the field of biblical studies, from the work of the early philologists on biblical languages, through to the more recent work of scholars like Moisés Silva, D. A. Carson, Stanley Porter, Buist Fanning and others.[3] Traditionally linguists considered the

---

[3] For biblical Hebrew see the useful summary of the history of study of the language in Bruce K. Waltke and M. O'Connor, *An Introduction to Biblical Hebrew Syntax* (Winona Lake, Ind.: Eisenbrauns, 1990), pp.

3

sentence to be the largest unit of language susceptible to useful analysis. But this view has been overturned during the past twenty-five years or so, as much progress has been made in analyzing how sentences, and groups of sentences, relate to one another, pass their information to one another, control and modify one another, and cohere in whole units that we call "texts" or "discourses."[4] This field of study is variously known as "discourse analysis" or "textlinguistics." The word "discourse" is used, in both common and academic language, in a wide variety of senses—from conversation or direct speech, through text, to rhetorical communication in a formal sense. Thus on the one hand discourse, as speech, is sometimes distinguished from narrative, while on the other it is often categorized as "scientific discourse," "feminist discourse" or the like, referring to particular kinds of high-level, academic communicative and persuasive

---

31-43; see also Nahum M. Waldman, *The Recent Study of Hebrew: A Survey of the Literature with Selected Bibliography* (Bibliographica Judaica 10; Cincinnati: Hebrew Union College Press, 1989). For early work on biblical Greek, see Georg B. Winer, *A Grammar of New Testament Diction Intended as an Introduction to the Critical Study of the Greek New Testament* (4th edn.; Edinburgh: T. & T. Clark, 1863); and A. T. Robertson, *A Grammar of the Greek New Testament in the Light of Historical Research* (3rd edn.; London: Hodder & Stoughton, 1919), especially pp. 3-30 and the bibliography on pp. 63-86. There is a convenient collection of classic papers by Adolf Deissman, James Moulton, Charles Torrey, Matthew Black and others in Stanley E. Porter, ed., *The Language of the New Testament: Classic Essays* (JSNTSup 60; Sheffield: JSOT Press, 1991) with Porter's valuable introduction to that volume, "The Greek of the New Testament as a Disputed Area of Research," pp. 11-38. For more recent studies on the linguistics of biblical Greek, see for example, Moisés Silva, *Biblical Words and Their Meaning: An Introduction to Lexical Semantics* (Grand Rapids: Zondervan, 1983); Peter Cotterell and Max Turner, *Linguistics and Biblical Interpretation* (Downers Grove, Ill.: InterVarsity Press, 1989); and the various contributions to Stanley E. Porter and D. A. Carson, eds., *Biblical Greek Language and Linguistics: Open Questions in Current Research* (JSNTSup 80; Sheffield: JSOT Press, 1993).

[4] The impetus toward the analysis of discourse is usually attributed to Zellig S. Harris, "Discourse Analysis," *Lang* 28 (1952): 1-30. The literature on discourse analysis is immense and growing rapidly. A small sample can be found in note 13 below.

behavior. I regard it as more or less equivalent to "text," which Gillian Brown and George Yule define as "the verbal record of a communicative act."[5] The corresponding range in the meaning of "discourse analysis" is less easily dismissed. This may be seen as a purely linguistic analysis of texts, as more specifically a study of the language of conversation, or as an analysis of what is being done, sociologically and politically speaking, with texts.[6] These disciplines are not unrelated and indeed all can be included under Brown and Yule's definition as "the analysis of language in use."[7] For my purposes I will take "discourse analysis" to mean the study of the syntactic and semantic structure of a text at levels higher than the sentence, and the way this is shaped by the pragmatics of real communication.[8]

It is outside the scope and intent of this study to describe the discipline of discourse analysis in any detail. However, we do need to clarify at this point the contribution that discourse analysis has made to biblical studies in general.

---

[5] Gillian Brown and George Yule, *Discourse Analysis* (Cambridge: Cambridge University Press, 1983), p. 6. Michael Stubbs, *Discourse Analysis: The Sociolinguistic Analysis of Natural Language* (Oxford: Basil Blackwell, 1983), p. 9, notes a number of conflicting distinctions that have been made between "discourse" and "text" and decides to treat them as essentially the same thing.

[6] This last is the sense in, for example, Elisabeth Schüssler Fiorenza, *Revelation: Vision of a Just World* (Proclamation Commentaries; Minneapolis: Fortress Press, 1991), p. 22: "Discourse analysis of Revelation understands rhetoric not as mere ornamentation and empty style but as the art of persuasion."

[7] Brown and Yule, *Discourse Analysis*, p. 1. It is interesting to note that the contributions to Teun A. van Dijk, ed., *Handbook of Discourse Analysis* (4 vols.; London: Academic Press, 1985) cover all three aspects of discourse analysis. Volumes 1 and 2 concentrate on syntactical and semantic studies, volume 3 on conversation, and volume 4 on the sociological dimensions of discourse.

[8] The distinction between "discourse analysis" and "textlinguistics" is sometimes seen in this way, such that textlinguistics focuses on the overt linguistic record, while discourse analysis has a potentially wider and more sociological scope, as we shall see. A similar point is made by Stubbs, *Discourse Analysis*, p. 10.

1.3 Discourse analysis in the study of the New Testament: A review of reviews

Although commentaries and exegetical studies of biblical texts have always included some statement on "structure," these have usually been based either on only the most obvious of markers on the text's surface or on some intuitive grasp of the theme of various subtexts, or else they have presented a formal analysis of the text with a view to locating its *sitz im leben*.[9] Our interest here, however, is in works that make more explicit use of discourse linguistics.

The impact of discourse analysis on biblical studies and the study of biblical languages (in particular NT studies and the NT Greek language) has been conveniently surveyed and evaluated in a number of articles that have appeared over the past several years.[10] I will therefore not

---

[9] There are some notable exceptions, particularly in the Word Biblical Commentary Series, where the regular section headed "Form/Structure/Setting," has allowed authors to go well beyond form critical or traditional structural approaches.

[10] See Stanley E. Porter and D. A. Carson, eds., *Discourse Analysis and Other Topics in Biblical Greek* (JSNTSup 113; Sheffield: Sheffield Academic Press, 1995), and especially Porter's introduction to that volume, "Discourse Analysis and New Testament Studies: An Introductory Survey," pp. 14-35. See also Simon Crisp, "Discourse Analysis and the Study of Biblical Greek: Part I," *TIC Talk* 37 (1997): 1-3; "Discourse Analysis and the Study of Biblical Greek: Part II," *TIC Talk* 38 (1997): 1-4. Crisp focuses on the impact of discourse analysis on the study of the Greek language and provides useful bibliographies that illustrate how much of this work takes place within the Bible translation community. Two helpful essays focusing on hermeneutical issues are Jeffrey T. Reed, "Modern Linguistics and the New Testament: A Basic Guide to Theory, Terminology, and Literature," in *Approaches to New Testament Study* (ed. Stanley E. Porter and David Tombs; JSNTSup 120; Sheffield: Sheffield Academic Press, 1995), pp. 222-65, and Jeffrey T. Reed, "Discourse Analysis as New Testament Hermeneutic: A Retrospective and Prospective Appraisal," *JETS* 39 (1996): 223-40. An even more recent collection, Stanley E. Porter and Jeffrey T. Reed, eds., *Discourse Analysis and the New Testament: Approaches and Results* (JSNTSup 170; Studies in New Testament Greek 4; Sheffield: Sheffield Academic Press, 1999), contains both

6

attempt a detailed review, but will extract some key points from these articles and supplement the references given.

Porter characterizes discourse analysis as a synthetic approach, integrating semantics, syntax and pragmatics.[11] It requires a two-way movement (described as "top-down" and "bottom-up," or macrostructural and microstructural), analyzing the whole discourse in terms of progressively smaller linguistic elements, and starting from the smallest elements, examining how they are built up to make the whole. Analysis of the discourse structure involves examination of

informational structure (e.g. lexical choice), cohesion (e.g. various connective devices), prominence (e.g. the ways in which significant material is highlighted), and linguistic cotext (e.g. the immediate textual environment) and context (the larger environment, including presuppositions and reference).[12]

Porter distinguishes four main schools of discourse analysis: the North American (chiefly represented by the Summer Institute of Linguistics), the English and Australian, the Continental European, and the South African schools.[13] The geographical labels given to these schools are

---

methodological essays and examples of the way in which discourse analysis has been approached by a range of scholars. For a more dated, but nevertheless useful, review of textlinguistic work on biblical texts in Sweden, see Birger Olsson, "A Decade of Text-Linguistic Analyses of Biblical Texts at Uppsala," *ST* 39 (1985): 107-126.

[11] Porter, "Discourse Analysis and New Testament Studies," p. 18.

[12] Porter, "Discourse Analysis and New Testament Studies," p. 19. Later in the same volume he speaks somewhat differently of the "three major components of discourse analysis" as discourse boundaries, prominence and coherence. See Stanley E. Porter, "How Can Biblical Discourse be Analyzed?: A Response to Several Attempts," in *Discourse Analysis and Other Topics in Biblical Greek* (ed. Stanley E. Porter and D. A. Carson; JSNTSup 113; Sheffield: Sheffield Academic Press, 1995), p. 114.

[13] Representative works from the various schools include the following: For **North American** there are Joseph E. Grimes, *The Thread of Discourse* (JLSMi 207; The Hague: Mouton, 1975); Kenneth L. Pike, *Language in Relation to a Unified Theory of the Structure of Human Behavior* (2nd edn.; JLSMa 24; The Hague: Mouton, 1967); Kenneth L. Pike and Evelyn G. Pike, *Grammatical Analysis* (rev. edn.; Dallas: SIL and University of

Texas at Arlington, 1982), pp. 226-303; Robert E. Longacre, "A Spectrum and Profile Approach to Discourse Analysis," *Text* 1 (1981): 337-59; Robert E. Longacre, *The Grammar of Discourse* (New York: Plenum Press, 1983); David A. Dawson, *Text-Linguistics and Biblical Hebrew* (JSOTSup 177; Sheffield: Sheffield Academic Press, 1994); Stephen H. Levinsohn, *Discourse Features of New Testament Greek* (Dallas: SIL, 1992); Kathleen Callow, *Discourse Considerations in Translating the Word of God* (Grand Rapids: Zondervan, 1974); and David A. Black, ed., *Linguistics and New Testament Interpretation: Essays on Discourse Analysis* (Nashville: Broadman, 1992). For **English-Australian**: there are Brown and Yule, *Discourse Analysis*; Stubbs, *Discourse Analysis*; M. A. K. Halliday and Ruqaiya Hasan, *Cohesion in English* (ELS 9; London: Longman, 1976); M. A. K. Halliday and Ruqaiya Hasan, *Language, context, and text: Aspects of language in a social-semiotic perspective* (Victoria, Australia: Deakin University, 1985); James L. Kinneavy, *A Theory of Discourse: The Aims of Discourse* (New York: W. W. Norton, 1971); Malcolm Coulthard, *An Introduction to Discourse Analysis* (London: Longman, 1977); and Malcolm Coulthard and Martin Montgomery, eds., *Studies in Discourse Analysis* (London: Routledge & Kegan Paul, 1981). For **Continental European** there are Robert-Alain de Beaugrande and Wolfgang U. Dressler, *Introduction to Text Linguistics* (London: Longman, 1981); Wolfgang U. Dressler, "Marked and Unmarked Text Strategies within Semiotically Based NATURAL Textlinguistics," in *Language in Context: Essays for Robert E. Longacre* (ed. Shin Ja J. Hwang and William R. Merrifield; Dallas: SIL and University of Texas at Arlington, 1992), pp. 5-18; Talmy Givón, ed., *Discourse and Syntax* (Syntax and Semantics 12; New York: Academic Press, 1979); David Hellholm, "The Problem of Apocalyptic Genre and the Apocalypse of John," *Semeia* 36 (1986): 13-64; and Teun A. van Dijk, *Text and Context: Explorations in the Semantics and Pragmatics of Discourse* (London: Longman, 1977). For **South African** there are Johannes P. Louw, "Discourse Analysis and the Greek New Testament," *BT* 24 (1973): 101-118; Johannes P. Louw "A Semiotic Approach to Discourse Analysis with Reference to Translation Theory," *BT* 36 (1985): 101-107; Johannes P. Louw "The Function of Discourse in a Sociosemiotic Theory of Translation," *BT* 39 (1988): 329-35; Eugene A. Nida, "Basic Elements of Discourse Structure," in *Language in Context: Essays for Robert E. Longacre* (ed. Shin Ja J. Hwang and William R. Merrifield; Dallas: SIL and University of Texas at Arlington, somewhat misleading, as exponents of each come from many different countries. It is a generalization, but perhaps a fair one, to say that Porter's "North American" and "South African" schools have been most influential in the field of Bible translation, while the other two are more closely linked with mainstream biblical studies.[14]

1992), pp. 47-50; and A. H. Snyman, "A Semantic Discourse Analysis of the Letter to Philemon," in *Text and Interpretation: New Approaches in the Criticism of the New Testament* (ed. P. J. Hartin and J. H. Petzer; NTTS 15; Leiden: E. J. Brill, 1991), pp. 83-99.

[14] Works that span the gap include Hendrikus Boers, *The Justification of the Gentiles: Paul's Letters to the Galatians and Romans* (Peabody, Mass.: Hendrickson, 1994); David J. Clark and Jan de Waard, "Discourse Structure in Matthew's Gospel," *Scriptura* S1 (1982): 1-97; Ernst R. Wendland, *The Discourse Analysis of Hebrew Poetic Literature: Determining the Larger Textual Units of Hosea and Joel* (Mellen Biblical Press Series 40; Lewiston, N.Y.: Mellen Biblical Press, 1995); and George H. Guthrie, *The Structure of Hebrews: A Text-Linguistic Analysis* (NovTSup 73; Leiden: E. J. Brill, 1994). The validity of the generalization can be demonstrated by an examination of journals and monographs. Articles relying largely on North American and South African schools are found in abundance in *The Bible Translator*, *Notes on Translation* and *Journal of Translation and Textlinguistics*, as an examination of their indexes will show. The large number of discourse analytic studies on biblical texts coming out of the translation community is significant. The demands of the task of translating the Scriptures into languages of vastly differing organization and structure have made discourse analysis a most necessary tool for translation. On the other hand, articles and monographs appearing in the wider biblical studies scene, showing more influence from the Contintental European and English-Australian schools, include David Hellholm, "Amplificatio in the Macro-Structure of Romans," in *Rhetoric and the New Testament: Essays from the 1992 Heidelberg Conference* (ed. Stanley E. Porter and Thomas H. Olbricht; JSNTSup 90; Sheffield: JSOT Press, 1993), pp. 123-51; Olsson, "A Decade of Text-Linguistic Analyses"; Jeffrey T. Reed, "To Timothy or Not? A Discourse Analysis of 1 Timothy," in *Biblical Greek Language and Linguistics: Open Questions in Current Research* (ed. Stanley E. Porter and D. A. Carson; JSNTSup 80; Sheffield: JSOT Press, 1993), pp. 90-118; Jeffrey T. Reed, "Identifying Theme in the New Testament: Insights from Discourse

9

Porter's article introduces three papers, each presenting a very different approach to discourse analysis, but all focusing on the book of Philippians.[15] Responses to these by Silva and Porter are equivocal, to say the least. Silva is particularly unconvinced:

> It is not totally unfair, I hope, to say that much of what goes under the rubric of discourse analysis involves one or more of the following: (a) restating the obvious using unnecessarily forbidding terminology; (b) giving expression to exceedingly general and vague ideas, the significance of which escapes at least this reader; (c) attempting to support particular interpretations with arguments that have no probative value whatever.[16]

Analysis," in *Discourse Analysis and Other Topics in Biblical Greek* (ed. Stanley E. Porter and D. A. Carson; JSNTSup 113; Sheffield: Sheffield Academic Press, 1995), pp. 75-101; Wolfgang Schenk, "Textlinguistische Aspekte der Strukturanalyse, dargestellt am Beispiel von 1 Kor XV.1-11," *NTS* 23 (1977): 469-77; Wolfgang Schenk "Hebräerbrief 4.14-16. Textlinguistik als Kommentierungsprinzip," *NTS* 26 (1980): 242-52; Folker Siegert, "Die Makrosyntax des Hebräerbriefs," in *Texts and Contexts: Biblical Texts in Their Textual and Situational Contexts: Essays in Honor of Lars Hartman* (ed. Tord Fornberg and David Hellholm; Oslo: Scandinavian University Press, 1995), pp. 305-316; and Bruce C. Johanson, *To All the Brethren. A Text-Linguistic and Rhetorical Approach to 1 Thessalonians* (ConBNT 16; Stockholm: Almqvist & Wiksell, 1987).

[15] George H. Guthrie, "Cohesion Shifts and Stitches in Philippians," in *Discourse Analysis and Other Topics in Biblical Greek* (ed. Stanley E. Porter and D. A. Carson; JSNTSup 113; Sheffield: Sheffield Academic Press, 1995), pp. 36-59; Stephen H. Levinsohn, "A Discourse Study of Constituent Order and the Article in Philippians," in *Discourse Analysis and Other Topics in Biblical Greek* (ed. Stanley E. Porter and D. A. Carson; JSNTSup 113; Sheffield: Sheffield Academic Press, 1995) pp. 60-74; Jeffrey T. Reed, "Identifying Theme in the New Testament," pp. 75-101.

[16] Moisés Silva, "Discourse Analysis and Philippians," in *Discourse Analysis and Other Topics in Biblical Greek* (ed. Stanley E. Porter and D. A. Carson; JSNTSup 113; Sheffield: Sheffield Academic Press, 1995), p.103.

Porter is more generous, though guarded in his evaluation of the particular efforts in question. He concludes:

> discourse analysis is probably much further along in establishing itself as a productive exegetical procedure than many have realized, although it still leaves a number of questions unasked and unanswered. It is not a magic wand that can be waved over significant exegetical issues to make all of their problems disappear or come clear. But any exegetical procedure that results in closer attention to the text itself, in particular to its grammatical phenomena, is to be welcomed.[17]

Jeffrey Reed reviews briefly the history of development of the discourse approach and outlines its major tenets, which could be summarized using his own words as follows:

> Discourse analysts take seriously the roles of the author, the audience, and the text in communicative events . . . [are] also guided by the tenet to examine language at a linguistic level larger than the sentence . . . discourse should be analyzed for its social functions and thus in its social context...discourse analysts emphasize the need to interpret natural occurrences of language—language as use.[18]

This is of particular interest because it defines discourse analysis not merely in terms of the level of language analyzed, but also with regard to the social function of the language and to the kind of data analyzed. Discourse analysis with this definition is closely related to the pragmatics of Speech-Act Theory, and concerned with how a text operates to produce effects in a real language community.[19] In the third aspect of his definition, and in the directions he suggests for further study, Reed appears to

---

[17] Porter, "How Can Biblical Discourse be Analyzed?" p. 116.

[18] Reed, "Discourse Analysis as New Testament Hermeneutic," pp. 229-34.

[19] For Speech-Act Theory, see J. L. Austin, *How to Do Things With Words* (Oxford: Clarendon, 1962); John R. Searle, *Speech Acts: An Essay in the Philosophy of Language* (Cambridge: Cambridge University Press, 1969). Its application to biblical studies was pioneered by Anthony C. Thiselton in his book *New Horizons in Hermeneutics* (Grand Rapids: Zondervan, 1992). See his note on p. 17.

11

subsume the "rhetorical" sense of discourse analysis within the linguistic approach. It is probably helpful to keep the two approaches somewhat distinct, though recognizing the relationship between them. Reed's fourth point emphasizes the fact that discourse analysis is analysis of actual texts, not an abstraction of linguistic theory. Although attempts are sometimes made to abstract markers of discourse function, these attempts are usually collections of specific occurrences rather than a true grammar of discourse.[20]

If Reed's essay is methodological and focuses on hermeneutics, Simon Crisp's is bibliographical and focuses on the contribution of discourse analysis to the study of the biblical Greek language.[21] Writing from within the Bible translation community, he reviews Porter's analysis and provides some counterbalance, in particular defending Stephen Levinsohn's "bottom-up" approach as necessary and significantly discourse-based (against Porter's accusation that he had retreated to the level of sentence grammar).[22] An examination of Crisp's extensive bibliography reveals that a large amount of the practical work on the application of discourse analysis to biblical texts has been done within the Bible translation community, in particular the Summer Institute of Linguistics (SIL), United Bible Societies (UBS) and other organizations within the Forum of Bible Agencies.[23] This underlines the point made by Reed that discourse analysis is most useful in the pragmatics of real, motivated communication and in the context of the believing community.

The two principal objections usually advanced by biblical scholars who are unconvinced of the usefulness of discourse analysis are (a) the variation and instability of both methodology and terminology and (b) the doubt that any useful results have been forthcoming which would not

---

[20] See, for example, Levinsohn, *Discourse Features of New Testament Greek*.

[21] Crisp, "Discourse Analysis: Parts I and II"; see note 10 above.

[22] Crisp, "Discourse Analysis: Part II"; cf. Porter, "Discourse Analysis and New Testament Studies," p. 26.

[23] See note 14 above. Note also the longer treatments in the Semantic Structure Analysis Series from the SIL; e.g., Ellis W. Deibler, *A Semantic and Structural Analysis of Romans* (Dallas: SIL, 1998); Robert H. Sterner, *A Semantic and Structural Analysis of 1 Thessalonians* (Dallas: SIL, 1998); Elinor M. Rogers, *A Semantic Structure Analysis of Galatians* (Dallas: SIL, 1989).

have been arrived at by other methodologies. The first of these is answered emphatically by Porter who takes biblical scholarship to task for methodological conservatism. Responding to Peter Cotterell and Max Turner's caveat that "at the present there are no firm conclusions, no generally accepted formulae, no fixed methodology, not even an agreed terminology," he says:

> If such criticism were taken as definitive, no discipline would ever develop . . . It is in the nature of humanistic and social-scientific investigation to be in the constant process of model-building and modification, while at the same time engaging in analysis of the data, allowing the data to influence the theory. It seems more like an example of special pleading to allow the state of flux of a discipline to constitute an insuperable barrier to using a method.[24]

In answer to the second criticism, Reed notes that "when linguistic analysis supports common belief, many respond that 'everyone knows that.' When it provides an unexpected finding, the response is that 'you can prove anything with linguistics.' "[25] For a substantive answer it would be necessary to examine the actual studies of biblical texts which have used discourse analysis and to ask whether they have made a contribution to the understanding of the text which is both significant and distinctive. Many discourse studies of biblical texts have been listed by Crisp and this is not the place for a detailed review.[26] However, to round off our discussion of the place of discourse analysis in biblical interpretation, we will briefly note the contributions of two works that Crisp has not mentioned.[27]

---

[24] Porter, "Discourse Analysis and New Testament Studies," p. 23; cf. Cotterell and Turner, *Linguistics and Biblical Interpretation*, p. 233. The same must be said also in defense of Relevance Theory.

[25] Reed, "Modern Linguistics and the New Testament," p. 264.

[26] See especially the works referred to in Part II of his survey (note 10), and also note 14 above.

[27] A number of significant publications on the book of Revelation which either explicitly use a discourse analytic methodology, or a method that approximates it either by accident or intent, will be reviewed in detail in chapter 2 below.

David Clark and Jan de Waard's discourse analysis of Matthew's Gospel starts with the observation, familiar at least since Bacon, that the book is structured around five blocks of teaching material.[28] Drawing on the work of Joseph Grimes, Robert Longacre, and M. A. K. Halliday and Ruqaiya Hasan, they proceed to discover many details of structure within and surrounding these blocks, using the perspective of a relatively naïve reader as a frame of reference.[29] These structuring patterns they describe as "too symmetrical and too aesthetically pleasing to be either accidental or imaginary."[30] While not all of their decisions on the boundaries of blocks or "scenes" are convincing, discourse analysis provides a way of understanding the coherence of stretches of text which have sometimes been treated simply as random collections.[31] The analysis sheds significant light on the tangled puzzle of Matt 24.[32] The overall structure discovered for the narrative passages demonstrates not only a progressive plot movement, but also an intertwining of motifs of rejection and recognition of the Messiah.[33] At the same time the discourse blocks are found to cohere around the Kingdom of Heaven, past, present and future.[34] Finally, and significantly for my purposes, discourse analysis facilitates the tracing of the role of participants both in large stretches of text and in smaller units.[35]

---

[28] See Warren Carter, *Matthew: Storyteller, Interpreter, Evangelist* (Peabody, Mass.: Hendrickson, 1996), pp. 149-75.

[29] For a defense of this perspective, see Clark and de Waard, "Discourse Structure in Matthew," p. 1.

[30] Clark and de Waard, "Discourse Structure in Matthew," p. 5.

[31] E.g., 8:1–9:38, treated in Clark and de Waard, "Discourse Structure in Matthew," pp. 17-20.

[32] Clark and de Waard, "Discourse Structure in Matthew," pp. 60-64.

[33] Clark and de Waard, "Discourse Structure in Matthew," pp. 73-75.

[34] Clark and de Waard, "Discourse Structure in Matthew," pp. 75-76.

[35] Clark and de Waard, "Discourse Structure in Matthew," pp. 79-81, 84. The work of Clark and de Waard has been noticed in the bibliography of W. D. Davies and Dale C. Allison, Jr., *A Critical and Exegetical Commentary on the Gospel according to Saint Matthew* (3 vols.; Edinburgh: T. & T. Clark, 1988), vol. I, pp. 58-72 . R. T. France, *Matthew, Evangelist and Teacher* (Exeter: Paternoster, 1989), pp. 141-53, gives it closer attention but finds it too subjective.

Closer to the mainstream of biblical studies, Hendrikus Boers uses a combination of linguistic discourse analysis, largely dependant on the colon analysis of the "South African" school, and structural exegesis, to locate what he considers to be the central focus of the books of Galatians and Romans.[36] It is of particular significance that the analysis of the surface-level linguistic structure of the book is necessary but only preliminary to an examination of the semantic "deep structure" in which Paul's value system is discovered. Thus Boers attempts discourse analysis at both ends of the spectrum. Reviewers have concentrated on the semiotic structural exegesis rather than the linguistic discourse analysis.[37] That both surface and deep structures impact and reflect meaning is affirmed by much contemporary scholarship, and Leander Keck, among others, notes Boers's contribution in this regard.[38]

To summarize this brief review, it is clear that discourse analysis in its several forms, ranging from textlinguistic analysis through to socio-rhetorical analysis, is a useful tool in the study of the New Testament, and is increasingly accepted and valued. Silva's criticism is both overstated and largely unwarranted and reflects a degree of methodological conservatism. If we accept that biblical texts are the linguistic records of real communicative events, each arising from a rhetorical situation, each intended to accomplish a rhetorical purpose, then it follows that the

---

[36] Boers, *The Justification of the Gentiles*. See Appendix I, pp. 229-39, for his description of the "Principles and Procedures in Discourse Analysis." In the body of the book, Section I focuses on the discourse structure, while Section II uses structural exegesis techniques to examine Paul's system of values.

[37] Jeffrey T. Reed in *JSNT* 60 (1995): 124, notices the discourse analysis but criticizes the narrowness of Boer's theoretical base in linguistics. Charles H. Cosgrove in *JBL* 115 (1996): 368-70, focuses entirely on the structural exegesis, with an overall positive evaluation. By contrast, Douglas J. Moo in *JETS* 39 (1996): 666-67, while noticing the semiotic basis, is more concerned that Boers contributes to the "trend away from the question of a human being's relationship to God toward the question of the relationship of human beings to one another."

[38] Leander E. Keck, "What Makes Romans Tick?" in *Romans* (ed. David M. Hay and E. Elizabeth Johnson; vol. 3 in *Pauline Theology*; ed. Jouette M. Bassler, David M. Hay, and E. Elizabeth Johnson; Minneapolis: Fortress Press, 1995), pp. 20-21, note 60.

attempt to discover their meaning will be significantly advanced by both textlinguistic and socio-rhetorical analysis.

1.4 Relevance Theory: A brief introduction

1.4.1 Background

Relevance Theory (RT) is a *pragmatic* theory, one that provides a description of human communication which is based on the realities of actual communication situations.[39] It takes into account the tendency towards efficiency in communication, which leads us to rely heavily on a shared communication environment and means that the text of our communication does not in itself contain all of the meaning of the communication. Meaning, instead, must be inferred by understanding the text within the appropriate context. RT is also a *cognitive* theory, in that it locates the process of understanding communication within the realm of human cognition, and describes the context that affects understanding as an internal, cognitive structure. In this section we will outline the background to RT and define some of the key terms used. Since one of the most frequent and pertinent criticisms of the theory is the complex terminology it uses, it will be as well to clarify these from the start.

The impetus for RT stems from the inadequacy of the code model to explain human communication. In the code model a sender encodes a thought in a linguistic message that is transmitted by some medium to a receiver, who decodes the message to produce a replication of the original thought.[40] Dan Sperber and Deirdre Wilson agree that encoding and decoding take place in communication but hold that these processes are

---

[39] The primary text is Dan Sperber and Deirdre Wilson, *Relevance: Communication and Cognition* (Oxford: Basil Blackwell, 1986). There is a second edition, which was printed in 1995. It differs only in having a "Postscript." A useful introduction with which to supplement this brief paragraph is found in Ernst-August Gutt, *Relevance Theory: A Guide to Successful Communication in Translation* (Dallas: SIL and UBS, 1992).

[40] See Claude E. Shannon and Warren Weaver, *The Mathematical Theory of Communication* (Urbana: University of Illinois Press, 1949), especially pp 5, 95-113. A modified version of their diagram is presented by Sperber and Wilson, *Relevance*, pp. 4-5.

inadequate to explain how communication works, unless supplemented by, or subordinated to, a process of implication and inference:

> the linguistic meaning of an uttered sentence falls short of encoding what the speaker means: it merely helps the audience infer what she means. The output of decoding is correctly treated by the audience as a piece of evidence about the communicator's intentions. In other words, a coding-decoding process is subservient to a Gricean inferential process.[41]

RT is grounded on the inferential theory of Paul Grice, who proposed a "cooperative principle" in conversation: "Make your conversational contribution such as is required, at the stage at which it occurs, by the accepted purpose or direction of the talk exchange in which you are engaged."[42] This he filled out with nine maxims setting guidelines for quantity, quality, relevance and manner of a conversational contribution. The importance of Grice's work is not that the various maxims provide rules or codes for successful communication but that they describe how communication creates the conditions for its own success. "Grice put forward an idea of fundamental importance: that the very act of communicating creates expectations which it then exploits . . . ."[43]

Successful communication depends on a context of shared information. But what is the nature of this shared information? Sperber and Wilson reject as impractical the idea that we consciously know not only the scope of our own knowledge but also how much we share with the person to whom we are communicating. Instead they focus on the looser concept of **manifestness** and use it to forge a more useful and rigorous definition of context, which in RT is called a **cognitive environment**.[44] Something is *manifest* to me if I can form a mental representation of it and accept that representation as true or probably true. I may not actually be thinking about it but I am capable of doing so. Facts can be more or less manifest,

---

[41] Sperber and Wilson, *Relevance*, p. 27. Note the convention of assuming a female speaker/author and male listener/reader.

[42] H. Paul Grice, "Logic and Conversation," in *Speech Acts* (vol. 3 of *Syntax and Semantics*; ed. Peter Cole and Jerry L. Morgan; New York: Academic Press, 1975), p. 45.

[43] Sperber and Wilson, *Relevance*, p. 37.

[44] See Sperber and Wilson, *Relevance*, p. 39.

depending on my situation and my mental abilities. My *cognitive environment* is the sum total of all facts that are manifest to me.

Two or more people can share a cognitive environment. A **mutual cognitive environment** then is the set of facts that are *mutually manifest.*[45] This does not imply that they *make* the same assumptions but that they *can* do so. Both speaker and listener are capable of representing these facts and are aware that the other is capable of representing them. There is no guarantee they will make a symmetrical choice of context and code to use in a communication situation. This asymmetry is inherent in communication, and allows the possibility that communication may fail. Sperber and Wilson describe the process of communication thus:

> It is left to the communicator to make correct assumptions about the codes and contextual information that the audience will have accessible and be likely to use in the comprehension process. The responsibility for avoiding misunderstandings also lies with the speaker, so that all the hearer has to do is go ahead and use whatever code and contextual information come most easily to hand.[46]

Communication is seen as the attempt to change the cognitive environment of another person, and thus to enlarge the scope of what is mutually manifest to both communicator and audience. When I receive a communication, I process it within a certain context and derive from it **contextual implications**, assumptions that result from the interaction of the new information with my already existing assumptions.[47] Clearly no audience can explore and classify all possible contextual implications of a given utterance. There must be a selecting and limiting process. Information that is totally new, with no connection to the audience's existing cognitive environment, will have no *contextual implications.*[48] Neither will old information. It is information that is new but has connections with the existing environment which will have the greatest **contextual effects**. These may include negating, strengthening, extending or enriching our existing assumptions. Such information is **relevant** information in Sperber and Wilson's terminology.

---

[45] Sperber and Wilson, *Relevance*, p. 42.

[46] Sperber and Wilson, *Relevance*, p. 43.

[47] See Sperber and Wilson, *Relevance*, pp. 107-108.

[48] It may have its own logical implications.

Before defining **relevance** more precisely, we need to specify more closely what sort of communication we are considering. A large black cloud in the sky communicates to me that it is likely to rain soon. But the cloud had no intention of communicating with me. While some human communication is like this, most is **ostensive communication**. When we communicate, we not only convey information, but we convey our intention to communicate. Our communication is self-conscious. This is not only true of structured propositional communication, but also of much weaker or non-verbal communication as well. Thus Sperber and Wilson define two levels of intention: *"Informative intention*: to make manifest or more manifest to the audience a set of assumptions . . . *Communicative intention*: to make it mutually manifest to audience and communicator that the communicator has this informative intention."[49] These ideas combine to give the following definition:

> *Ostensive-inferential communication*: the communicator produces a stimulus which makes it mutually manifest to communicator and audience that the communicator intends, by means of this stimulus, to make manifest or more manifest to the audience a set of assumptions {*I*}.[50]

1.4.2 The principles of relevance

If the idea of relevance is to explain why we pick one interpretation of a given communication and not another, then it must be defined in a quantifiable way. Different contextual effects and implications have to be able to be judged more or less relevant. This does not require an absolute scale of relevance, but a comparative one, based on the two factors of contextual effects and processing effort. Thus Sperber and Wilson assert that an assumption is *more relevant* in a particular context if it produces greater contextual effects. It is also more relevant when the effort required to process it is small.[51]

---

[49] Sperber and Wilson, *Relevance*, pp. 58, 61.

[50] Sperber and Wilson, *Relevance*, p. 63. A similar idea was stated much earlier (1969) by Quentin Skinner, "Meaning and Understanding in the History of Ideas," in *Meaning and Context: Quentin Skinner and His Critics* (ed. James Tully; Cambridge: Polity Press, 1988), p 63.

[51] Sperber and Wilson, *Relevance*, p. 125.

These two conditions illustrate the fundamental insight of Relevance Theory—that human communication takes place in a balancing act between processing effort and contextual effect. Communication works because the audience makes the assumption that the communicator intends to communicate and intends to be relevant. The audience does not need to determine in advance the context within which to process a communication. Sperber and Wilson suggest that the choice of an appropriate context is ongoing through the communication process and governed by the search for relevance. They note "there is nothing in the nature of a context, or of comprehension, which excludes the possibility that context formation is open to choices and revisions throughout the comprehension process."[52] In fact, the immediate context in which an utterance occurs is only an initial context, and in the process of interpretation it can be supplemented in one or more different ways:

(1) short term memory of previous parts of the conversation (indicated by anaphoric pronouns);
(2) encyclopedic entries;
(3) environmental factors (indicated by deictic pronouns).[53]

According to Sperber and Wilson, "These factors determine not a single context but a range of possible contexts. What determines the selection of a particular context . . . is . . . the search for relevance."[54]

Thus in understanding a communication, the audience does not take a particular context as given and proceed to assess the relevance of the communication. Instead relevance is taken as given and a context selected to justify that assumption.

This leads Sperber and Wilson to enunciate what they called "the presumption of optimal relevance," which, as modified in the second edition of *Relevance*, states:

Presumption of optimal relevance (revised)
(a) The ostensive stimulus is relevant enough for it to be worth the addressee's effort to process it.
(b) The ostensive stimulus is the most relevant one compatible with the communicator's abilities and preferences.[55]

---

[52] Sperber and Wilson, *Relevance*, p. 137
[53] See Sperber and Wilson, *Relevance*, pp. 140-41
[54] Sperber and Wilson, *Relevance*, pp. 141.

An audience understands a communication by bringing to it the most accessible elements of the mutual cognitive environment and deciding on the meaning that produces the best contextual effects for the least processing effort. The communicator, knowing this, produces the stimulus that will lead the receptor to his intended meaning. This explanation is summarized by two principles of relevance.[56] The "First (or Cognitive) Principle" is the fundamental claim: "Human cognition tends to be geared to the maximisation of relevance." The "Second (or Communicative) Principle" encapsulates the nature of ostensive communication: "Every act of ostensive communication communicates a presumption of its own optimal relevance."

1.4.3 Developments and implications for discourse analysis

Sperber and Wilson proceed from this platform to explain many subtle features of human communication which depend on the hearer inferring the author's intended meaning, including a wide range of imagery, poetic language, and the structuring of the text of a communication. In order to do this, they distinguish between the explicit and implicit assumptions conveyed by an utterance. Explicit assumptions (**explicatures**) are only those that are a development of the logical form encoded in the utterance, the text of the utterance itself. All others are implicit (**implicatures**).

The search for relevance by a trade-off between contextual effects and processing effort can explain the way in which stylistic features of an utterance affect the meaning. Sperber and Wilson examine such features as word order and placement of focal stress, backgrounding and foregrounding, and structural features such as topic-comment, given-new, and focus-presupposition distinctions. They conclude:

---

[55] Sperber and Wilson, *Relevance*, 2nd edn., p. 270. Compare the original statement in the first edition of *Relevance*, p. 158. The modified statement allows that the actual relevance may not be the absolute maximum, but may be influenced by the speaker's aims, priorities, and abilities.

[56] Sperber and Wilson, *Relevance*, 2nd edn., pp. 260-61. In the first edition, *Relevance*, p. 158, there was only one principle, the second of these. The first was an underlying assumption. The change is "expository and not substantive" (p. 271). By the "principle of relevance," I normally intend the second.

Given that utterances have constituent structure, internal order and focal stress, and given that they are processed over time, the most cost-efficient way of exploiting these structural features will give rise to a variety of pragmatic effects. There is a natural linkage between linguistic structure and pragmatic interpretation, and no need for any special pragmatic conventions or interpretation rules: the speaker merely adapts her utterance to the way the hearer is going to process it anyhow, given the existing structural and temporal constraints.[57]

In a development very significant for our interpretation of text including the Bible, Sperber and Wilson assert that there is no sharp division between strong implications of an utterance which are clearly intended by the speaker and weak implications for which the hearer "takes the entire responsibility."

Clearly, the weaker the implicatures the less confidence the hearer can have that the particular premises or conclusions he supplies will reflect the speaker's thoughts, and this is where the indeterminacy lies. However, people may entertain different thoughts and come to have different beliefs on the basis of the same cognitive environment. The aim of communication in general is to increase the mutuality of cognitive environments rather than guarantee an impossible duplication of thoughts.[58]

This sliding scale of implicatures with corresponding movement of responsibility from speaker to hearer is interestingly illustrated by the spectrum of contemporary hermeneutic strategies. But it should be noted that it is only in the limiting cases that the hearer assumes full responsibility. Weak implicatures are significantly exploited by the communicator to achieve, among other things, a wide range of poetic effects. This too is a reflection of the principle of relevance, as a speaker can often achieve a large degree of relevance "through a wide array of weak implicatures."[59]

Although the theory was largely developed in relation to immediate verbal communication, the authors clearly saw its implications for an understanding of the way in which written texts are produced and

---

[57] Sperber and Wilson, *Relevance*, p. 217.

[58] Sperber and Wilson, *Relevance*, pp. 200.

[59] Sperber and Wilson, *Relevance*, p. 222.

understood.[60] A number of writers have applied the theory to the understanding of discourse structure. Fundamental to this direction of development is the work of Diane Blakemore, who argued that neither the coherence of utterances, nor attention to topic, is an adequate basis for explaining the organization of discourse.[61] The fact that RT takes into account extralinguistic factors in constructing contexts, and the fact that the analysis (and the content of contexts) is based not on utterances themselves but on the propositions they represent, recommend RT as the theoretical basis required. Relevance, rather than coherence, explains the way discourse is organized. Furthermore, the contexts within which relevance is found by the hearer are related but constantly evolving:

> within a planned discourse there is a continuity of context, that is, information made accessible by the interpretation of the first utterance is used in establishing the relevance of the second . . . and so on . . . In this way discourse provides the hearer with a continually changing background against which new propositions are processed.[62]

We will look later at the way these ideas on the importance of relevance for discourse analysis are developed in some detail by Regina Blass, with illustrative material from a West African language.[63]

---

[60] See Sperber and Wilson, *Relevance*, pp. 61, 75, 168. For a more detailed treatment of the way in which RT relates to the interpretation of literary texts, see Pattemore, "The People of God," Chapter 2.

[61] Diane Blakemore, "Organisation of Discourse," in *Language: The Socio-Cultural Context* (vol. 4 of *Linguistics: The Cambridge Survey*; ed. Frederick J. Newmeyer; Cambridge: Cambridge University Press, 1988), p. 234.

[62] Blakemore, "Organisation," p. 241. See also Diane Blakemore, *Semantic Constraints on Relevance* (Oxford: Basil Blackwell, 1987); Diane Blakemore, " 'So' as a constraint on relevance," in *Mental Representations: The interface between language and reality* (ed. Ruth M. Kempson; Cambridge: Cambridge University Press, 1988), pp. 183-95.

[63] Regina Blass, *Relevance relations in discourse: A study with special reference to Sissala* (Cambridge: Cambridge University Press, 1990), pp. 7-42. See section 1.9, pp. 52-58, when we consider the implications of RT for discourse analysis.

To sum up, RT suggests that when we hear or read an act of deliberate (ostensive) communication, we assume that the communicator not only intended us to understand the communication, but also shaped it to be optimally relevant. We interpret it within the context of ideas already present in our minds which, when we add the new information, will yield a flow of good results for acceptably low processing effort. Central to this is the understanding that the context which shapes our understanding of a communication is a context in our minds, a cognitive construction. Our physical and social environment, the history and geography of the world, our life history, and the history of our relationship with the communicator all affect the way we understand a communication, but they do so by affecting our minds.

1.5 Relevance Theory and literary texts

Relevance Theory appears on the surface to be little more than a common-sense notion. Yet by closely defining relevance and the nature of manifestness and cognitive environments, it has proved to be a powerful explanatory tool in investigating the process of communication. It claims not so much to be a "better theory" for the understanding of human cognition but to provide the underlying pathway for all theories. But before exploring in greater detail the contribution of RT to textlinguistics or discourse analysis, we must first consider a prior question. Is RT applicable to written texts, and in particular to ancient texts?

Sperber and Wilson developed RT largely with reference to short utterances of spoken language, in face-to-face contexts, and their spontaneous interpretation. Our interests are in the study and interpretation of (ancient) texts, extended written documents. The use of RT on such material involves a leap in the scale, medium and communication situation and raises questions of the validity of relevance in this new environment. A few quotes illustrate the fact that the authors of the theory saw no intrinsic problem with making this leap:

> Where communication is non-reciprocal, there are various possible situations . . . The communicator may be in a position of such authority over her audience that success of her informative intention is mutually manifest in advance. Journalists, professors, religious or political leaders assume, alas often on good grounds,

that what they communicate automatically becomes mutually manifest.[64]

When a representation is stored not as a basic factual assumption but by being embedded under an expression of attitude, it is often processed in a self-conscious, non-spontaneous way. This . . . is true of speculatively held opinions, religious beliefs, or scientific hypotheses . . . We assume, for instance, that the lengthy and highly self-conscious processes of textual interpretation that religious or literary scholars engage in are governed just as much by the principle of relevance as is spontaneous utterance comprehension.[65]

The addressees of an act of ostensive communication are the individuals whose cognitive environment the communicator is trying to modify . . . they may be individuals falling under a certain description, as when we address the present paragraph to all individuals who have read the book so far and found it relevant to them. In broadcast communication, a stimulus can even be addressed to whoever finds it relevant. The communicator is then communicating her presumption of relevance to whoever is willing to entertain it[66]

The change in scale would appear to present no intrinsic obstacle to the applicability of RT given the power of human cognition to grasp and conduct a sustained argument. Nor is the change to text as medium a problem—the main implication is that the text itself becomes the most accessible context (or concentric set of contexts) within which the search for relevance takes place.[67] It is the change to a communication situation that is non-immediate and non-reciprocal which presents the greatest challenge to the pertinence of relevance. The central issue is to establish in what ways the author and audience can be said to have a mutual

---

[64] Sperber and Wilson, *Relevance*, p. 63.

[65] Sperber and Wilson, *Relevance*, p. 75.

[66] Sperber and Wilson, *Relevance*, p. 158.

[67] Recall also that Skinner had much earlier treated texts as examples of ostensive communication. See note 50, p. 19 above. The importance of the structure of the text itself as context will be discussed in more detail in sections 1.8–1.9, pp. 45-59 below.

cognitive environment and for the author to be communicating ostensively. We will consider this briefly in the following paragraphs.[68]

It is necessary in considering literary texts to distinguish three different communication situations. There is the original communication event in which the author transmitted her writings to a particular audience (which may or may not be explicitly defined). There is the situation of subsequent ordinary readers of the text, cut off from the original context. And there is the position of the scholar studying either of the previous two situations.[69] The problem in each case is to establish whether there is a mutual cognitive environment within which the search for relevance can be seen to guide both author and audience.

In the original communication event there can be little doubt of the existence of a large number of shared cognitive contexts, beginning from the text itself and widening to include the life situations of the audience and author (some, though not all, aspects of these will be mutually manifest), and an array of other texts (oral and written) to which the author can assume the audience has access. Relevance is most certainly an operating principle in the author's construction of the text and in the audience's interpretation of it.

By virtue of committing a text to writing an author implicitly offers it to a wider and less clearly defined audience, or indeed to "anyone who finds it relevant." Nevertheless there may well be a greater degree of shared cognitive environment than is at first apparent. Once again it begins with the text itself but this context can be widened (contra Paul Ricoeur). The author will assume her wider audience shares assumptions derived from membership in a particular linguistic, cultural, or national community. These may be quite specific, as in the case that will concern us in this study of a community of faith, where other texts, beliefs, traditions and practices may well be assumed. Ostensive reference within such contexts is possible though deixis may at times be problematic.[70]

---

[68] A more detailed treatment and more extensive references can be found in Pattemore, "The People of God," pp. 29-46.

[69] The first situation may be termed *synchronic*, as it assumes that the writing and reading take place within a limited time span. The second and third situations may therefore be termed *diachronic*.

[70] *Deixis* is a characteristically pragmatic concept, which Stephen C. Levinson, *Pragmatics* (Cambridge: Cambridge University Press, 1983), p. 54, defines in the following way: "The term is borrowed from the Greek

The more removed the audience, the smaller is the extent of the mutual cognitive environment. This will not diminish the importance of the search for relevance in the audience's interpretation of the text, but it will mean a progressive loss in confidence that the derived meaning in any way represents the author's intentions.[71] Contemporary secular use of apocalyptic language would appear to be a case in point.

The scholar or critic is a special case of the "subsequent ordinary reader." As such, the considerations of shared context just noted apply. Scholars are more self-conscious in their search for meaning, but are nonetheless guided both directly and indirectly by the principle of relevance.[72] Indirectly, the assumption that the communication to original or subsequent ordinary readers operated by the principle of relevance reaffirms the fundamental importance of historical-critical research, in order to discover the nature of the mutual cognitive environments within which the communication and its interpretation took place.[73] Directly, relevance

---

word for pointing or indicating, and has as prototypical or focal exemplars the use of demonstratives, first and second person pronouns, tense, specific time and place adverbs like *now* and *here*, and a variety of other grammatical features tied directly to the circumstances of utterance.

Essentially, deixis concerns the ways in which languages encode or grammaticalize features of the **context of utterance** or **speech event**" (emphasis his).

[71] The limiting case is when the audience's interests dominate, subvert, or eliminate the author's. This is called "eisegetical interpretation" by Anne Furlong, "Relevance Theory and Literary Interpretation" (Ph.D. thesis, University College London, 1996), pp 199-204.

[72] This is true even though the author may have had no intention to communicate to later scholars, nor to subject her communication to their scrutiny. G. B. Caird, *New Testament Theology* (ed. L. D. Hurst; Oxford: Clarendon, 1994), p. 2, comments on the biblical authors: "They never dreamt that what they wrote would, centuries later, be subjected to the microscopic scrutiny of modern biblical scholarship, providing in every unusual phrase and every unexpressed assumption matter for a doctoral dissertation."

[73] Again this interest that RT both exemplifies and explains was anticipated by Skinner, "Meaning and Understanding," p. 63: "The essential question which we therefore confront, in studying any given text, is what its author, in writing at the time he did write for the audience he

influences the work of scholars and critics even if they are unaware of it, because their conclusions will be those that, in their opinion, best explain the data available, that is, are optimally relevant to them. This suggests the need for caution when the text appears to yield no adequate meaning as it stands. Rather than quickly proposing textual emendations or attributing the current text to the work of editors or redactors, it may be necessary to admit that there is a failure of relevance on the diachronic level rather than on the synchronic.[74] But even more directly, to use RT in the interpretation of texts is to bring to conscious focus a factor that is operative whether or not the interpreter is aware of it. It involves examining how the form of the text might have achieved optimal relevance, interacting with the reader's cognitive environment(s) to produce good cognitive effects. It will involve careful analysis of the output of historical-critical research to determine which cognitive environments may have been more accessible than others, yielding good cognitive effects without gratuitous processing effort. Thus by investigating the "readers' meaning," and with the assumption that the author is aiming for optimal relevance with respect to his intended meaning, the scholar is provided with the best possible clues to the author's intentions.[75]

---

intended to address, could in practice have been intending to communicate by the utterance of this given utterance."

[74] Note the comment by historian R. G. Collingwood, *The Idea of History* (Oxford: Clarendon, 1946), pp. 218-19: "When he finds certain historical matters unintelligible, he has discovered a limitation of his own mind; he has discovered that there are certain ways in which he is not, or no longer, or not yet, able to think. Certain historians, sometimes whole generations of historians, find in certain periods of history nothing intelligible, and call them dark ages; but such phrases tell us nothing about these ages themselves, though they tell us a great deal about the persons who use them, namely that they are unable to rethink the thoughts which were fundamental to their life."

[75] There is yet another level at which relevance considerations influence the scholar, but which does not directly impact on the focus of my study. This is in the communication of his or her work. I presume, for example, that anyone reading this present volume is prepared to expend considerably more processing effort in the pursuit of fruitful cognitive effects than the average reader. I also assume a mutual cognitive environment that includes not only a vast array of texts, but also sets of

1.6 Relevance and translation

Relevance Theory has had a mixed reception within the Bible translation community, being strongly championed in some quarters and dismissed as theoretically suspect, or pragmatically irrelevant, in others. In this section I will discuss the attempt by Ernst-August Gutt to assert relevance as the single theoretical basis for translation, and, more particularly, the subsequent criticism of this position by Ernst Wendland.[76] Although this present study is not *directly* concerned with translation, it is ultimately motivated by translation needs, and the debate over RT in translation is nevertheless pertinent because it represents the point of closest approach of RT to biblical studies.[77] Furthermore, some of the

conventions for referring to them, and a specialized semantic domain. The responsibility for inferring my intentions, however, lies with the reader, who is entitled to access these environments in such a way as to achieve optimal relevance.

[76] Ernst-August Gutt, *Translation and Relevance: Cognition and Context* (Oxford: Basil Blackwell, 1991); Ernst-August Gutt, *Relevance Theory: A Guide*; Ernst R. Wendland, "A Tale of Two Debtors: On the Interaction of Text, Cotext, and Context in a New Testament Dramatic Narrative (Luke 7:36-50)," in *Linguistics and New Testament Interpretation* (ed. David A. Black; Nashville: Broadman, 1992), pp. 101-143; Ernst R. Wendland, "A Review of 'Relevance Theory' in Relation to Bible Translation in South-Central Africa: Part I," *JNSL* 22 (1996): 91-106; Ernst R. Wendland, "A Review of 'Relevance Theory' in Relation to Bible Translation in South-Central Africa: Part II," *JNSL* 23 (1997): 83-108. Note also the earlier publications by Gutt on the application of relevance principles to translation: Ernst-August Gutt, "Relevance Theory and Increased Accuracy in Translation," *NOT* (1985): 29-31; Ernst-August Gutt, "Unravelling Meaning: An Introduction to Relevance Theory," *NOT* (1986): 10-20; Ernst-August Gutt, "Matthew 9.4-17 in the Light of Relevance Theory," *NOT* (1986): 13-20.

[77] Cotterell and Turner, *Linguistics and Biblical Interpretation*, appear to have been the first to appropriate Sperber and Wilson's insights for biblical interpretation (especially with regard to conversation, p. 270-71, but also anticipated in their discussion of presupposition pools, pp. 90-92), but the implications were not worked out in any detail. For works in the translation field, other than those of Gutt listed above, see Tim

most important criticisms Wendland levels at Gutt's approach are, in fact, criticisms of RT itself, rather than its application to translation, and as such deserve careful consideration.[78]

Gutt begins with a survey of the failure of various attempts, both descriptive and evaluative, to provide an adequate theoretical account of translation.[79] His own choice of a relevance-theoretic framework is influenced by the fact that it addresses not external factors but the mental processes involved in understanding language, by its explanatory rather than descriptive orientation, and by its potential for treating translation as real communication.[80] His appropriation of RT is then focused on the

---

Farrell and Richard Hoyle, "Translating Implicit Information in the Light of Saussurean, Relevance, and Cognitive Theories," *NOT* 9 (1995): 1-15; Fritz Goerling, "Relevance and Transculturation," *NOT* 10 (1996): 49-57; Christoph Unger, "Types of Implicit Information and Their Roles in Translation," *NOT* 10 (1996): 18-30; Tim Farrell and Richard Hoyle, "The Application of Relevance Theory: A Response," *NOT* 11 (1997): 19-26. Others to use RT in biblical interpretation are (explictly) P. J. Maartens, "The Relevance of 'Context' and 'Interpretation' to the Semiotic Relations of Romans 5:1-11," *Neot* 29 (1995): 75-108; and (implicitly) A. J. P. Garrow, *Revelation* (New Testament Readings; London: Routledge, 1997). For an application of RT to the function of Greek particles, see Marlon Winedt, "The Narrative and Communicative Function of ἀλλά in the Gospel of Luke: A Relevance-Theoretic Perspective" (paper presented at the UBS Triennial Translation Workshop; Malaga, Spain, June 2000). This is a sample of the work Winedt has presented in his Ph.D. dissertation: "A Relevance-Theoretic Approach to Translation and Discourse Markers: With Special Reference to the Greek Text of the Gospel of Luke" (Free University of Amsterdam, 1999).

[78] In the course of personal discussions, Wendland has indicated that he now considers his earlier critiques to be "too negative." Nevertheless the issues he raised in the reviews listed above are significant ones and I will continue to use them as a framework for discussion. For another careful evaluation of the debate between Gutt and Wendland, see David van Grootheest, "Relevance Theory and Bible Translation" (Ph.D. thesis, Free University of Amsterdam, 1996).

[79] Gutt, *Translation*, pp. 1-20.

[80] Gutt, *Translation*, pp. 20-21. Note especially his following comment: "no external factor has an influence on either the production or

concept of *interpretive resemblance* of thoughts and utterances, and the "guarantee of faithfulness," which RT claims accompanies any utterance.[81] Since not all natural language utterances can be said to have propositional forms, Gutt departs from Sperber and Wilson's formulation by considering interpretive resemblance between utterances, rather than propositional forms.[82] Thus "interpretive resemblance" becomes not only a theoretical notion but a criterion of faithfulness of translation, and by implication of any intra-lingual interpretation as well.

From this basis Gutt critiques the related but distinct approaches to Bible translation advocated by UBS and SIL and finds both wanting. His test case for these two methods of translation is Matt 2, especially as treated by R. T. France, and here he makes some very significant observations for the application of relevance to biblical interpretation.[83] France distinguishes between "the 'surface meaning', which any reasonably intelligent reader might be expected to grasp, and what we may call a 'bonus' meaning accessible to those who are more 'sharp-eyed', or better instructed in Old Testament scripture" and concludes that Matthew may well have been deliberately composing his narrative with these layers of

---

interpretation of a translation unless it has entered the mental life of either the translator or his audience. Its mere existence 'out there' is not enough to influence the translation." This is equally applicable to intra-lingual interpretation and is a consequence of RT's more rigorous definition of context.

[81] Gutt, *Translation*, pp. 34, 39-44. See Deirdre Wilson and Dan Sperber, "Representation and relevance," in *Mental Representations: The interface between language and reality* (ed. Ruth M. Kempson; Cambridge: Cambridge University Press, 1988), pp. 138-39.

[82] See Gutt, *Translation*, p. 44: ". . . two utterances, or even more generally, two ostensive stimuli, interpretively resemble one another to the extent that they share their explicatures and/or implicatures.

This notion of interpretive resemblance is independent of whether or not the utterances in question have a propositional form, but at the same time it is context-dependent, since the explicatures and implicatures of the utterance are context-dependent."

[83] Gutt, *Translation*, pp. 70-72; R. T. France, "The Formula-Quotations of Matthew 2 and the Problem of Communication," *NTS* 27 (1981): 233-51.

available meaning.[84] Gutt observes that such a view of multiple intended meanings "is quite consistent with relevance theory" but does not elaborate in what way this is so.[85] From the readers' perspective, the different meanings are arrived at because the stimulus of the text interacts differently with the different cognitive environments that they bring to the text. The author, knowing that this is potentially so, deliberately structures the text to allow for optimal relevance to be found at different levels by different people. This observation significantly modifies the concept which is often implicit and occasionally explicit in discussions of relevance, that there is a unique interpretation of an utterance consistent with the principle of relevance. This is only so for a specific audience at a specific time. Note also that the layers of meaning suggested by France and Gutt are determined by the author. They are strong implicatures. There are also potentially large numbers of weak implicatures, for which the author takes less responsibility. It is these that cause the greatest difficulty in translation (and in other interpretive tasks).

Gutt's development of his relevance-based account of translation need not detain us long. He considers translation as interlingual interpretive usage, a definition that allows for both indirect and direct translation (which correspond to indirect and direct quotation), depending on the requirements of the environment and audience. He concludes:

> In all instances we were able to account for the phenomena in question without reliance on descriptive-classificatory theory . . . principles, rules and guidelines of translation are applications of the principle of relevance . . . Thus the main contribution of this book is a reductionist one on the theoretical level—issues of translation are shown to be at heart issues of communication.[86]

---

[84] France, "Formula-Quotations," p. 241. In fact what France has called the "surface meaning" is already dependent on a knowledge of OT texts and connotations associated with Messiahship (p. 249). So there is an even more basic layer of meaning, that of a simple narrative with perhaps unnoticed intertextualities. (This would be a "spontaneous interpretation" in Furlong's terminology.)

[85] Gutt, *Translation*, p. 72.

[86] Gutt, *Translation*, p. 188. Gutt is currently working on a more detailed exposition of translation theory from an RT perspective.

It is the reductionism acknowledged here that is at the heart of Wendland's criticism of Gutt and of RT in general.[87] In particular he is concerned for the implications of such reductionism for the practice of translation:

It is neither credible nor convincing to assert that RT alone provides the sole solution for all of the problems of discernment, assessment, and choice that every serious translator must continually wrestle with.[88]

But it should be noted that what Gutt admits to is reductionism "on the theoretical level," namely that translation is a type of communication and as such the theory (in this case RT) developed for communication is applicable, with appropriate elaboration as Gutt has done.[89] Whether or not Gutt has been successful in demonstrating a unitary treatment of translation, this does not eliminate the need to wrestle with "problems of discernment, assessment, and choice."[90] RT claims to explain the processes of human understanding at a fundamental, cognitive level, a level that underlies the more immediate linguistic processing of semantics, syntax and discourse. The "reductionism" is that relevance becomes a criterion for understanding the contribution made by each of these levels of language. I will return to this point again in the discussion below.

Wendland finds both sides of the RT equation, processing effort and contextual effects, as well as the concept of "context" itself, to be problematic. His criticism of the cognitive environment definition of context as idiosyncratic has some point.[91] But in fact "context" has been such an ill-defined concept in both linguistic and biblical studies that the more

Unfortunately, maintaining a focus on RT in *interpretation* prevents us from exploring this further.

[87] Wendland, "Two Debtors," pp. 136-41; Wendland, "Review: Part I," pp. 91-92, 98-99.

[88] Wendland, "Review: Part I," pp. 98-99; see also his personal irenic note 1, p. 92.

[89] A similar point is made by van Grootheest, "Relevance Theory and Bible Translation," p. 92.

[90] I share many of Wendland's hesitations with regard to the adequacy of Gutt's account of translation. See Wendland, "Review: Part I," pp. 99-103; "Review: Part II," pp. 83-88.

[91] Wendland, "Review: Part I," pp. 95-96.

precise definition of RT is a major step forward.[92] It is only as the wider "context" features as part of a person's mental life that it affects his understanding of linguistic and other stimuli.[93] Further, the fact that context in RT includes not only the contributions of text and co-text, but also of extralinguistic context, makes it more comprehensive as well as being precise.[94]

On the processing effort side of the equation, Wendland is concerned that RT implies an "easy listening" approach to all communication and ignores the case of "literarily competent individuals" and texts designed for such readers.[95] Some proponents of RT appear to imply this, and if it were a necessary consequence of RT it would fail to account for the bulk of the literary heritage of any language. But it is precisely by the definition of context in terms of an individual's cognitive environment that RT does in fact account for sophisticated and complex literature. Readers and hearers, both individuals and communities, have varying degrees of literary experience and varying abilities to process linguistic stimuli. Authors and speakers are aware of this and construct their messages so as to optimize relevance for the audience they have in mind. Furthermore the structure of the message may be deliberately such as to have different cognitive effects for different audiences, as is clear in the treatment of Matt 2 above (pp. 31-32). But even competent readers will weigh processing effort against potential benefits in further contextual effects.[96]

On the contextual effects side of the equation, Wendland has a number of significant concerns. Central to these is the apparent limitation of the theory to "cognitive" effects. On the one hand this is seen as involving logical, propositional processing of stimuli and ignoring the more intuitive and evocative effects of poetic imagery. And on the other hand it is seen to exclude the emotional and volitional effects that an author may have intended.

---

[92] I will address this issue in more detail in section 1.8. See pp. 45-51.

[93] See note 80, pp. 30-31 above.

[94] Wendland's careful, multilevel analysis of Luke 7:36-50 ("Two Debtors") makes use of precisely the kind of complex but well-defined context that RT assumes—text, co-text and context.

[95] Wendland, "Review: Part I," p. 94.

[96] See also Furlong's treatment of spontaneous and literary readings in "Relevance Theory and Literary Interpretation," and the discussion in Pattemore, "The People of God," pp. 32-35.

The "contextual effects" which play such a prominent role in the RT approach to verbal interaction cannot be confined to matters involving the intellect alone, especially where recognized literary and religious works are concerned. Instead, the perspective needs to be broadened considerably to incorporate associated feelings, attitudes, values, moods and desires.[97]

I believe this concern, though valid in itself, to be without foundation in respect to RT, and to stem from too narrow a definition of cognition, restricted to conscious intellectual processing. In fact cognitive processes are arguably behind all changes in mental states and certainly behind all behavioral modification.[98] Poetic effects work because they stimulate cognitive, but not necessarily conscious, processes.[99] Changes in behavior begin in the mind. Thus RT is quite correct to focus on cognitive effects of communication. They form the layer that underlies all other effects and determine all responses.[100] It is somewhat ironic to note that Wendland,

---

[97] Wendland, "Review: Part II," p. 83; see also "Review: Part I," pp. 103-105.

[98] Thus Sperber and Wilson, *Relevance*, 2nd edn., pp. 261-62, attribute the tendency to maximize relevance to the biological evolution of the human mind.

[99] RT does not require either the elements of the cognitive environment or the cognitive processes to be fully on the level of the conscious. This is the point of the rejection of a "mutual knowledge" definition of context, outlined above, pp. 17-18. Without reference to RT, Thiselton has expressed the same consideration when, in speaking of the limits of our "horizons" of understanding, he says, "these boundaries embrace not only what we can draw on in conscious reflection, but also the pre-cognitive dispositions or competences which are made possible by our participation in the shared practices of a social and historical world" (*New Horizons*, p. 46).

[100] It must be said that RT is radically naturalistic—witness Dan Sperber's attempt, in *Explaining Culture: A Naturalistic Approach* (Oxford: Basil Blackwell, 1996), to use it to write a naturalistic account of culture, and Sperber and Wilson's comments on the evolution of cognition in note 96. As such it will give no account of the "spiritual effects" of biblical literature, if by that we mean effects which are caused, not by the processes of comprehension and inference and a person's responses to the

35

having expressed concern that RT does not leave room for the pragmatics of poetic effects, then finds that the way it does so, by assigning them to indeterminate weak implicatures. This allows *too much* liberty in this area.[101] His apparent preference is for a singular, author-determined implicature to be drawn. But RT does more justice to poetry than this, while at the same time providing a (relevance-determined) limit to the extent that any poetic text will be processed.[102] Which implicatures should be reflected in translation (and, by extension, in intra-lingual interpretation) will also be a function of relevance and context.

Wendland's criticism of the "contextual effects" side of the equation includes the observation that apart from the three contextual effects allowed by RT (the derivation of contextual implications, the strengthening of an existing assumption, and the elimination of an existing assumption) there should also be the possibility of the gradual weakening of an existing assumption.[103] This is a frequently raised question and such cases are handled by RT, not as a distinct type of effect, but as the elimination of an *underlying* assumption.[104]

One further observation of Wendland's is worth noticing because of its importance for biblical texts. He is concerned that RT's reader-centered, relevance-driven approach to understanding (and to translation) would mean that "translators as a matter of principle ought to try to accent the familiar and downplay what is alien in order to produce a message which manifests the highest 'consistency' . . . within the target language-culture

---

outcomes of these processes, but by some "spiritual" force which acts (mystically or irrationally) through the sacred text. On the other hand, the question of whether God, as the presumed ultimate author of the biblical text, must also adhere to the principle of relevance is a significantly important one and will be addressed in the following section.

[101] Wendland, "Review: Part II," pp. 88-91.

[102] See also the work of Furlong and especially Adrian Pilkington, "Poetic Thoughts and Poetic Effects: A Relevance Theory Account of the Literary Use of Rhetorical Tropes" (Ph.D. thesis, University College London, 1994), both reviewed in Pattemore, "The People of God," pp. 31-35.

[103] Wendland, "Review: Part I," p. 96.

[104] See, for example, I. Higashimori and D. Wilson, "Questions on Relevance," *UCLWPL* 8 (1996): 114.

setting."[105] This appears to reflect a misunderstanding of both the concept of relevance and the nature of contextual effects. Relevant contextual effects do not simply consist in confirming existing assumptions, but may even overturn them.[106] A relevant stimulus is not one that duplicates what is already in the cognitive environment of the hearer, but it must have some point of contact if it is to be processed.[107] Any concern that receptor-centeredness might lead to the superimposition on the biblical text of traditional, modernistic or denominational biases is somewhat ironic, since RT is more often criticized for being too concerned with

---

[105] Wendland, "Review: Part I," p. 102.

[106] RT thus provides a theoretical grounding for Thiselton's hermeneutical approach, dependent at this point on the concept of a "horizon of expectations," as proposed by Hans R. Jauss, *Toward an Aesthetic of Reception* (trans. Timothy Bahti; Theory and History of Literature 2; Brighton: Harvester Press, 1982), especially pp. 3-45. So Thiselton, *New Horizons*, p. 34, writes: "Every reader brings a horizon of expectation to the text. This is a mind-set, or system of references, which characterizes the reader's finite viewpoint amidst his or her situatedness in time and history. Patterns of habituation in the reader's attitudes, experiences, reading-practices, and life, define and strengthen his or her horizon of expectation . . . A text, however, can surprise, contradict, or even reverse such a horizon of expectation." See also Jauss, *Aesthetic*, p. 44.

[107] Wendland, "Two Debtors," p. 138, rightly observes that the full understanding of Jesus' parables requires the reader/hearer to "adopt Christ's own central core of cognitive assumptions." But his conclusion that RT fails in this regard does not follow. The parables are in many ways similar to Matt 2, discussed above. A surface-level meaning is readily available based on few contextual assumptions and involving little processing effort. And the true, or inner, understanding does indeed require a premium of processing effort. But so long as there are contextual clues to indicate that an inner meaning, with more significant contextual effects, is to be had, there is no reason why the search for optimal relevance will not proceed. Christ's cognitive assumptions can only be adopted if they are present in the cognitive environment and if there are indications that it is worth the processing effort to adopt them. Such indications may be within the relationship of teacher and disciple, or they may be inherent in the surface-level meaning of the parable itself, such as its apparent banality, or absurdity.

the author's intentions. Anne Furlong has suggested that impositions such as Wendland fears result from a search for maximal rather than optimal relevance, and should be classed as eisegetical.[108] Wendland's criticisms stem from a serious concern for faithfulness to the biblical message in the translation task. His suggestions for a broader-based approach reflect the high degree of both scholarship and skill that he brings to the task.[109] Nevertheless I believe the criticism he has advanced against RT and its importance for biblical interpretation and translation to be unwarranted. RT does not supplant semantic, syntactic, structural or literary analysis. It both undergirds and guides them. And Gutt's work is important for bringing it to bear on biblical text.

1.7 Relevance and Scripture

Relevance Theory is an explanatory theory of human communication from an essentially naturalistic perspective. As such it attempts to account for the communication of meaning between humans in terms of human cognitive processes. But to use it to analyze the book of Revelation is to apply it to a text that, by any standard of judgment, is no "ordinary" text. Whether or not the scholar chooses to regard it as "inspired," or to have in any sense a "divine" origin, it is undoubtedly *intended* to be so read and so heard, indeed much more explicitly so than many other parts of the New Testament. This raises two questions for the application of RT, one relatively trivial and the other much more profound. Both have implications for each of the two dimensions of communication to which I have referred, the synchronic and the diachronic, relating respectively to

---

[108] See Furlong, "Relevance Theory and Literary Interpretation," pp. 199-204.

[109] Note also Ernst R. Wendland's comment in another review of RT, "On the Relevance of 'Relevance Theory' for Bible Translation," *BT* 47 (1996): 134: ". . . the RT approach is extremely useful for Bible translators to become familiar with—*if* modified, or perhaps rephrased . . . and carefully integrated *within* a more explicitly comprehensive text-context oriented, structure-functional methodology" (emphasis his). As will be seen, this is precisely the role that I see RT taking within the process of exegesis.

the original hearers and to subsequent readers and students.[110] First, what are the implications of the *claim* to inspiration or divine origin, for the search for relevance? And secondly, is it possible for RT to accommodate the real possibility of divine communication? Or to put it more bluntly, can God be, and does God have to be, relevant?

The first question is trivial because in allowing for the claim to inspiration we are still treating the text as an example of natural language communication, suspending judgment on whether or not the communication has *in fact* any other source than the mind of John. Sperber and Wilson have already allowed for this kind of communication:

> Where communication is non-reciprocal, there are various possible situations . . . The communicator may be in a position of such authority over her audience that success of her informative intention is mutually manifest in advance. Journalists, professors, religious or political leaders assume, alas often on good grounds, that what they communicate automatically becomes mutually manifest.[111]

One of the features of Revelation, as with other apocalyptic literature, is its explicit self-authentication.[112] From the perspective of the first readers/hearers, this claim to be authentic prophecy and a Spirit-inspired vision will have been evaluated not only on the basis of the content and claims of the text itself, but also on the life-context and relationship of the recipients and author. If the claim was accepted (and the preservation of the text suggests it was), then a high degree of relevance will have been assumed for it.[113] The hermeneutic task would have been to identify correctly the contexts that optimize relevance, and this task would not have been abandoned lightly. It is also likely that even if no significant immediate contextual effects were found for a particular part of the text, it would still have been preserved on the assumption of its relevance, in the expectation that at some future time, or with some further help, it

---

[110] See above, pp. 25-28.

[111] Sperber and Wilson, *Relevance*, p. 63.

[112] See David E. Aunes's definition, in "The Apocalypse of John and the Problem of Genre," *Semeia* 36 (1986): 86-87; and other articles in *Semeia* 36 (1986) and *Semeia* 14 (1979).

[113] On the reception of the Apocalypse in the early church, see Pattemore, "The People of God," p. 1, note 1.

would yield its results. Extended diachronically on the level of the ordinary reader, this factor may also help to explain the continuing place in the canon of Scripture of a much neglected and misunderstood book.[114] From the perspective of the scholar studying the first century A.D. communication event, the presumption of authenticity and inspiration must be clearly identified as a significant component of the mutual cognitive environment. If we are to discover how it was the first recipients understood the text, we must do this against the background of their reception of it as an inspired document. And it is against the same background that we must understand Revelation's subtext of intertextual allusion. The hermeneutic task then is to identify contexts for the first hearers of the book which include their understanding of its origins and status, and hence to identify the contextual effects that result.

But can RT cope with the reality of a God who speaks? For there are no *a priori* grounds that require us to exclude this possibility, or indeed to exclude it from the field of scholarly debate.[115] The very fact that I am interested in the study of John's Apocalypse is because I belong to a community which has consistently affirmed for millennia that God does speak, and that he has spoken through this particular text. Does God, if God speaks, communicate by optimizing relevance? And how should this affect the way in which we read and study Revelation in the twenty-first century? To answer these questions fully would require a long detour into the realms of theology and epistemology. My remarks will, by contrast, be

---

[114] In fact few generations of the church have been without those who have confidently claimed to have discovered the key to the relevance of the Apocalypse. See, for example, Henry B. Swete, *The Apocalypse of St John* (London: Macmillan & Co., 1911), pp. ccvii-ccxix; Isbon T. Beckwith, *The Apocalypse of John* (1919; repr., Grand Rapids: Baker Book House, 1967), pp. 318-36; Norman Cohn, *The Pursuit of the Millennium* (New York: Oxford University Press, 1961); Rodney L. Petersen, *Preaching in the Last Days: The Theme of 'Two Witnesses' in the Sixteenth and Seventeenth Centuries* (New York: Oxford University Press, 1993).

[115] John Webster, in a recent lecture, has questioned the division since Kant, between theology as a discipline governed by hermeneutic rules of "general theory," and reading the Bible as Scripture. He calls for a reprioritizing of the "local interpretation" by reading Scripture to hear the voice of God. See John Webster, "Texts: Scripture, Reading, and the Rhetoric of Theology," *Stimulus* 6 (1998): 10-16.

brief and will focus on two ideas—the implications of divine speech for understanding the nature and stance of biblical text, and the responsibility this lays on the person who reads the Bible as Scripture, as divine speech.

Nicholas Wolterstorff has argued on the basis of Speech-Act Theory that it is meaningful to claim that God speaks, and therefore to consider the implications for divine authorial responsibility.[116] Different modes of discourse offer useful analogies for divine discourse—not only "double agency" discourse or deputized discourse, which is appropriate to prophecy, but also "appropriated discourse," which may be more appropriate for other forms of Scripture.[117] If God can be thought to intervene, as Wolterstorff argues, either to deputize someone to speak on his behalf, or to appropriate someone's speech as his own, then God also has the rights and obligations of an author/speaker.[118] Against Ricoeur, Wolterstorff affirms that we can read texts not just to discover their "sense," in relation to a text-created world, but also to understand the authorial discourse.[119] Either way, in the biblical text human discourse has become an instrument of divine discourse. Scripture can thus be considered divine discourse, but it is never unmediated, it is always *incarnated* divine discourse. The divine author, both by delegating and by appropriating, accepts the conditions of *human* communication, with its rights and responsibilities. These include the responsibilities to be relevant and to respect the audience's context, and the rights to be heard and understood.

Any model of Scripture as divine discourse incarnate in human language must do justice to both halves of the formula. Thus first we must

---

[116] Nicholas Wolterstorff, *Divine Discourse: Philosophical reflections on the claim that God speaks* (Cambridge: Cambridge University Press, 1995). For Speech-Act Theory, see note 19, p. 11 above.

[117] Wolterstorff, *Divine Discourse*, pp. 37-57.

[118] Wolterstorff, *Divine Discourse*, pp. 95-129.

[119] Wolterstorff, *Divine Discourse*, pp. 130-52. See Paul Ricoeur, *Hermeneutics and Human Sciences: Essays on Language, Action, and Interpretation* (ed. and trans. Paul B. Thompson; Cambridge: Cambridge University Press, 1981), pp. 131-44; Paul Ricoeur, *Essays on Biblical Interpretation* (ed. Lewis S. Mudge; Philadelphia: Fortress Press, 1980), pp. 99-100; cf. Kevin J. Vanhoozer, *Biblical Narrative in the Philosophy of Paul Ricoeur: A Study in Hermeneutics and Theology* (Cambridge: Cambridge University Press, 1990), p. 109, note 7.

affirm the validity of searching for the meaning of Scripture by optimizing relevance. God has chosen to speak in human language. God's eternal and effective word has undergone a *kenosis*, and therefore the normal rules of communication can be applied. Both the original audience and the later readers and students are obliged to optimize the relevance of the text within mutual cognitive environments. As Richard Hays has suggested for Paul's letters, so for any Scripture, we must first read it as "not-Scripture," as ordinary human communication embedded in a relevance-creating context, and in particular, attend to its use of its own prior Scripture. Only then will we be able to hear it as the voice of God.[120]

Yet if we are content with the human dimension of Scripture's text, the search for relevance remains an academic exercise, the text itself inert marks on paper, powerless to reach, let alone move us. We have accounted only for the responsibility of the divine author to be relevant and our corresponding right to use a human hermeneutic. The complementary dimensions are equally, or even more, important: the divine right to be heard, and our responsibility to optimize the cognitive effects of the divine message. John Webster suggests that we should be less concerned about how God communicates, and more about who it is that speaks to us, that we should locate our understanding of the nature of Scripture first in the doctrine of God as trinity—because of the work of the Father in the freedom of his communication, because of the Son who is the Word, because of the Spirit who makes real God's self-utterance.[121] Such an understanding of Scripture echoes harmonically through the whole intertextual space of the church's historical existence. Further, it revitalizes the ostensive dimension of Scripture's communication for subsequent generations, including our own. Where Ricoeur denies to any text the power to refer ostensively, Kevin Vanhoozer has rightly pointed out that Ricoeur's "hermeneutical philosophy lacks an adequate approximation for

---

[120] Richard B. Hays, *Echoes of Scripture in the Letters of Paul* (New Haven: Yale University Press, 1989), p. 5, says: "If we approach Paul's letters a priori as Scripture in their own right, we run the risk of distortion through a hieratic reading that loses sight of their historical contingency and hermeneutical innovation. Paradoxically, we learn how rightly to read Paul's letters as Scripture only by first reading them as not-Scripture and attending to how he read the Scripture he knew."

[121] Webster, "Texts," p. 12. The second location he suggests is in the doctrine of the church (p. 13).

the Christian teaching about the Holy Spirit."[122] The God who "spoke to our ancestors in many and various ways by the prophets," who "has spoken to us by a Son," who deputized men and women to speak and appropriated their words, this God, I would argue, continues to speak to us by the present activity of the Holy Spirit who again appropriates the words of an ancient text and uses them to deliberately and ostensively communicate to us.[123] Mark Hargreaves comments helpfully:

> The Bible's referential potential lies in its themes. It is supported by the Holy Spirit who works in the area of thematic resonance. He brings about a recognition of the thematic relevance of Scripture. This is the common Christian experience of Scripture addressing a contemporary situation.[124]

The work of the Holy Spirit provides a continuity between the origins of Scripture among the ancient people of God and the understanding of Scripture in the contemporary Church. And this continuity of the Church/Spirit community provides a means by which Scripture can refer to the past and transform the present. The Holy Spirit is an ostensive, relevance-creating communicator, the bridge between the author's intentionality and the modern reader's life. That this is no new insight is evident from Scripture itself: "For whatever was written in former days was written for our instruction, so that by steadfastness and by the encouragement of the scriptures we might have hope."[125]

The recognition of this "divine right" of speech by the student of Scripture entails corresponding responsibilities. It requires an accountability in our hermeneutical practice, not only, as Daniel Patte has helpfully suggested, to the academy and to ordinary readers of Scripture, but also to the authors of Scripture and the divine, relevance-creating Author.[126] Their ostensive communication carries the force of their intentionality.

---

[122] Vanhoozer, *Ricoeur*, p. 278; cf. Paul Ricoeur, *Interpretation Theory: Discourse and the Surplus of Meaning* (Fort Worth: Texas Christian University Press, 1976), p. 30; Ricoeur, *Hermeneutics*, p. 145.

[123] Heb 1:1-2.

[124] Mark Hargreaves, "Telling Stories: The Concept of Narrative and Biblical Authority," *Anvil* 13 (1996): 134.

[125] Rom 15:4; cf. 1 Cor 9:10; 10:11.

[126] Daniel Patte, *Ethics of Biblical Interpretation: A Reevaluation* (Louisville: Westminster John Knox, 1995), p. 107 and passim.

This accountability in turn entails a commitment not to readily abandon the search for relevance (either to the original audience, or to ourselves), but to search for cognitive environments within which the flow of cognitive effects is optimized. It entails the renunciation of any attempt to manipulate, control or colonize the text for our own ideological purposes.

What does all this imply for our use of RT in the present study of John's Apocalypse? An understanding of Scripture as divine discourse incarnate in human communication implies that the study of the Apocalypse as the text of a human communication event, governed by the optimization of relevance, is a *necessary*, but not *sufficient*, condition for understanding it. It is necessary because of the incarnational nature of divine discourse, and it will involve incorporating the presumption of divine origin as a part of the ordinary *human* context within which it was sent and received. It is not sufficient because of the divine origin of the incarnate discourse. The book of Revelation could be seen to participate in both of Wolterstorff's categories of deputized and appropriated discourse. And within it the reader/hearer is explicitly addressed, either "directly" or "indirectly," by God (Rev 1:8; 21:5-8), by the exalted Christ (Rev 1:11; 2:1–3:22; 22:7, 12-13, 16, 20), and by the Spirit (Rev 2:7, 11, 17, 29; 3:6, 13, 22).[127] Any approach based on the assumption that "unbiased reason" is the only tool needed for understanding, cannot hope to detect more than one dimension of the text. To ignore the function of the Apocalypse as Scripture is to limit the contexts in which relevance can be found, to attempt to shut out the voice of the Spirit. Yet even when we read the biblical text as Scripture, within a believing community, relevance plays a significant role. We read to hear the voice of the God whom, in some measure, we have come to know, and that (partial and probably flawed) knowledge is also part of our cognitive environment. Thus we will search for contexts that optimize God's relevance (remembering that relevance is not the same as confirming our existing beliefs) and will at times prefer open agnosticism to radical cynicism.

To return to the point from which I began this section, it may be helpful to consider an analogy between RT and the Theory of Evolution. In

---

[127] The terms "directly" and "indirectly" are both relative to the narrative context. Of course all the communication is really indirect in the sense that it is through John. And equally obvious is the fact that the whole book is implicitly a communication from God through Jesus and John (Rev 1:1).

fact the analogy is by no means an arbitrary one.[128] As evolution is a principle that may be employed on the basis of atheistic presuppositions, but which in itself does not exclude God as the active agent, so relevance may be used to exclude the divine voice, but it may equally be used with an acknowledgment of the relevance-creating power of an eloquent God. God's works and God's words—both find expression in processes open to human investigation and both are sufficiently self-effacing that the divine voice may not be heard nor the divine hand seen.[129]

1.8 Discourse analysis and Relevance Theory: The problem of context

The previous two sections have been a digression from the main line of our argument, through which we have sought to establish the validity of applying Relevance Theory to biblical text. We now return to consider specifically how RT can contribute to the study of the discourse structure of a text. There are several ways in which discourse analysis is closely related to a relevance-directed study of a text. In the first place Porter leads into his introduction to discourse analysis by stressing the importance of context. Noting the "appreciable distance between the world of the New Testament and the modern world," he comments:

> Whereas there is increasing awareness in many subdisciplines of New Testament study regarding the importance of understanding the complexities of context, many of these studies have not addressed the attendant linguistic issues.[130]

In a footnote on the word "context," he states: "Context itself is a difficult term to define, but here is meant to include at least the sociological, literary, historical, theological and, certainly, linguistic worlds out of which the text(s) emerged."[131]

---

[128] See note 98, p. 35, and note 100, pp. 35-36 above.

[129] This possibility is reflected in the statement of Jesus, quoting Isaiah, that some will "indeed listen, but never understand . . . indeed look, but never perceive" (Matt 13:14; cf. Isa 6:8-9).

[130] Porter, "Discourse Analysis and New Testament Studies," pp. 14-15. The lead-in quote is on p. 14.

[131] Porter, "Discourse Analysis and New Testament Studies," p. 15, note 3.

It is this interest in total context that he finds discourse analysis to address. Speaking of different models of textlinguistic analysis he says:

each defines language usage in terms of its social-semiotic function. In other words, language is seen as an instrument or tool for communication and social interaction. Within a framework of actual usage, language establishes a reciprocal relationship with its setting or context.[132]

Similarly Reed's description of discourse analysis stresses its importance as a study of language in use and focuses on its pragmatic and socio-rhetorical force.[133]

These interests (in context, real language usage, and the pragmatic effects of text) are all shared by RT. But at the heart of all pragmatic analysis is the issue of context, and it is here that many conventional discourse approaches have difficulties. The thesis that RT complements and completes conventional discourse approaches can be supported by an examination of two of the standard and frequently quoted texts on discourse analysis: Brown and Yule's *Discourse Analysis,* and Robert-Alain de Beaugrande and Wolfgang Dressler's *Introduction to Text Linguistics.* Both are extremely interested in the role of context in the interpretation of texts and yet struggle to pin down the way in which context acts, and the limits of its expansion. Both address the pragmatic processes involved in the production and reception of texts and stress the importance of non-textual knowledge, but fall short of a satisfactory explanatory framework. After looking at these approaches more closely, we shall return to examine in further detail the ways in which RT fills the gaps in existing discourse theory and methodology.

1.8.1 Brown and Yule – the identification of context (1983)

Brown and Yule locate their interest firmly in the pragmatics of real communication:

the discourse analyst treats his data as the record (text) of a dynamic process in which language was used as an instrument of

---

[132] Porter, "Discourse Analysis and New Testament Studies," p. 20.
[133] Reed, "Discourse Analysis as New Testament Hermeneutic," pp. 233-35, 237.

communication in a context by a speaker / writer to express meanings and achieve intentions (discourse).[134]

Thus context is of central importance for the understanding of discourse. They distinguish "context of situation" from co-text. The former is described in terms of the real or supposed world within which the communication takes place, and the practical and physical dimensions of the discourse.[135] But the special importance of co-text is underlined:

the main point we are concerned to make is to stress the power of co-text in constraining interpretation. Even in the absence of information about place and time of original utterance, even in the absence of information about the speaker / writer and his intended recipient, it is often possible to reconstruct at least some part of the physical context and to arrive at some interpretation of the text. The more co-text there is, in general, the more secure the interpretation is. Text creates its own context.[136]

Yet context presents the discourse analyst with a problem, namely that in theory it has no limits. There is no rigorous way of limiting how much context needs to be invoked, or of identifying which aspects of context are important for interpretation.[137] The authors handle this problem by appeal to two principles: "local interpretation," which "instructs the hearer not to construct a context any larger than he needs to arrive at an interpretation"; and "analogy," which tells us that what we hear can be expected to conform to our previous experience, or at least can be

---

[134] Brown and Yule, *Discourse Analysis*, p. 26.

[135] Brown and Yule, *Discourse Analysis*, pp. 38-39.

[136] Brown and Yule, *Discourse Analysis*, pp. 49-50. Note that "co-text" is that part of "context" which is formed by the text itself. In view of the confusion sometimes resulting from this terminology, the value of RT's term "cognitive environment" becomes clear.

[137] So, Brown and Yule, *Discourse Analysis*, p. 50, write: "A problem for the discourse analyst must be, then, to decide when a particular feature is relevant to the specification of a particular context and what degree of specification is required. Are there general principles which will determine the relevance or nature of the specification, or does the analyst have to make *ad hoc* judgements on these questions each time he attempts to work on a fragment of discourse?"

interpreted by appeal to types of situation, to analogies.[138] The interaction of these normative human assumptions with the flow of a text is held to constrain and channel the role of context in discourse interpretation, and hearers and readers of a text naturally "attribute relevance and coherence to the text they encounter until they are forced not to."[139]

This discussion is very close to Relevance Theory and yet falls short of the precision and comprehensiveness of Sperber and Wilson's handling of the comprehension process. RT, as has been noted above, provides a definition of context which includes the effect of the situational context, cotext and previous knowledge, but only as each has entered the cognitive processes of the text hearer/reader. Further, the principle of relevance combines and sharpens the two criteria proposed by Brown and Yule.

Similar difficulties are encountered in their handling of the idea of the *topic* of a discourse, which they admit to be highly ambiguous.[140] Their suggested solution is to define a "topic framework" thus:

> Those aspects of the context which are directly reflected in the text, and which need to be called upon to interpret the text, we shall refer to as *activated features of context* and suggest that they constitute the contextual framework within which the topic is constituted, that is, *the topic framework*.[141]

---

[138] Brown and Yule, *Discourse Analysis*, pp. 58-67 (quote from p. 59).

[139] Brown and Yule, *Discourse Analysis*, p. 66. The quote continues: "The normal expectation in the construction and interpretation of discourse is, as Grice suggests, that relevance holds, that the speaker is still speaking of the same place and time, participants and topic, unless he marks a change and shows explicitly whether the changed context is, or is not, relevant to what he has been saying previously. Similarly the normal expectation is that the discourse will be coherent . . . human beings do not require formal textual markers before they are prepared to interpret a text. They naturally assume coherence, and interpret the text in the light of that assumption."

[140] Brown and Yule, *Discourse Analysis*, p. 74, state that "for any practical purposes, there is no such thing as the one correct expression of the topic for any fragment of discourse. There will always be a set of possible expressions of the topic."

[141] Brown and Yule, *Discourse Analysis*, p. 75.

Yet this formulation continues to be somewhat problematical for the discourse topic since the topic framework has been so defined as to exclude elements that are not "directly reflected in the text." Once again the difficulties are overcome by the RT concept of a "mutual cognitive environment." What a discourse, or a part of a discourse, is "about" will be determined by the interaction of the text of the discourse with the hearer/reader's cognitive environment.

Again, in their discussion of the role of previous knowledge and of inference in the understanding of discourse, Brown and Yule foreshadow some important concepts that would be developed by RT, but still fall short of the analytical and predictive power of the idea of relevance. Thus, on the question of how much previous knowledge is used, they say:

> The outstanding problem . . . for the discourse analyst who wishes to represent the interaction between previous knowledge / experience and the comprehension of the discourse at hand, is to reach a working compromise. In this compromise representation, there should be enough richness of detail to capture the potential complexity of our preexisting knowledge / experience, but there should also be a constraint on how much of this richness of detail we actually use in our processing of the discourse we encounter.[142]

And inference produces its own special problems:

> Given [this] 'open-ended' feature of inferencing, it is extremely difficult to provide, for any naturally occurring text, the single set of inferences that an individual reader has made in arriving at an interpretation . . . In other words, the analyst may be left with no secure basis for talking, in analytic as opposed to intuitive terms, about the inferences involved in the comprehension of texts.
>
> This rather bleak conclusion is not intended as a suggestion that the nature of inference is beyond description.[143]

The search for optimal relevance, the balance of processing effort against cognitive effects, would seem to be the way forward which would enable these concepts to be used with precision and power.

---

[142] Brown and Yule, *Discourse Analysis*, pp. 255-56.
[143] Brown and Yule, *Discourse Analysis*, p. 269.

1.8.2 De Beaugrande and Dressler – the limitation of context (1981)

While de Beaugrande and Dressler are also concerned with the role of context in text interpretation, they highlight the way in which syntax, as an autonomous code system for unpacking meaning, produces unmanageable and unreasonable demands on processing time and effort. They propose seven "constitutive principles" for textuality: cohesion, coherence, intentionality, acceptability, informativity, situationality, and intertextuality.[144] But to these must be added the regulative principles of efficiency, effectiveness, and appropriateness:

> The EFFICIENCY of a text depends on its use in communicating with a minimum expenditure of effort by the participants. The EFFECTIVENESS of a text depends on its leaving a strong impression and creating favourable conditions for attaining a goal. The APPROPRIATENESS of a text is the agreement between its setting and the ways in which the standards of textuality are upheld.[145]

Clearly their term "efficiency" relates (inversely) to the Relevance Theory concept of processing effort, while "effectiveness" is close to the idea of cognitive effects, and "appropriateness" describes something of the relevance relationships of the text to the cognitive environment of the hearer. Yet de Beaugrande and Dressler perceive a fundamental opposition between efficiency and effectiveness:

> Procedurally, **efficiency** contributes to *processing ease*, that is, the running of operations with a light load on resources of attention and access. **Effectiveness** elicits *processing depth*, that is, intense use of resources of attention and access on materials removed from the explicit surface representation. **Appropriateness** is a factor determining the correlation between the current occasion and the standards of textuality such that reliable estimates can be made regarding ease or depth of participants' processing. Notice that efficiency and effectiveness tend to work against each other . . . Hence, appropriateness must mediate between these opposed factors to indicate the proper balance

---

[144] de Beaugrande and Dressler, *Text Linguistics*, pp. 3-10.
[145] de Beaugrande and Dressler, *Text Linguistics*, p. 11.

between the conventional and the unconventional in each situation.[146]

While this is in many ways similar to the analysis proposed by Sperber and Wilson, RT does not see efficiency and effectiveness as quite so clearly opposed to each other. Efficiency may in fact create effectiveness. The ease with which a text can be processed may increase the cognitive effects obtained and thus contribute to the text a high degree of relevance.

With regard to the actual processes involved in understanding a text, de Beaugrande and Dressler emphasize the rapid, unwieldy expansion of possible pathways of interpretation, given only the constraints of syntax:

> Tests show that a language model in which syntax is autonomous cannot function in real time because of COMBINATORIAL EXPLOSION: an immense over-computation of alternative structures and readings that run into astronomically vast operating times . . . The production and reception of a text of greater length, if they had to be done without interaction of language levels and cognitive or situational factors, would seem to be little short of a miracle.[147]

This miracle is made somewhat more credible when context is defined as cognitive environment and relevance made the guiding criterion for discourse interpretation. Hence, as we saw with Brown and Yule, de Beaugrande and Dressler deal with exactly the same problems as are addressed by Sperber and Wilson, and while in some ways they come closer to RT, they are still left with unresolved tensions in understanding the way discourses are interpreted, tensions that RT focuses on and brings to more precise theoretical and explanatory resolution.[148]

---

[146] de Beaugrande and Dressler, *Text Linguistics*, p. 34 (emphasis theirs).

[147] de Beaugrande and Dressler, *Text Linguistics*, pp. 32-33. The autonomy of syntax would mean that the meaning of a text is derived from its syntactic form, unconstrained by considerations of context or by any limits to the time and effort expended in analyzing it.

[148] The similarities between de Beaugrande and Dressler on the one hand, and Sperber and Wilson on the other, extend to a number of other considerations and may be due to the fact that they too work with cognitive theories of text processing. Note especially de Beaugrande and

1.9 Relevance Theory in discourse analysis

Regina Blass has developed the application of Relevance Theory to discourse analysis pioneered by Blakemore.[149] Blass begins from the same point as Sperber and Wilson, namely the importance of the entire cognitive context for understanding communication. But instead of single utterances, her focus is now on the interpretation of entire discourses, including the contribution of discourse structure to discourse meaning. She argues that discourse meaning and discourse structure are not inherent in the text, thought of as a set of linguistic signs (words spoken or marks on paper), but in the interaction between the text and the context.[150]

It is precisely because cohesion (surface-level, grammatical relationships) and coherence (deeper, meaning-based relationships) fail to take adequate account of context that neither can give a satisfying explanation of the way discourses are understood:

> the existence of coherence relations is neither necessary nor sufficient for comprehension. The appeal to coherence is superfluous: coherence relations, like cohesion relations, are merely a superficial symptom of something deeper, which is itself the key to comprehension . . . what is crucial to discourse comprehension is the recognition of relevance relations, which are relations between the content of an utterance and its context.[151]

Neither is "topic" (which as we have already seen is acknowledged even by discourse analysts to be a problematic concept) a feature of discourses which can be identified from within the text of the discourse and used as a means of analyzing its structure or content:

Dressler's (*Text Linguistics*) treatment of intentionality (p. 123), situationality (pp. 163, 179), and the interaction of stored-knowledge and text-presented knowledge (pp. 202-206).

[149] Blass, *Relevance relations*; see Blakemore, *Semantic Constraints*; Blakemore, "Organisation."

[150] Blass, *Relevance relations*, pp. 9-10: "Discourse analysis can therefore not be a purely linguistic matter; it necessarily involves an analysis of the role of context in the interpretation process."

[151] Blass, *Relevance relations*, p. 24-25.

Brown and Yule seem to see discourse analysis like a jigsaw puzzle . . . However, Brown and Yule seem to forget that in the case of text there are two "pictures" involved. One is in the mind of the speaker, the other will be in the mind of the hearer, and they are not necessarily the same. In processing a text, the speaker is concerned about which picture the hearer will construct, and takes his assumptions into account. It cannot be assumed that every text provides enough content for anyone who reads it to activate the right context, so that a discourse analyst will be able to complete the puzzle. Neither picture nor context is fixed in advance, and there is no reason to think that the text itself provides all the necessary clues. There is no one-to-one relation between the content of the text and the intended context, and . . . the identification of a topic depends on context as well as on content.[152]

Now it is undeniable that all discourse analysts emphasize the importance of context, as we have seen in the two cases discussed above. What they appear to lack is an adequate definition of context and an adequate model to describe and predict the choice and limitation of context, which clearly takes place in any communication. Here Blass repeats for extended discourse what Sperber and Wilson established in the case of shorter utterances, and which may be summed up as follows:

(1) Context is neither simply the "context of situation" (a vague and ill-defined notion) nor simply the co-text, but the sets of mental representations (including mental representations of situation and co-text) that form the cognitive environment within which a text is processed.

Notice that I am not rejecting the view that physical, social and cultural factors play a major role in utterance interpretation. Of course they do. I am claiming, however, that they affect interpretation by affecting the individual's assumptions about the world. Physical, social and cultural assumptions are just some of the many types of assumptions of which the context for utterance interpretation is composed.[153]

---

[152] Blass, *Relevance relations*, pp. 28.
[153] Blass, *Relevance relations*, p. 31.

(2) This cognitive environment is not preselected or given, but is constructed in the course of the hermeneutic process in order to maximize relevance.

The notions of contextual effect and processing effort are very important for discourse analysis. As a discourse proceeds, the hearer works out the contextual effect of the newly presented information in a context retrieved or derived from memory and perception. These contextual effects and new assumptions then become part of the context in which later stretches of the discourse are processed. Selection of a context will be affected by the twin aims of minimising processing effort and maximising contextual effect. Thus relevance theory suggests an answer, not only to the traditional pragmatic problems for which Grice's maxims have been used, but also for the problem of context selection, which . . . has defeated so many pragmatic theories.[154]

(3) The initial context gives access to ever widening circles of context as parts of the discourse are processed and they in turn give access to further assumptions and to knowledge derived from both perception and memory. This expansion of context, however, is not unrestrained but subject to the principle of relevance. Just sufficient context will be activated to obtain optimal relevance for the text being processed. This allows for the importance of co-text and yet at the same time both expands and limits the potential sources of contextual assumptions used in understanding the text.

A cognitive and dynamic understanding of context combined with the principle of relevance therefore provides precisely what was lacking in the previous discussions of discourse analysis.

It needs to be noted here that we have moved, with Blass and RT, from a narrow to a broader understanding of what is meant by "discourse analysis." Rather than a concern simply for the surface structure of a discourse, Blass argues that discourse analysis is a process of retracing the hearer's steps in understanding the text:

I do not share Brown and Yule's view that data-based discourse analysis is something quite different from the investigation of the hearer's task in processing . . . Although Brown and Yule

---

[154] Blass, *Relevance relations*, p. 53.

criticise analyses which look only at texts, they seem to assume that there is a way of analysing discourse without reference to what the hearer does in understanding it . . . However, to me, discourse analysis is nothing else *but* tracing the hearer's part in understanding utterances, and I claim that any other approach either yields uninteresting statements of statistical frequency, or is like going on a journey without a destination in mind.[155]

When it comes to the question of how to "do discourse analysis" within the framework of RT, Blass is tantalizingly brief. Her own study is mainly concerned with the discourse function of certain particles in a West African language and she only begins to open the door on the wider possibilities of her theoretical position. However, she does provide certain important starting points, largely made with respect to narrative discourses, but which clearly have wider validity.

First, bringing RT to bear on the understanding of discourse does not involve abandoning previous ways of looking at and analyzing text, but instead sharpens their focus. For example, discourse analysts will talk of the "staging" of a discourse, or the way in which the parts of a discourse are ordered in order to produce a variety of effects such as climax, and the ways in which this staging process can be used to partition the discourse.[156] Blass says:

It is the aim of the speaker to optimise relevance over a discourse; that is, to achieve adequate contextual effects for the minimum justifiable processing effort. This makes it reasonable to introduce all contextual assumptions needed to establish the main point of the discourse before the climax itself is reached; where there are several peaks of relevance, perhaps culminating in a single, overall peak, the result should be the sort of paragraph structure so often noted in narrative texts.[157]

Thus, secondly, it is meaningful to talk of the paragraph structure of a discourse and the connectivity that creates it, including both cohesion

---

[155] Blass, *Relevance relations*, p. 11 (emphasis hers).

[156] On "staging" see Brown and Yule, *Discourse Analysis*, pp. 125-52; Grimes, *Thread of Discourse*, pp. 117-35, 323-36.

[157] Blass, *Relevance relations*, p. 77.

and coherence, but more as well. What defines text units is now identity or similarity of cognitive environment. Text units are units of relevance.

> Typically, within a paragraph of narrative, there is a continuity of context in the following sense: information made easily accessible by the interpretation of the first utterance is used in establishing the relevance of the second . . . and so on indefinitely . . . [This information consists of] first, the contextual assumptions used in establishing the relevance of an utterance, second, the content of the utterance itself, and third, its contextual effects.[158]

Finally, we can examine a whole discourse for its relevance. This is both a unifying concept for the discourse and an orienting principle for its various component parts:

> In the case of a planned narrative, for example, it seems reasonable to assume that the speaker tries to optimise relevance over the narrative as a whole. In this case one could talk of the narrative as a whole as consistent or inconsistent with the principle of relevance . . . every part of a narrative must be there for a reason, and within relevance theory there are only a few possible reasons to consider: either it must be relevant in its own right, or it must contribute to the relevance of later stretches of discourse.[159]

In one sense then, using Blass's description, the whole effort of biblical exegesis and hermeneutics could be described as discourse analysis—an attempt to follow the cognitive processes of the earliest readers. But in this work we are particularly concerned with the structuring of a text. What makes certain parts of the discourse cohere with each other more than with other parts? Using the insights of RT it is now clear that the structural units which contribute to meaning at every level, from the smallest to the whole text, can be defined as sections of text over which there is an optimization of relevance. Hierarchical and coordinate relationships between structural units will also be such as to optimize relevance for the complex of such units being considered.

---

[158] Blass, *Relevance relations*, p. 78.
[159] Blass, *Relevance relations*, p. 79.

Discourse analysis, then, is inherently pragmatic and it is this drive to understand texts within the pragmatics of real communication which leads us to the principle of relevance as the primary criterion for discourse structure.[160] In searching for optimal relevance over the various levels of discourse structure of a biblical text, it needs to be clearly understood that we are primarily seeking to uncover the relevance to the original readers, which I have earlier called synchronic relevance. However, we do it, of necessity, from within our own cognitive environment and there are considerations of this diachronic relevance which inevitably affect our view. The hope of insights into the relevance perceived by the original readers rests on a number of assumptions. Fundamentally we assume that human thought processes, in particular logical and inferential processes, are to some degree universal and unbounded by local and temporal conditioning. Thus what appears to us as a logical or inferential relationship we assume would have appeared so to first century A.D. readers/hearers as well. Second, we assume that we can reconstruct a sufficient amount of the cognitive environment of the first readers/hearers to make meaningful statements about their probable perceptions of relevance. But Blass has argued correctly that in the absence of contextual information it is valid to construct a hypothetical context if we can show that this leads to optimal relevance for the text.[161] In fact we will most often be working with cognitive environments that are a mix of evidenced and hypothetical contextual assumptions. The test of our hypotheses will be the degree of relevance obtained for the text.[162] There remains an unavoidable degree of opacity of the original context, however, in that we don't know what we are lacking about it. We can

---

[160] These ideas will be pressed into the service of discourse analysis in chapters 3–5 below. On the application of RT to discourse analysis, see further Christoph Unger, "The scope of discourse connectives: implications for discourse organization," *JLing* 32 (1996): 403-438. For a defense of the RT approach to the study of discourse structure, see Deirdre Wilson, "Discourse, coherence and relevance: A reply to Rachel Giora," *JPrag* 29 (1998): 57-74, who writes in reply to criticisms by Rachel Giora, "Discourse coherence and theory of relevance: Stumbling blocks in search of a unified theory," *JPrag* 27 (1997): 17-34.

[161] Blass, *Relevance relations*, p. 31.

[162] The validity of this test rests, of course, on the fundamental assumption described above.

construct positive aspects of contexts with a greater or lesser degree of probability, but we have no way of knowing what additional parameters, whether features of the situational environment, or earlier texts, or relational assumptions, have simply disappeared without trace.

These considerations have some implications for the way we analyze discourse:

(1) The context within which the structure of a text is understood is the mutually manifest cognitive environment. This is composed of the co-text, the situational context, the intertextual relationships, as they have become a part of both the author's and audience's mental geography.

(2) Text units, or integral text sequences, are units over which relevance is optimized. This applies to both large and small units.

(3) Relationships perceived between text units are those relationships that optimize relevance. This means that significant contextual effects are experienced for acceptably low processing effort.

(4) More complex relationships should only be postulated where there is a failure to account for the presence of a particular feature by means of linking to the most readily accessible cognitive environment.

(5) The significance of discourse markers is always that which optimizes relevance. This means, for example, that in Revelation μετὰ ταῦτα ("after these things") does not always operate on the same level. The referent of "these things" will be such as to maximize cognitive effects for minimal processing effort.

These general remarks will suffice for the present. The more specific ways in which considerations of relevance affect an understanding of discourse structure will become apparent when we approach the text in chapters 3–5. It will be seen then that, far from replacing conventional discourse analytic techniques, an appreciation of relevance enhances them and gives added assurance of their validity.

58

Chapter 2

The Structure of the Apocalypse: A Selective Review

2.1 Introduction: The relevance of discourse analysis

It is a consequence of the basic premises of Relevance Theory that a relevance-theoretic study of an extended text should begin with an analysis of the discourse structure of that text. Both RT and discourse analysis are pragmatic accounts of language, rooted firmly in the realities of actual, situational discourse, and they stress the importance of context (or "cognitive environment" in RT terms) for discourse interpretation. Co-text, though only one of the possible sources of contextual assumptions, is nevertheless an extremely important one. But how much of the co-text is accessed in constructing meaning? How far back does the audience roam in searching for clues to the identity of a referent? Are there natural boundaries in the text beyond which the search will not normally stray without a significant increase of processing effort? Can a much earlier text segment form the context for interpreting a later one if the two are clearly linked by markers of surface-level cohesion or semantic coherence? Questions such as these are central to the reconstruction of cognitive environments, which is a prerequisite for interpreting the text using RT. Such questions in turn, require us to look at the syntactic and semantic structure of the text, to "do discourse analysis." In particular we will be interested in a discourse segmentation approach that analyses the text into hierarchically linked segments and explores the relationship between these segments.[1]

---

[1] For an example of this approach on another NT book, see Guthrie, "Cohesion Shifts." It is the primary approach, as we shall see shortly, of Hellholm, "Problem," and is also the approach reflected in (or assumed

But more specifically still, the overall focus of my studies in the book of Revelation is the role played by the people of God in the book. I want to explore the way in which the listeners of the book found themselves addressed and the ways in which they might have related to the characters in the vision narratives. How were they attracted to listen, what personal relevance might they have perceived in the visions, and how were they motivated by the vision accounts? In order to answer these questions, it is necessary to identify the participants of each communication level of the text, and of each scene within the vision narrative.[2] Pronominal reference is a notorious source of ambiguity in text, and in studying Revelation there is the added difficulty of the cryptic and varied nature of much of the language.[3] A discourse approach that focuses on the role and relationship of participants in the text is thus a necessary starting point.[4] Such an approach cannot be divorced from the kind of segmentation analysis already proposed. Participant structure contributes to discourse segmentation and is in turn affected by it.[5] Thus although they are two theoretically distinct approaches, I will make no attempt to keep the two separate.

In this chapter I will review several structural studies on the Apocalypse which are of particular interest, before attempting in the succeeding chapters to elucidate the semantic-pragmatic structure of Revelation,

---

by) the "Discourse Segmentation Analysis" level of footnotes in *The Greek New Testament* (ed. Barbara Aland et al.; 4th rev. edn.; Stuttgart: Deutsche Bibelgesellschaft and United Bible Societies, 1993).

[2] I use "participant" here in the sense of a human or other intelligent being, rather than in the broader linguistic sense in which any nominal or pronominal entity can be considered a participant.

[3] It is worth noting too that pronouns are only one manifestation of the more general class of "pro-forms," which stand in for other words and may include pro-verbs, pro-adjectives, etc. See de Beaugrande and Dressler, *Text Linguistics*, pp. 60-66. The referential function of any of these pro-forms may be problematical, but will be closely dependent on context, and thus requires relevance-guided discourse analysis.

[4] For an example of this type of discourse analysis, see Reed, "To Timothy or Not?"

[5] For the first direction of influence, note that Hellholm, "Problem," p. 47, includes among his markers of discourse segmentation "changes in (grouping of) agents."

with special regard to participants, using the principle of relevance as a significant criterion.

2.2 Previous structural studies

The structure of the book of Revelation has both intrigued and frustrated generations of commentators and scholars, justifying G. K. Beale's comment, "The diverse proposals are a maze of interpretative confusion."[6]

---

[6] G. K. Beale, *The Book of Revelation* (NIGTC; Grand Rapids: Eerdmans, 1999), p. 108. Beale's commentary provides a comprehensive and helpful review of structural work on the Apocalypse (pp. 108-135, 141-44), as well as advancing his own proposal (pp. 135-41, 152-70), which will be examined later. For another useful analysis of structural approaches based around 13 different "organising principles," see Ekkehardt Müller, *Microstructural Analysis of Revelation 4-11* (AUSDDS 21; Berrien Springs, Mich.: Andrews University Press, 1996), pp. 13-27. Apart from the commentaries, significant works consulted in the course of this study, which relate to the overall structure of the book, include: Richard Bauckham, *The Climax of Prophecy: Studies on the Book of Revelation* (Edinburgh: T. & T. Clark, 1993), pp. 1-37; G. K. Beale, "The Influence of Daniel upon the Structure and Theology of John's Apocalypse," *JETS* 27 (1984): 413-23; G. K. Beale, "The Interpretive Problem of Rev. 1:19," *NovT* 34 (1992): 360-87; John W. Bowman, "The Revelation to John: Its Dramatic Structure and Message," *Int* 9 (1955): 436-53; Austin Farrer, *A Rebirth of Images: The Making of St. John's Apocalypse* (Westminster: Dacre Press, 1949); Charles H. Giblin, "Recapitulation and the Literary Coherence of John's Apocalypse," *CBQ* 56 (1994): 81-95; M. D. Goulder, "The Apocalypse as an Annual Cycle of Prophecies," *NTS* 27 (1981): 342-67; Lars Hartman, "Form and Message: A Preliminary Discussion of 'Partial Texts' in Rev 1–3 and 22, 6ff." in *L'Apocalypse johannique et l'Apocalyptique dans le Nouveau Testament* (ed. J. Lambrecht; BETL 53; Gembloux, Belgium: J. Duculot, 1980), pp. 129-49; Hellholm, "Problem"; Jan Lambrecht, "A Structuration of Revelation 4, 1–22, 5," in *L'Apocalypse johannique et l'Apocalyptique dans le Nouveau Testament* (ed. J. Lambrecht; BETL 53; Gembloux, Belgium: J. Duculot, 1980), pp. 77-104; Ralph J. Korner, " 'And I Saw . . .' An Apocalyptic Literary Convention for Structural Identification in the Apocalypse," *NovT* 42 (2000): 160-83; Michelle V. Lee, "A Call to Martyrdom:

61

Analyses of the structure of Revelation earlier in the twentieth century tended to be distracted by the concerns of source and tradition criticism.[7] Elisabeth Schüssler Fiorenza has highlighted the inadequacies of such approaches.[8] Redaction and composition criticism have the advantage of treating the work as a deliberate construction, rather than an arbitrary compilation, and yet the focus is often still on the individual components and the way they have been put together, rather than on the artistry of the whole.[9] Schüssler Fiorenza moves the discussion forward by attention to explicit linguistic markers, and by suggesting the patterns of seven and the techniques of "intercalation" and "interlude" as fundamental structural devices in the book.[10] Finding John Gager's attempts at a

---

Function as Method and Message in Revelation," *NovT* 40 (1998): 165-94; James L. Resseguie, *Revelation Unsealed: A Narrative Critical Approach to John's Apocalypse* (Biblical Interpretation Series 32; Leiden: E. J. Brill, 1998), pp. 160-66; Elisabeth Schüssler Fiorenza, "Composition and Structure of the Book of Revelation," *CBQ* 39 (1977): 344-66; Christopher R. Smith, "The Structure of the Book of Revelation in Light of Apocalyptic Literary Conventions," *NovT* 36 (1994): 373-93; L. C. Spinks, "A Critical Examination of J. W. Bowman's Proposed Structure of the Revelation," *EvQ* 50 (1978): 211-22; Kenneth A. Strand, "Chiastic Structure and Some Motifs in the Book of Revelation," *AUSS* 16 (1978): 401-408; Kenneth A. Strand, "The Eight Basic Visions in the Book of Revelation," *AUSS* 25 (1987): 107-121; Robert Surridge, "Redemption in the Structure of Revelation," *ExpTim* 101 (1990): 231-35; Ugo Vanni, *La struttura letteraria dell' Apocalisse* (2nd edn.; Aloisiana 8a; Brescia, Italy: Morcelliana, 1980); Ernst R. Wendland, "7 X 7 (X 7): A Structural and Thematic Outline of John's Apocalypse," *OPTAT* 4 (1990): 371-87; Adela Yarbro Collins, *The Combat Myth in the Book of Revelation* (HDR 9; Missoula, Mont.: Scholars Press, 1976), pp. 5-55. Other works, dealing with individual sections, will be listed as they are encountered.

[7] For further bibliographical information, see Schüssler Fiorenza, "Composition," pp. 345-50, and the notes there. Note that this essay can also be found as chapter 6 in Elisabeth Schüssler Fiorenza, *The Book of Revelation: Justice and Judgment* (Philadelphia: Fortress Press, 1985), pp. 159-80. The page numbers given here are for the *CBQ* article.

[8] Schüssler Fiorenza, "Composition," pp. 344-58.

[9] See, e.g. Schüssler Fiorenza, "Composition," pp. 350-54.

[10] Schüssler Fiorenza, "Composition," pp. 358-66. It is not entirely clear how she distinguishes between "interludes" and "intercalations," so the

structuralist approach inadequate, she proposes her own, which focuses on the central importance of the "small prophetic scroll," whose contents she finds in 10:1–15:4.[11] The final outcome of her analysis is a chiastic pattern which underscores that the main function of Revelation "is the prophetic interpretation of the political and religious situation of the community."[12] Whether or not her analysis is accepted, the significance of this work is that it anchors the purpose of the book firmly in the very structural framework.[13] Yet even this important work pays inadequate attention to the actual linguistic discourse structure of the text. In common with most other commentators and scholars, Schüssler Fiorenza passes lightly over the linguistic markers on the way to higher levels of semantic patterning, and the chiastic structure she arrives at requires a

---

name intercalation perhaps should be reserved for what she call a "double intercalation" (p. 361). An intercalation is a construction in which two text sequences, A and B, are interlocked (the term used by Yarbro Collins, *Combat Myth*, pp. 16-19), so that the concluding part of A occurs after the opening of B. This could be diagrammed in the form [A___A][B][A][B___B].

[11] Schüssler Fiorenza, "Composition," pp. 354-55, 362-64; cf. John G. Gager, *Kingdom and Community: The Social World of Early Christianity* (Englewood Cliffs, N.J.: Prentice-Hall, 1975), pp. 49-57. For a discussion of the relationship of structuralist and historical exegesis with respect to the book of Revelation, see P. Prigent, "L'Apocalypse: exégèse historique et analyse structurale," *NTS* 26 (1979): 127-37.

[12] Schüssler Fiorenza, "Composition," p. 366. Overall chiastic structures are also proposed for Revelation by Nils W. Lund, *Chiasmus in the New Testament: A Study in the Form and Function of Chiastic Structures* (Chapel Hill: University of North Carolina Press, 1942; repr., Peabody, Mass.: Hendrickson, 1992), pp. 321-30; Strand, "Chiastic Structure"; Strand, "Eight Basic Visions"; and Lee, "Call to Martyrdom."

[13] Lee, "Call to Martyrdom," similarly emphasizes the importance of structure for meaning and function, in this case the centrality of two segments, Rev 13:1-18 and 14:1-20, each of which represents a "Moment of Decision" (p. 174). Note, however, that a significantly different type of structural analysis is possible, represented by Lambrecht, "Structuration," in which later septets are embedded within earlier ones. We shall return to this issue in our detailed examination of the structure in the following chapter.

rearrangement of text units which seriously undermines its credibility.[14] The processing effort required to benefit from the proposed structure appears to outweigh the cognitive effects produced. There are only a few exceptions to this general tendency to undervalue the surface structure of the text. We will examine in some detail the work of David Hellholm on the textlinguistic structure of Revelation (largely a macrosyntactic exercise) and that of Ekkehardt Müller on the microstructure of the book. To these must be added briefer notes on Lars Hartman's work, which anticipates Hellholm, on Eugene Boring's examination of the voices in Revelation, on a paper by Wendland, and on the contributions of recent commentaries by David Aune and Beale.[15]

2.3 Hellholm's textlinguistic approach

Hellholm's work is directed toward a definition of the apocalyptic genre, seeking to amplify the earlier definition of John Collins by adding a description of the function of an apocalypse.[16] But he approaches the subject from a textlinguistic perspective in which the aspects of form, content and function are represented by syntactics, semantics and pragmatics respectively. Among the significant results which emerge is the fact that individual text sequences are related not merely syntagmatically but also hierarchically to one another. This is paralleled by a hierarchy of communication levels. The most deeply embedded level of the text of Revelation, which is also at the highest communication level, is

---

[14] Lee's analysis avoids the problem of rearrangement, but still appears to ignore certain overt structuring signals.

[15] David E. Aune, *Revelation 1–5* (WBC 52A; Dallas: Word, 1997); Beale, *Revelation*.

[16] For the original definition, see John J. Collins, "Introduction: Towards the Morphology of a Genre," *Semeia* 14 (1979): 9. Hellholm, "Problem," proposes to extend the definition by adding, *"intended for a group in crisis with the purpose of exhortation and/or consolation by means of divine authority* (p. 27)." Aune, "Problem of Genre," finds Hellholm's definition of function inadequate. While the details of his argument are not central to our purpose at this point, it should be noted that his article provides a relatively easy way into Hellholm's work, which he rightly characterizes as "exceedingly complex" (p. 70). See also the discussion of genre in Pattemore, "The People of God," pp. 7-8.

21:5-8, the speech of God from the throne, which thus contains the central message of the book.[17]

While there has been recognition of the importance of Hellholm's work, one of the striking features of the literature is the almost complete silence regarding either the detail of his method, or the result of his text delimitation.[18] It seems necessary, therefore, to give some more detailed attention to Hellholm's methods and results.

Hellholm adopts (conceptually if not terminologically) Kurt Baldinger's helpful distinction between "semasiological" and "onomasiological" approaches to text, corresponding to the receiver's and the sender's perspective respectively.[19] While the scholar must be able to account for both

---

[17] Hellholm, "Problem," pp. 43-44. Having previously found a similar structure in *The Shepherd of Hermas*, Hellholm concludes that this kind of embeddedness is characteristic of the genre, and is part of its strategy of authentication. For his work on *Hermas*, see David Hellholm, *Das Visionenbuch des Hermas als Apokalypse: Formesgeschichtliche und texttheoretische Studien zu einer literarischen Gattung* (vol. 1 of *Methodologische Vorüberlegungen und makrostrukurelle Textanalyse*; ConBNT 13:1; Lund, Sweden: CWK Gleerup, 1980).

[18] Note comments by Aune, "Problem of Genre," pp. 70-78; and John M. Court, *Revelation* (NT Guides; Sheffield: JSOT Press, 1994), pp. 80-81. A decade and a half since she wrote it, the assessment of Adela Yarbro Collins, "Introduction: Early Christian Apocalypticism," *Semeia* 36 (1986): 4, remains pertinent: "Hellholm's text-linguistic analyses of *Hermas* and Revelation have not yet received the close scrutiny which they deserve. His analysis of the book of Revelation especially is abbreviated and preliminary. Before it can be taken as definitive, he must show that it is actually based on scientific linguistic criteria and not, at crucial points, on intuitive criteria similar to those used in previous analyses of the composition and structure of Revelation."

[19] Kurt Baldinger, *Semantic Theory: Towards a Modern Semantics* (ed. Roger Wright; trans. William C. Brown; Oxford: Basil Blackwell, 1980), p. 132, says of the distinction between the sender's and receiver's tasks that it "correspond[s] exactly to the opposition . . . between semasiology and onomasiology. The hearer receives from his interlocutor forms, the meaning of which he must determine in order to understand them. Thus, the hearer's task is semasiological. The speaker, on the other hand, has to communicate mental objects (concepts). He must select designations from the vocabulary placed at his disposal by his memory; he must link

aspects, there is a degree of priority accorded to the semasiological because even the scholar finds himself confronted not with a structural analysis, still less an insight into the mind of the sender, but simply the text. Thus for the scholar as well as the original receiver the

> macro-structure must be recognizable on the surface level, since the receiver 'obtains from the author neither a macro-structure nor a text deep structure but a text *tel quel*. Consequently there must exist signals—called delimitation markers—by means of which the reader or listener can arrive at such a macro-structure.'[20]

Thus Hellholm's approach recognizes the fundamental importance of "the delimitation of texts into *functional text-sequences* of different ranks . . . by means of hierarchically ranked delimitation markers on the surface level."[21]

Hellholm describes text as a woven fabric (*textus* = web) with warp and woof. The warp is the micro-syntagmatic structure. The woof is the macro-syntagmatic structure, which itself is made of two components that must be independently determined: hierarchically arranged communication levels and hierarchically arranged text sequences of different ranks.[22] Together these require a three dimensional analysis of text.

Hellholm proceeds to define the markers that delimit text sequences and distinguishes the levels on which they operate in ascending order as text-level, abstraction-level and meta-level. Those at the meta-level, signaling information about the text itself, are highly significant for

---

concepts to acoustic images, so converging them into *significants*; that is, his task is onomasiological." See Hellholm, "Problem," pp. 29-31.

[20] Hellholm, "Problem," p. 32, quoting Elisabeth Gülich and Wolfgang Raible, *Linguistische Textmodelle: Grundlagen und Möglichkeiten* (Uni-Taschenbücher 130; Munich: Fink, 1977), p. 163. At this point Hellholm, and the textlinguists he quotes, must be criticized from a relevance-theoretic standpoint, because they fail to take into account the context within which the text is both sent and received. This does not diminish the importance of the surface-level text delimitation, but does question the basis on which this is done. See the earlier discussion of the importance of RT to discourse analysis, pp. 45-58 above, and further below, pp. 189-91.

[21] Hellholm, "Problem," p. 32 (italics his).

[22] Hellholm, "Problem," p. 36.

delimiting the text into not just a sequence of text units but a hierarchically arranged sequence. They include, most importantly, substitutions on the meta-level, such as μετὰ ταῦτα, where a whole text unit is substituted by a pronoun. Other delimitation markers are classed as changes in the "set of worlds," episode markers (both temporal and spatial), changes in the grouping of agents (which he sees as more significant than changes in individual actors), renominalization, and connectors (such as adverbs and conjunctions).[23]

Within the text of Revelation, Hellholm identifies the six most important communication levels, which act as meta-levels for other levels, as those between the author and the general Christian audience, between the author and the seven churches, between otherworldly mediators and the author, between the "heavenly scroll" and the author, between otherworldly mediators and the author within the "heavenly scroll," and between God and the author within the "heavenly scroll."[24] He proceeds to discuss the most embedded text, 21:5-8, which turns out to coincide with the highest ranking of text sequence and thus is the focal point of the whole Apocalypse, functioning to authorize the text and to provide for the recipients of the book both the promise of vindication and the threat of exclusion from the holy city.

This analysis calls for some immediate response. First, we may ask whether in fact the communication levels Hellholm lists are truly embedded within one another. In particular it is not obvious that the later events of communication between otherworldly mediators and the author occur *within* the communication level between the scroll and the author. And does the scroll really communicate with the author at all? To test his analysis we have only one place to go—to the text itself, to examine how the passages in question are linked together. But here we are already venturing into Hellholm's second, and supposedly independent, macrosyntagmatic axis, that of hierarchically arranged text sequences. The communication levels cannot be determined without regard to the delimitation of text sequences. Nor, for that matter, can the text sequences be delimited and arranged without regard to the communication situations envisaged. The two axes are not independent. These two significant features of the text interact with each other so as to make the coincidence of

---

[23] Hellholm, "Problem," pp. 38-42. By "set of worlds" he intends locations within which the text can function: this world, either as it really is or in a fictional extension, or other worlds (see pp. 40-41).

[24] Hellholm, "Problem," pp. 43-44.

deep embedding with high text-rank not as significant as Hellholm supposed. We shall return to this point in the course of examining the text-sequential analysis.

Hellholm displays, without detailed justification, his analysis of the macrostructure of the Apocalypse into hierarchically ranked text sequences.[25] While the display itself is not easy to follow, it does provide a compact overview of the proposed structure.[26] Perhaps the best way to appreciate both the strengths and weaknesses of Hellholm's analysis is first to collapse the display to the lowest grade and then expand it step by step to include progressively higher grades of text sequences.[27]

---

[25] Hellholm, "Problem," pp. 47-52. The displays that follow in my critique are all simplifications of Hellholm's display on these pages and no further references will be given. For the sake of clarity I have left out some detail and exaggerated the indentation. Note that while Hellholm uses the neologism "textsequence" I will normally keep the two words separate, unless directly quoting.

[26] Few attempts to display the detailed structure of large sections of text end up being easily readable. Hellholm's display suffers from a double redundancy. *First*, there is the constant repetition of "TS," standing for "textsequence." But because every part of the text is a text sequence it plays no discriminatory role and, in a later work, Hellholm uses a similar methodology, but his abbreviation is "ST," which this time stands for "Sub-text" (Hellholm, "Amplificatio"). *Second*, the number to the left of TS is the rank of the text sequence, which is also given by the length of the string of numbers to the right of TS, and by the indentation of the text. Thus it conveys no new information and yet contributes to the complexity of the display. To these redundancies we might add the complaint that the string of numbers after the TS becomes almost unreadable after about 5 levels; for example, a ninth-grade text sequence is displayed as: $9TS^{222226221}$ New Heaven and New Earth (21:1-8).

We may be glad that he has not given us any higher grades, though he must suppose them since the section he classifies as of highest rank, 21:5-8, is obviously a higher grade within this one.

[27] A certain ambivalence of spatial metaphor becomes apparent here. It seems to me most natural to think of progressive embedment as "deeper," and of minor text sequences as being "below" the major ones in which they are included. Hellholm's analysis is typical of the "top-down" approach as defined by John Beekman and John Callow, *Translating the Word of God* (Grand Rapids: Zondervan, 1974), pp. 278-81. But Hellholm

The lowest grade encompasses the entire Apocalypse, but whereas one would expect this text sequence to be composed of a series of higher-grade text sequences, which together make up the whole, it is deficient at the next level, where there is only one entry:

^{00}TS Apocalypse 1:1–22:21
  ^{0}TS Prologue 1:1-3

The "first-grade" sequences, which comprise the rest of the Apocalypse, are thus hierarchically subordinated to the Prologue. There is no difficulty in envisaging this from the point of view of communication situations since the Prologue stands as title over, and introduces, the embedded letter. But this means that communication levels are being made determinative for the text sequence hierarchy, and Hellholm has claimed them as independent ways of analyzing the text. In terms of text sequences proper, we would expect the whole Apocalypse to be composed of two first-degree text sequences in this way:

^{0}TS Apocalypse 1:1–22:21
  ^{1}TS^1 Prologue 1:1-3
  ^{1}TS^2 Letter 1:4–22:21

Everything else would then be embedded one further level.[28]
Reverting to Hellholm's numbering, we expand the display as far as the first-grade sequences:

^{00}TS Apocalypse 1:1–22:21
  ^{0}TS Prologue 1:1-3
      ^{1}TS^1 Epistolary prescript 1:4-8
      ^{1}TS^2 Visionary part 1:9–22:5
      ^{1}TS^3 Epilogue in form of vision authentication 22:6-20
      ^{1}TS^4 Epistolary postscript 22:21

This analysis into first-grade text sequences is relatively uncontroversial, with the exception of the boundary between ^{1}TS^2 and ^{1}TS^3, which ignores the obvious parallels between 17:1–19:10 and 21:9–22:9.[29]

---

regards the whole book as the "lowest" and the finest divisions as the "highest," inverting the pyramid. To avoid confusion we will use his perspective throughout this section.

[28] This is similar to the proposal put forward by Hartman, "Form and Message," p. 140.

Expanding our summary display to include the second-grade text sequences reveals a number of further problems and underlines some old ones:

⁰⁰TS Apocalypse 1:1–22:21
  ⁰TS Prologue 1:1-3
    ⁰TS¹ Title proper 1:1-2
    ⁰TS² Macarism 1:3
  ¹TS¹ Epistolary prescript 1:4-8
    ²TS¹¹ Address 1:4-5b
    ²TS¹² Doxology 1:5c-6
    ²TS¹³ Motto in form of prophetic saying 1:7
    ²TS¹⁴ God's self-predication 1:8
  ¹TS² Visionary part 1:9–22:5
    ²TS²¹ Revelation without otherworldly journey 1:9–3:22
    ²TS²² Revelation with otherworldly journey 4:1–22:5
  ¹TS³ Epilogue in form of vision authentication 22:6-20
    ²TS³¹ Attestation of book and motto 22:6
    ²TS³² Verification of the seer 22:8-9
    ²TS³³ Paraenesis with citation of motto 22:10-15
    ²TS³⁴ Christ's statement of revelatory transmission 22:16
    ²TS³⁵ Prophetic pneumatic saying 22:17
    ²TS³⁶ Canonization formula 22:18-19
    ²TS³⁷ Final citation of motto and response 22:20
  ¹TS⁴ Epistolary postscript 22:21

Once again the independence of the two macrocosmic dimensions must be questioned, and the sequence break before 22:6 remains problematic. But, in addition, note that the nil-grade text sequence has subcomponents. This demonstrates an inconsistency in Hellholm's nomenclature, where otherwise the *grade* (to the left of TS) equals the number of sublevels (the length of the digit string to the right of TS). There is also an imbalance with respect to the relationship of the higher-grade text sequences to the whole Apocalypse. If the structure contributes towards meaning, then it is strange that the very minor subsections of ¹TS³ (²TS³¹,

---

[29] This is an issue we will address in greater detail in chapter 5 below, pp.165-87. See Charles H. Giblin, "Structural and Thematic Correlations in the Theology of Revelation 16-22," *Bib* 55 (1974): 487-504; Aune, *Revelation 1–5*, pp. xcv-xcvii.

$^2TS^{32}$, etc.) should stand in the same relationship to the whole Apocalypse as does the bulk of the book ($^2TS^{22}$).[30]

We expand the display one stage further, restricting ourselves to the analysis of only $^1TS^2$, but including all of the fourth-grade and a few of the fifth-grade text sequences:

$^1TS^2$ Visionary part 1:9–22:5
  $^2TS^{21}$ Revelation without otherworldly journey 1:9–3:22
    $^3TS^{211}$ Pneumatic rapture at place of revelation 1:9-10a
      $^4TS^{2111}$ Situation report 1:9
      $^4TS^{2112}$ Report of rapture 1:10a
    $^3TS^{212}$ Revelation of message to 7 churches 1:10b–3:22[31]
      $^4TS^{2121}$ Commissionary revelation 1:10b-20
      $^4TS^{2122}$ Message to seven churches 2:1–3:22
  $^2TS^{22}$ Revelation with otherworldly journey 4:1–22:5
    $^3TS^{221}$ Pneumatic enrapture to place of revelation 4:1-2a
      $^4TS^{2211}$ Situation report 4:1
      $^4TS^{2212}$ Report of enrapture 4:2a
    $^3TS^{222}$ Revelation of that which is to come 4:2b–22:5
      $^4TS^{2221}$ Throne room revelation as introduction to
              Heavenly Scroll 4:2b–5:14
      $^4TS^{2222}$ The revelation of the heavenly scroll 6:1–22:5
        $^5TS^{22221}$ Scriptura exterior 6:1–7:17
        $^5TS^{22222}$ Scriptura interior 8:1–22:5

Notice here a significant feature of the structure of Revelation, namely its "bottom-heavy" nature, where the largest subsections of major sections are the last ones. The fifth-grade text sequence $^5TS^{22222}$ contains approximately 79% of either $^3TS^{222}$ or $^2TS^{22}$ and 66% of $^1TS^2$.

But there are a number of unanswered questions about the criteria on which important decisions have been made. On what ground is the whole of 6:1–22:5 taken as the revelation of the heavenly scroll? On what further grounds is this section subdivided between the exterior and the interior scrolls? These questions are significant because the whole of 8:1–22:5 is now embedded within level 5 and it is precisely this that leads to the "speech from the throne" (21:5-8) being the text sequence of highest

---

[30] This would be somewhat alleviated if we considered an alternative structure in which the Visionary part (1:9–22:20 or at least to 22:9) is embedded within the letter as a part of the letter body.

[31] This is presumably a misprint for 3:22.

THE STRUCTURE OF THE APOCALYPSE: A SELECTIVE REVIEW

degree, the result on which so much of Hellholm's argument rests. It should also be noted, however, that even in Hellholm's full diagram it is not clear precisely how 21:5-8 attains its supposedly unique status. Hellholm describes this delimitation of the text of Revelation as "preliminary" and promises a more "definitive textlinguistic analysis" in the second volume of his studies on *The Shepherd of Hermas*.[32] It is unfortunate that this has not yet appeared. Yet this is already a significant advance on more traditional approaches to outlining the structure of the book of Revelation (or indeed of any biblical text). First, he treats structure as contributing to meaning. This is one of the primary contributions of discourse analysis to the understanding of texts. In his case it is genre recognition that is at issue, while in my relevance-theoretic approach genre recognition is a preliminary step, a cognitive effect that contributes to the relevance of the whole, and thus to the elucidation of meaning. Second, Hellholm has argued that it is the text as we have it, not some hypothetical precursor or rearrangement of it, which must be analyzed. Furthermore, he rightly focuses on surface-level linguistic markers to delimit the text, and his description and analysis of these is both well defined and linguistically significant. Finally, his commitment to a hierarchical arrangement of text sequences, with strong emphasis on the communication situations involved, is theoretically sound from the point of view of both discourse analysis and Relevance Theory.

Over against this, three major criticisms need to be made. First, Hellholm has concentrated on "the text, the whole text and nothing but the text." While the first two of these are laudable, the third is challenged by RT. The text itself is only a clue (even if the most important one) in the search for the structure and hence the meaning of a communication event. Thus a relevance-guided elucidation of structure will need to take explicit account of extra-textual factors that may contribute to the perception of structure by the receptors of the text. Second, I have strongly questioned the independence of the text sequence hierarchy from the embedding of communication levels. I believe there is a complex interplay between communication level and text sequence such that it is not possible to trace either independently. Finally, there remain serious questions about the criteria by which the higher levels of text sequence have been delimited.

Before leaving Hellholm, it is worth noting his comments on the significance of certain sixth-grade text sequences that we have not

---

[32] See Hellholm, "Problem ," p. 47, note 50.

examined in this critique.[33] Among these he identifies three "intercalations" (7:1-14; 10:1–11:14; 12:1–14:20) and an "addendum" (17:1–22:5). The effect of these "Supplementary visions" is twofold. They result in the first two septets being open-ended, and they focus attention on the microcosmic situation of the church, where the author's major interest lies.[34] If the extent and relationship of these sequences can be confirmed, then they may prove to be important locations for closer attention in investigating the role of the people of God in the Apocalypse.

2.4 Müller's microstructural analysis

Müller begins from an analysis of the diversity of structural studies and theories on the Apocalypse and proposes "a thorough microstructural analysis of the Book of Revelation based on a more objective method which mainly concentrates on literary features rather than on pure content analysis."[35] The outcome of his analysis is a display of the text of Revelation in which major sections are delimited, the text is displayed clause by clause with indentation to show various levels of dependence, and the repetition or echoing of words or phrases is highlighted. He has provided an immense amount of valuable raw material for the study of the text and its structure, and probably the most systematic portrayal in print of the repetition of vocabulary and phrases, together with comparisons of their usage between different parts of the book. Nevertheless, there are a number of issues regarding his methodology which must be investigated and clarified if his data is to be used with confidence.

His distinction between macrostructure (Hellholm's primary interest) and microstructure is unexceptionally concerned with the scale of the structures involved. But the aim in both cases is, according to Müller, to discover the "line of thought" and "intention" of the author.[36] This contrasts with the priority Hellholm gives to the perspective of the reader/hearer.[37] While Relevance Theory does not dismiss the possibility of access to the author's intention, it does suggest that the most defensible assumption that can be made about the author is that s/he intended

---

[33] There are two in ⁵TS²²²²¹ and six in ⁵TS²²²²².
[34] Hellholm, "Problem," p. 53.
[35] Müller, *Microstructural Analysis*, p. 8.
[36] Müller, *Microstructural Analysis*, pp. 10-11.
[37] Hellholm, "Problem," p. 32.

to maximize relevance for the receptor, and thus the best way to the author's intention is to investigate the text from the point of view of the audience first.[38]

Müller's brief but detailed review of scholarly contributions to the study of the macrostructure of Revelation highlights at least 13 different "organizing principles" that have been found by various writers to hold the key to the structure.[39] Of particular interest, because in some ways it forms the opposite pole to the structure that will eventually be outlined by Müller, is that proposed by Jan Lambrecht, in which the seven trumpets arise out of the seventh seal, and the seven bowls in turn out of the seventh trumpet.[40] There is also a significant omission from the works with which he regularly interacts, namely Hellholm's study that I have critiqued above, the most important work prior to Müller's to explicitly and deliberately apply linguistic techniques to the book of Revelation.[41]

The outcome of such a diversity of opinion is that "[t]he multiplicity of proposed macrostructures for the Book of Revelation contributes to the criticism of structural studies as being purely subjective."[42] Müller claims that his own study avoids this kind of subjectivity, largely because it is interested in the surface-level text only, and in fact the grammatical form of the text rather than the semantic content.

> No attention is given to questions of introduction (author, place, and time of writing etc.), textual criticism, genre, sources, or social-historical context.[43]

In other words, it is the text as text, an isolated string of marks on paper, which is in view. He explicitly sets aside the influence of the OT, or indeed any prior sources, together with any attempt to ascertain

---

[38] See the discussion in chapter 1 above, pp. 26-28.

[39] Müller, *Microstructural Analysis*, pp. 13-27.

[40] Lambrecht, "Structuration," pp. 85-88.

[41] Though Müller notes Hellholm's work (*Microstructural Analysis*, p. 10, note 1), he scarcely interacts with him either in terms of methodology or over structural decisions. He does cite Wendland, "7 X 7."

[42] Müller, *Microstructural Analysis*, p. 26. Note also the comment on p. 46: "One only has to look at the multiplicity of proposed macrostructures for the Book of Revelation to wonder if the missing consensus is not due to a certain subjectivity inherent already in the approach of the respective scholar [*sic*]."

[43] Müller, *Microstructural Analysis*, p. 43.

conceptual "deep structures."[44] By deliberately refusing to attend to content, he seems to be trying to isolate one clue to meaning from the others.[45] RT understands the communication of meaning (of which structure is a contributing part) as a multi-stranded cord that cannot be untwined without destroying the cord itself. Relevance is created by a combination of the text as verbal signs (Müller's focus), the semantic content it evokes, and the "cognitive environment," the mental representation of both the co-text and situational context. To isolate one strand is to unravel the cord. It is further questionable whether Müller is really interested, as he claims, in *literary* forms or whether his method really has anything to do with *literary* criticism.[46] His concern is solely with syntactic forms.

Subjectivity is a major concern for Müller and he proposes a number of safeguards to ensure that his work does not suffer from the problem he has perceived in others.[47] A number of these are both sound and helpful. He emphasizes the priority of the biblical text over any preconception of its structure, and thus precludes the use of additions, omissions, emendations or relocations in order to force a structure on the text. He urges caution whenever large-scale structures are postulated. And he does not expect to find perfect structures in the text. But once again he emphasizes internal factors to the exclusion of external ones, and what he terms a "literary approach which pays attention to grammatical and syntactical constructions, to semantic patterns, and to compositional patterns" as

---

[44] Müller, *Microstructural Analysis*, pp. 45-46.

[45] By contrast, Beekman and Callow, *Translating the Word of God*, pp. 267-71, argue for the importance of dealing with semantic rather than surface-level structure. While Müller's analysis bears a degree of visual resemblance to the "Semantic Structure Analysis" diagrams that have been the outcome of discourse analysis based on Beekman and Callow, the resemblance is only superficial. See further C. Bartsch, "The SSA Approach to Understanding Discourse," *NOT* 3 (1989): 55-58. Examples of the SSA approach to whole books of the NT include Rogers, *Galatians* and Deibler, *Romans*.

[46] Müller, *Microstructural Analysis*, p. 43, comments: "In a certain sense, the method used in this study is related to literary criticism and close reading, insofar as its focus is on the final form of the text, its unity, and its artistic design." This might be a fair statement if it read *"only* insofar . . ."* and omitted the reference to artistic design.

[47] Müller, *Microstructural Analysis*, pp. 47-49.

opposed to a "pure content analysis."[48] These assumptions we have already found to be questionable, particularly from a relevance-theoretic perspective.

His final safeguard is that "Macrostructures must not provide a straightjacket for microstructural analysis."[49] He appeals to Edgar McKnight's *Post-Modern Use of the Bible* for the movement from letter to word to sentence to literary unit.[50] McKnight claims that coherence is the key to structure. But we should note, first, that coherence operates as much on a macrosyntactic (or discourse) level as on a microsyntactic level, and secondly, that we have already seen that coherence relations alone are not sufficient to explain discourse structure.[51] Indeed there may be a sense in which a book like Revelation does prioritize its macrostructures, as these would be the ones most noticeable on a first reading/hearing. Microstructural patterns, which require more detailed study, would then be found within a cognitive environment that already includes some idea of the macrostructure.

Müller describes in some detail his own method of diagramming text in a syntactical display called "sentence flow," which arises out of methodologies proposed by Gordon Fee, Walter Kaiser, Scot McKnight and J. Ramsey Michaels.[52] None of these have come from an explicitly linguistic standpoint. Müller does note the work of the "South African" school of discourse analysts, with their emphasis on "colon analysis."[53] He describes this method as helpful but says "sentence cola do not seem to clarify the syntactical data of a sentence and their relationship as clearly

---

[48] Müller, *Microstructural Analysis*, p. 48.

[49] Müller, *Microstructural Analysis*, p. 49.

[50] Edgar V. McKnight, *Post-Modern Use of the Bible: The Emergence of Reader-Oriented Criticism* (Nashville: Abingdon, 1988), p. 220.

[51] See chapter 1, pp. 52-58 above.

[52] Müller, *Microstructural Analysis*, pp. 50-58. See Gordon D. Fee, *New Testament Exegesis: A Handbook for Students and Pastors* (Philadelphia: Westminster Press, 1983), pp. 60-76; Walter C. Kaiser, *Toward an Exegetical Theology: Biblical Exegesis for Preaching and Teaching* (Grand Rapids: Baker Book House, 1981), pp. 87-104, 175-81; Scot. McKnight, "New Testament Greek Grammatical Analysis," in *Introducing New Testament Interpretation* (ed. Scot McKnight; Grand Rapids: Baker Book House, 1989), pp. 89-94; J. Ramsey Michaels, *Interpreting the Book of Revelation* (GNTE 7; Grand Rapids: Baker Book House, 1992).

[53] See the references in note 13, pp. 7-9 above.

as a sentence flow does." [54] This is a rather subjective comparison and does not do justice to the linguistic sophistication of "colon analysis." Combined with his inattention to Hellholm's textlinguistic approach, this is evidence of how little Müller draws on the work of linguistic discourse analysts.

Turning to the kind of display generated by Müller's method, there are two notable and helpful features. First, clauses are indented according to a set of rules, largely dependent on their level of subordination.[55] This progressive indentation is a useful way of ensuring a display of the text that is hierarchical at least on the microstructural level. However, there remains an element of subjectivity even in this, as he says, "*If necessary or helpful* for the sake of clarification, objects, the genitive, adverbial phrases, and prepositional phrases *may be but need not be* indented."[56]

The second feature of the display is an intricate system of marking words and phrases, which enables many of the subtleties of the structure to be clearly shown. Thus closed and open boxes mark repeated formulae and phrases and a variety of type styles similarly mark repeated words. These formulae, words and phrases are further linked within individual subsections by vertical lines. Subsections and paragraphs are delimited by means of horizontal lines. The text display is supplemented by tables, which indicate a comparison of usage of terms and phrases between the major subsections of the text.

Although Müller produces a display for the whole book of Revelation, his main focus is on chapters 4–11 and for these he describes his method in detail, justifies the decision he has made over ambiguities, and explores some of the implications of his structural analysis.[57] He considers that the ambiguities which affect the syntactical display are few, although those that do are important for the exegesis.[58] This is significant as it confirms the role of structure in meaning. But conversely it illustrates the fact that decisions on ambiguities in structure cannot be taken with respect to structure alone. It is the overall relevance that is the determining factor. Notice also that where decisions on ambiguities in structure had to be made "[t]hese decisions were mainly based on John's usage of terms and phrases in the rest of Revelation—in other words on

---

[54] Müller, *Microstructural Analysis*, pp. 55-56.

[55] Müller, *Microstructural Analysis*, p. 56.

[56] Müller, *Microstructural Analysis*, p. 60 (italics mine).

[57] Müller, *Microstructural Analysis*, pp. 152-97, 198-434.

[58] Müller, *Microstructural Analysis*, pp. 196-97.

the context and on John's language, as well as partly also on his presumable sources."[59] It is not possible to escape the influence of context, nor is it desirable to do so. Müller's text displays are of considerable help in elucidating the fine structure of the text. Nevertheless, a number of important criticisms need to be made.

First, what Müller calls "structuring formulae" (such as μετὰ ταῦτα and εἶδον, καὶ ἰδού) are in fact syntagmatic markers on a higher level. But his display cannot account for this. Μετὰ ταῦτα in particular is a "substitution on the meta-level," to use Hellholm's terminology, and scarcely functions at the microsyntactic level.[60] Εἶδον, καὶ ἰδού is a cataphoric marker but still delimits the whole section, not just the clause or sentence to which it is immediately connected. Müller's horizontal lines hide the rank of these markers.[61]

Second, by grouping conjunctions, prepositions and adverbs with the clause or phrase they introduce, he also masks the structuring function of these particles.[62] They themselves could be used to form a skeleton of the structure of the section. Müller ranks these particles with the phrase or clause rather than seeing them acting at paragraph or section level.[63]

Third, the decision not to attend to content but only to linguistic form results in the hierarchical nature of the text not being fully clear. For example, the display of 4:4 is:

4. (1) καὶ κυκλόθεν τοῦ θρόνου θρόνους εἴκοσι τέσσαρες,
   (2) καὶ ἐπὶ τοὺς θρόνους εἴκοσι τέσσαρας πρεσβυτέρους
       καθημένους περιβεβλημένους ἐν ἱματίοις λευκοῖς
   (3) καὶ ἐπὶ τὰς κεφαλὰς αὐτῶν στεφάνους χρυσοῦς.[64]

Here phrase 2 is clearly semantically subordinate to 1, and 3 to 2. RT would assert that the thrones in phrase 2 are immediately interpreted as the thrones in phrase 1 and phrase 2 is thus clearly structurally subordinated to it. Similarly the αὐτῶν of phrase 3 must be interpreted in terms

[59] Müller, *Microstructural Analysis*, p. 196.
[60] See Hellholm, "Problem," p. 39.
[61] Note especially the line below 4:1, p. 157 of *Microstructural Analysis* by Hellholm.
[62] This criticism is similar to the first one, but at a slightly lower level.
[63] For examples in Hellholm, *Microstructural Analysis*, see the occurrences of καὶ in 4:1 (p.157) and εὐθέως in 4:2 (p.158).
[64] Müller, *Microstructural Analysis*, p. 159.

of the πρεσβυτέρους in phrase 2. The overall effect of this is like a zoom lens moving from a distant to a closeup shot.[65] Likewise, the assertion, regarding Rev 6:9 and 6:11, that whether καὶ is epexegetic or not "the syntactical display remains the same" demonstrates a serious shortcoming in the method, as once again the hierarchical nature of the text is obscured.[66]

Finally, marking the repetition of words and phrases is helpful but still does not give any clue to the way in which these repetitions function. Are they merely a kind of verbal percussion section? Or do they function to structure the text and if so in what way? Do they function within the microstructure only? Or are some repetitions macrostructural (on the abstraction or meta-levels of Hellholm)? The paragraphing that Müller proposes (by means of double spaces and horizontal lines) seems to cut across the strong vertical lines linking repetitions. In the display of 5:6-14, six to nine vertical lines cut across the horizontal section divisions.[67] I suspect that maximum relevance in terms of the structure has not yet been obtained. But at least the display alerts us to this kind of linkage and the hints are there that more processing effort will release greater cognitive results.

Müller suggests that his study provides data with which to establish a macrostructure for the text.[68] It is certainly true that he is able to identify some of the major structural questions posed by the Apocalypse. But the success he has in answering those questions is dependent to some extent on the reliability of his methodology. And it is precisely at the point where the methodology is most lacking, namely in accurately describing the hierarchy of the text, that it is most tested by the macrostructural questions. Most of the questions have to do with the relationship of large sections of text to each other—whether they are linked in parallel or hierarchical structure. The details of Müller's

---

[65] A similar example occurs on p. 185 (display on p. 143) of Müller's *Microstructural Analysis*: Whether the breastplates belong to the horses or the riders in 9:17 *should* affect the display in some way, contrary to Müller's assertion. The same kind of zoom-lens effect is created, this time with a subsequent widening back to take in the horses that are renominalized in the second half of the verse. The true semantic structure clearly involves subordination rather than coordination of the phrases.

[66] Müller, *Microstructural Analysis*, p. 182.

[67] Müller, *Microstructural Analysis*, pp. 81-82.

[68] Müller, *Microstructural Analysis*, pp. 198-99.

arguments, and a detailed response, will have to wait until we examine the text ourselves. In brief, in contrast to both Hellholm and Lambrecht, he finds the major sections of the text to be related but distinct units. For example, he claims 4:1–8:1 and 8:2–11:18 are distinct units on the same level, where both the others find that the rest of the book, starting from 8:2, is a part of the description of the seventh seal, and thus hierarchically subordinate. While Müller convincingly demonstrates the internal unity and coherence of these two units, it does not necessarily follow that the second is on the same level as the first.[69]

Müller appears to be at least partly motivated by a desire to allow for recapitulation in the successive septets. Thus he stresses the importance of delimiting the section of the seven seals by saying, "This question, however, is of vital importance, for it has to do with the issue of recapitulation and it decisively affects the interpretation of Revelation."[70] At issue is whether the seventh seal is concluded by the silence or whether this is only transitional and the rest of the book (at least to 22:5) is the contents of the seventh seal. Müller argues that if the seventh seal extends to 8:5 or 6 (and by extension then to the rest of the book) then "there is not much room for recapitulation."[71] But this mistakenly supposes that the sequence of **structures** necessarily reflects a sequence of **time**. It is quite conceivable that there might be an embedded text sequence structure, which nevertheless portrayed a recapitulating sequence of events in the narrative world. On the other hand, there is the strong possibility that the relationship between the seals and the trumpets and between the trumpets and the bowls involves some sort of interlocking or intercalation relationship, rather than being directly coordinate.[72]

Apart from the issues already mentioned, Müller also identifies another question that will have significant implications for the text structure and for my study in particular. This is the question of the status of the interruptions to the sequences of seals and trumpets (Rev 7 and 10:1–11:14). Are they expansions of the sixth member of each sequence, or intercalations relatively unrelated to the sequences in which they occur?

---

[69] See Müller, *Microstructural Analysis*, pp. 239-40. This issue will be dealt with in more detail in chapter 4 below.

[70] Müller, *Microstructural Analysis*, p. 233.

[71] Müller, *Microstructural Analysis*, p. 235.

[72] See Yarbro Collins, *Combat Myth*, pp. 16-19; Spinks, "Examination of Bowman's Proposal"; Schüssler Fiorenza, "Composition," pp. 170-73.

These passages, together with Rev 12–14, are among the sixth-grade sequences whose significance was highlighted by Hellholm and in which the people of God figure most prominently.

Müller's microstructural study provides a wealth of well-presented data with which to analyze the structure of the book of Revelation. The limitations I have highlighted, in particular the lack of attention to semantic questions, the lack of attention to context and the weakness in the hierarchy of the text, must, however, be taken into account when using the data.

2.5 Other contributions to the discourse structure of the Apocalypse

It remains to examine briefly a number of other contributions to the study of the structure of Revelation which relate to a discourse analysis perspective.

One of the earliest contributions to the textlinguistic analysis of Revelation is Hartman's study of Rev 1–3 and 22:6-21.[73] He uses the same methodology and terminology as Hellholm, derived largely from the work of Elisabeth Gülich and Wolfgang Raible. Without denying the validity of source-critical analysis, he treats the text as it stands as the record of a communicative event located in a particular situational and literary context. And he explicitly affirms that this context may influence the perception of structure and meaning. For example, regarding a possible change from a traditional baptismal confession in 1:5, he says:

> this change . . . becomes significant only in so far as we find it reasonable to assume that the traditional formula belonged to the common background of both author and reader. If so, this background formed part of the referential frame which determined and conditioned the communication.[74]

---

[73] Hartman, "Form and Message."

[74] Hartman, "Form and Message," p. 130. Note also the following statement, p. 131: "The most important devices for demarcating a passage as a unit, a paragraph, are signals on the text's surface which organize the text (*Gliederungsmerkmale*). But this organisation of a text can also be dependant upon or even mainly controlled by text-external conventions, e.g., literary 'form'—conventions, which make it natural for a reader to delimit a partial text in a certain way."

Such considerations are not only good textlinguistics but are in keeping with the extra-textual interests that Relevance Theory insists must influence the understanding of the structure and meaning of a text. Hartman proceeds to examine each of the "partial texts" he discerns in the beginning and ending of the Apocalypse in the light of three sets of questions, relating respectively to the delimitation and form of the text, to its literary function, and to the way in which form and function impact the message of the text. Here again he comments that "we will have to take into consideration not only Rev but also material that presumably belongs to or bears witness to the referential background of author and reader."[75] Leaving aside the details of his analysis to be interacted with later, it is worth noting further that Hartman, like Hellholm, not only analyzes the text into "partial texts" but also insists that these partial texts be hierarchically arranged.[76] Though he appears less convinced of his tentative hierarchy for the final section, his proposal for 1:1-9 is similar to that of Hellholm but with the advantage of treating the whole text as composed of two first order partial texts, 1:1-3 and 1:4–22:21.[77]

Wendland's proposed discourse structure for Revelation is based on the thesis that the chief organizing principle in the book is the number seven.[78] The prominence of the number is in itself neither new nor controversial. Wendland, however, finds seven sets of seven in the central section of the book (4:1–22:5), with a further set both before and after this, and embedded sets of seven in nearly every subsection. His analysis is in many ways similar to that of Adela Yarbro Collins who is in turn dependent on Austin Farrer.[79] While the precise delimitation of the sets of seven

---

[75] Hartman, "Form and Message," p. 132 (abbreviation his).

[76] Hartman, "Form and Message," pp. 140, 148-49.

[77] Hartman, "Form and Message," p. 140. See my criticism of Hellholm's analysis on pp. 64-73 above. In Hartman's analysis the whole text is the zero order; the first order partial texts are 1:1-3 and 1:4–22:21; the second order are 1:1-2; 1:3; 1:4-8; and 1:9–22:21.

[78] Wendland, "7 X 7," p. 372.

[79] Yarbro Collins, *Combat Myth*, pp. 14-16, 19; Farrer, *Rebirth of Images*, pp. 55-58. For another structural outline based on sevens, see Charles H. Talbert, *The Apocalypse: A Reading of the Revelation of John* (Louisville: Westminster John Knox, 1994), p. 12. Against the tendency to find septenaries other than the numbered ones, see Giancarlo Biguzzi, *I settenari nella struttura dell'Apocalisse: Analisi, storia della ricerca,*

varies slightly, he identifies (it would appear independently) both of Yarbro Collins's "unnumbered sevens" and in addition finds that what she calls the "Babylonian appendix" and the "Jerusalem appendix" are also patterned in sevens.[80] The details will be dealt with in the following chapters, but two things stand out in Wendland's presentation. First, his analysis of the text is based on a sophisticated array of discourse markers that involve both surface-level syntactical markers and semantic and rhetorical devices.[81] Second, he finds a strong correlation between the numbered structures and the message of the book, arguing that "the author must have had some reason (other than pure generic constraints, i.e. apocalyptic literature) for their inclusion."[82] Both of these features, the attention to explicit syntactic and semantic structuring, and to the impact of structure on meaning, are characteristic of the best discourse analytic approaches to texts. On the negative side there are numerous uncertainties and ambiguities over both his broad structure (1:1-3; 1:4–3:22; 4:1–22:21) and the fine details (e.g., in 19:11–20:15), and he does not reflect as well as Yarbro Collins the clear parallels between the Babylon and New Jerusalem segments. But once again the greatest weakness, from an RT perspective, is that the book is largely treated in a vacuum, without regard to its contextual and intertextual situation. The remark quoted above, for example, implies that "purely generic constraints" would not be determinative for meaning. Yet at the same time his own understanding of the significance of the number seven (and other numbers) must be conditioned by extra-textual factors, including the conventions of the genre.

Boring has suggested a completely different basis on which to analyze the text of Revelation, one that is just as important to our purpose as the delimitation of textual units. This is the identification of the speaking

---

interpretazione (RivBSup 31; Bologna: Edizione Dehoniane, 1996), pp. 33-35.

[80] Yarbro Collins, *Combat Myth*, p. 19; Wendland, "7 X 7," pp. 380, 383-85. While the detailed breakdown of the first unnumbered series is identical, the second differs significantly, especially towards the end.

[81] Wendland, "7 X 7," p. 373. He identifies *kai* parataxis/asyndeton, parallel syntactic constructions, lexical-semantic sets, patterned recursions, anaphora, epiphora, anadiplosis, inclusion, and, to a lesser extent, introversion or chiasmus.

[82] Wendland, "7 X 7," p. 374.

voices that communicate to the hearer of the text.[83] There is clearly a relationship between this approach and Hellholm's attention, already noted, to communication situations.[84] Boring proposes, "The text of Revelation can be thought of as several layers of quotation marks, hierarchically arranged."[85] Three sets of these quotation marks surround the complete text, representing the words of the lector, of the written text, and of John himself. But thereafter the picture rapidly becomes more complicated as John speaks in several roles, reports the words of voices he hears, occasionally uses a messenger formula, and sometimes throws his own comments directly to the audience.[86] Not all the voices proposed by Boring are immediately distinguishable. An issue that is potentially important for our discourse analysis is whether there is a distinction between John speaking as a commentator, John speaking directly to the audience as a prophet, and "Interjectory Direct Address." But the fact that he draws attention to this type of statement is in itself helpful to my purpose of identifying the ways in which the hearers are involved and motivated by the text. Boring examines the confusion of voices in 1:1-2 and 22:6-20a in some detail. Setting aside various theories of compilation and redaction, he finds more help from Hartman's textlinguistic approach and Ugo Vanni's liturgical theory, yet finds each wanting.[87] His own solution begins from the assumption that the book is a real letter, in the tradition of the Pauline Epistles, which actualizes the writer's presence when it is read to the assembled audience. But he adds to this the concept of Christian prophecy (itself influenced by OT prophetic modes), in which the voice of the prophet and the voice of God, the voice of Christ and the voice of the Spirit, fade into each other and are often indistinguishable. Seen from this perspective the apparent confusion of voices in the Apocalypse is a deliberate fusing of the levels of communication in which the reading of the text makes present the voice of the triune God. Thus Trinitarian theology is not logically formulated but expressed

---

[83] See M. Eugene Boring, "The Voice of Jesus in the Apocalypse of John," *NovT* 34 (1992): 334-59.

[84] See the discussion above, pp. 65-68.

[85] Boring, "The Voice of Jesus," p. 335.

[86] Boring, "The Voice of Jesus," pp. 336-41.

[87] Boring, "The Voice of Jesus," pp. 343-49; cf. Hartman, "Form and Message"; Ugo Vanni, "Un esempio di dialogo liturgico in Ap 1,4-8," *Bib* 57 (1976): 453-67.

through the voices of the text.[88] This study is significant from a relevance point of view, in that it has moved the discussion of structure of the text out beyond the text itself into the communication situation in which it occurs, with structure, context and content mutually interacting.

Aune's recent commentary contains a number of features that are important from both discourse analysis and RT perspectives, not so much in his introductory section on literary structure as in the body of the commentary. The introduction reviews a number of contentious issues in the study of the structure of the Apocalypse.[89] His source-critical and redaction-critical view of the history of the text leads him to reject all recapitulation theories, as he considers that vision accounts of diverse origin have been brought together to form "*a single chronological narrative of the eschatological events that will soon begin to unfold.*"[90] This leads him to treat phrases like καὶ εἶδον as functioning paratactically to superimpose a secondary temporal sequence. Examining the focus on the series of sevens stressed by Farrer and Yarbro Collins, he brings the discussion back to the key question as to whether or not the series recapitulate each other.[91] He endorses Charles Giblin's presentation of the close structural parallels between Rev 17:1–19:10 and 21:9–22:9 and suggests that the second is deliberately patterned on the first.[92] While the abbreviated outline found in the introduction is unexceptional, the detailed outlines for each section in the commentary under the heading "Form/Structure/Setting" come much closer to providing a microstructural discourse analysis of the text concerned.[93] Although this is not done using the words of the text but with summary headings, the minuteness of detail is such that the result is very close to the "colon analysis" proposed by Johannes Louw and others of the South African school of discourse analysis, with perhaps a greater weighting given to the semantics rather than the syntax. It therefore provides a comparable and useful alternative to Müller's microstructure. The second feature of these "Form/Structure/Setting" sections, which is of particular use to my

---

[88] Boring, "The Voice of Jesus," pp. 349-56.

[89] Aune, *Revelation 1–5*, pp. xc-cv.

[90] Aune, *Revelation 1–5*, p. xciii (italics his).

[91] Aune, *Revelation 1–5*, pp. xciii-xcviii.

[92] Aune, *Revelation 1–5*, pp. xcv-xcviii; cf. Giblin, "Structural and Thematic Correlations."

[93] Aune, *Revelation 1–5*, pp. c-cv; compare, for example, the detailed outline of 1:9-20 on pp. 68-70.

purpose, is the background material compiled in the subsections entitled "Literary Analysis" and "Literary Form."[94] Whether or not one accepts his source-critical proposals, the compilation of generically related texts and potential sources is extremely helpful in constructing the kind of extra-textual cognitive environments that RT requires us to take into account.

Beale's commentary is itself somewhat less structurally organized than Aune's and consequently more difficult to navigate. He presents no detailed structural outline, either for the whole book of Revelation or for individual sections. But his particular interest in the OT background to Revelation has resulted in a large number of excursuses in the body of the commentary which catalogue the relationship of the text to the OT. This wealth of background from OT cultic and literary contexts complements the more wide-ranging and eclectic contexts detailed by Aune, and both must be evaluated for their accessibility from an RT perspective.

Beale's introductory section on the structure of the Apocalypse reviews a wide range of views, particularly with regard to the question of recapitulation.[95] While he himself approves of the basic recapitulationist idea, his own view is that the book of Daniel, and in particular Dan 2:28-29, 45, is the fundamental key to the structure.[96] He argues that the phrase ἃ δεῖ γενέσθαι ἐν τάχει and its variants, in Rev 1:1, 19; 4:1; 22:6, are deliberate allusions from Daniel which alert the reader/hearer to regard the book of Daniel as the primary interpretive framework for understanding both the structure and the meaning of Revelation.

This leads to a structural outline in which these four references form the literary hinges, setting off an introduction (1:1-8) and a conclusion (22:6-21) from the main body of the text. The text itself is then formed by

---

[94] E.g., Aune, *Revelation 1–5*, pp. 70-75, for 1:9-20.
[95] Beale, *Revelation*, pp. 108-135. For futurist views see pp. 108-121; for recapitulationist views see pp. 121-35.
[96] This is in line with his earlier publications; for example, G. K. Beale, "The Use of Daniel in the Synoptic Eschatological Discourse and in the Book of Revelation," in *The Jesus Tradition Outside the Gospels* (ed. David Wenham; Gospel Perspectives 5; Sheffield: JSOT Press, 1984), pp. 129-53; Beale, "The Influence of Daniel"; and Beale, "The Interpretive Problem." In fact, a section of the commentary, "The Disputed Significance of Revelation 1:19 as an Interpretive Key to the Book," pp. 152-68, is a slight revision of the article mentioned last. This has led to an unfortunate and admitted degree of repetition, which should nevertheless not be allowed to detract from the strength of the point being made.

an envelope relating to the church, at first imperfect on earth (1:9–3:22) and then perfect in glory (21:9–22:5), surrounding a five-part central section of visions (4:1–21:8) with its own hinge at 4:1.[97] Speaking of the ἐν τάχει in 1:1, which has been changed from Daniel's ἐπ' ἐσχάτων τῶν ἡμερῶν, he says:

> What Daniel expected to occur in the far-off "latter days," the defeat of cosmic evil and the ushering in of the divine kingdom, John expects to begin in his own generation, if it has not already started to happen. Therefore, John may be asserting that Daniel 2 (and its parallel, Daniel 7ff.) is one of the primary literary frameworks within which the following contents of the whole Apocalypse are to be conceived.[98]

And again, a little further on:

> If it can be concluded that these Daniel 2 allusions are intentional and draw with them the contextual idea of Daniel 2, then there is a basis for proposing that this provides a significant framework of thought for the whole Apocalypse, that is, end-time judgment of cosmic evil and consequent establishment of the eternal kingdom.[99]

Beale has rightly pointed out that the perception of structure is equally affected by the inferential process of access to extra-textual (in this case intertextual) contexts. This is thoroughly consistent with and supported by RT. [100]

This selective review of structural studies on the Apocalypse has highlighted a number of works which analyze, in more or less detail, the linguistic discourse structure of the text of the Apocalypse considered as an isolated entity (Hartman, Hellholm, Müller, Wendland) and others which open up the structural discussion to the kind of extra-textual influences that RT requires, but which give less than adequate attention to the syntactic and semantic discourse markers in the text itself (Boring, Aune, Beale). It will be my aim in the remainder of this study to bring these two

---

[97] Beale, *Revelation*, p. 136.

[98] Beale, *Revelation*, p. 137.

[99] Beale, *Revelation*, p. 141.

[100] Compare the discussions in chapter 1 above, on the influence of RT on discourse analysis, pp. 45-58. See also the discussion on "Relevance and Intertextuality," in Pattemore, "The People of God," pp. 59-73.

dimensions together and to attempt a relevance-guided discourse analysis of the Apocalypse.

Chapter 3

Discourse Structure of the Apocalypse
Part 1: Large-scale structures

In this chapter we will examine the structure of the Apocalypse on the largest scales, covering the whole book, and in a little more detail at the beginning and ending of the book.

3.1 The integrity of the Apocalypse as a single discourse unit

"A unit of text is a unit of relevance if relevance is optimised over it."[1] Blass's summary of "discourse analysis within relevance theory" leads us first to examine the Apocalypse as a whole unit. The assumption of its integrity as a text entails the assumption that relevance is optimized by considering the unit of communication begun in Rev 1:1 to proceed continuously and finish at Rev 22:21. Both the integrity and the completeness of this text unit could conceivably be challenged. Is it a single unit or some kind of a composite, whether by juxtaposition or interpolation of independent text units?[2] Is it complete in itself, or is it part of a larger text?

Neither the integrity nor the completeness of the text of the Apocalypse is significantly threatened by any external textual evidence.[3] For the

---

[1] Blass, *Relevance relations*, p. 80.

[2] An *edited* text, even if it is a composite, and even if some component parts can be shown to have their own self-contained integrity, will presumably still exhibit a degree of relevance over the whole text, due to the editor's communicative intent.

[3] See Aune, *Revelation 1–5*, pp. cxxxiv-clx, for a detailed treatment of the text of Revelation. Fragmentary manuscripts clearly cannot be taken

purposes of discourse analysis, we focus on the internal evidence of integrity.[4] Few scholars today accept highly speculative source-critical analyses such as those proposed by R. H. Charles, Massyngberde Ford or M.-E. Boismard, yet the question must still be asked as to whether the whole text coheres as a unit.[5] The first and most significant challenge to this is the shift in communication situation between 1:3 and 1:4. In 1:1-3 an anonymous author addresses an equally anonymous audience, referring to John in the third person, whereas 1:4–22:21 presents, at least formally, a unified communication situation in which a specific person (John) himself addresses a specific group of people (the Asian churches)

---

as evidence of a text whose limits, on the scale of the whole book, are different from the text we assume.

[4] That Revelation should be treated as a complete unit on its own might perhaps be challenged from two directions: its place within "Johannine literature" and its place in the canon of the NT. While the former may have implications for relevance relations, it is too controverted to take into account in any systematic way in this study. See R. H. Charles, *The Revelation of St. John* (2 vols.; ICC; Edinburgh: T. & T. Clark, 1920), vol. I, pp. xxix-l, and Stephen S. Smalley, *Thunder and Love: John's Revelation and John's Community* (Milton Keynes, England: Word, 1994), pp. 57-73, for two quite different discussions. As far as its place in the canon is concerned, we may assume, given its unique textual history, that it stood alone for some considerable period. For references see Pattemore, "The People of God," p. 1, note 1. Nevertheless its canonical position will considerably affect the way its relevance is perceived today. It is the canonical context that gives rise to the first text sequence listed by Hellholm, "Problem," p. 47: [00]TS [*APOKALYPSIS IŌANNOU*]. This superscription will form no part of my investigation.

[5] Charles, *Revelation*, vol. I, pp. l-lix; vol. II, pp. 144-54; M.-E. Boismard, "<<L'Apocalypse>>, ou <<Les Apocalypses>> de S. Jean," *RB* 56 (1949): 507-541; J. Massyngberde Ford, *Revelation* (AB 38; Garden City, N.Y.: Doubleday, 1975), pp. 39-46. Aune, *Revelation 1–5*, pp. cv-cxxxiv, provides an updated summary of source-critical hypotheses and presents his own. This is effectively critiqued by Adela Yarbro Collins, "Source Criticism of the Book of Revelation," *BR* 43 (1998): 50-53. However one judges the likelihood of any of these hypotheses, the immediate task is to examine the coherence of the text as it has reached us.

90

by means of a well-known form of communication, the letter.[6] It is, however, unlikely for a number of reasons that 1:1-3 is simply added on to a pre-existing letter.

First, notice that although there is no closing section with the same communication situation as 1:1-3, the semantic content of the initial verses is strongly echoed in 22:6-7.[7] Even if 1:1-3 was deliberately composed to reflect 22:6-7, this would still argue that the text as we have received it is a carefully edited unit. The fact that this closure is on a different communication level only serves to emphasize the integration of the two levels. Furthermore, there are occasional text sequences within the body of the Apocalypse, relatively unconnected to their immediate environment, which appear to belong to the same communication level as 1:1-3, namely that of author to audience.[8]

One feature of the opening words echoed in 22:6 which strongly increases the relevance obtained by considering the text to be a unified whole is the point emphasized by Beale, concerning the structuring role of the phrase ἃ δεῖ γενέσθαι ἐν τάχει as an allusion to Dan 2:28-29, 45.[9]

---

[6] J. M. Ross, "The Ending of the Apocalypse," in *Studies in New Testament Language and Text: Essays in Honour of George D. Kilpatrick* (ed. J. K. Elliott; Leiden: E. J. Brill, 1976), pp. 338-44, tentatively suggests that the epistolary closing may not be original, and, even more tentatively, prefers the reading of 2329, which ends the book with Ἀμήν, ἔρχου κύριε Ἰησοῦ, μετὰ τῶν ἁγίων σου. ἀμήν. The manuscripts certainly witness to a large degree of uncertainty on the precise wording, but most scholars accept that some form of an epistolary ending is original. See, for example, Bruce M. Metzger, *A Textual Commentary on the Greek New Testament* (2nd edn.; Stuttgart: Deutsche Bibelgesellschaft and UBS, 1994), pp. 690-91; David E. Aune, *Revelation 17–22*, (WBC 52C, Dallas: Word, 1998), pp. 1239-41.

[7] See Aune, *Revelation 17–22*, pp. 1148-49. Analyses that treat 1:1-3 (or 1:1-8) as prologue and 22:6-21 as epilogue ignore the difference in communication situation. Such, for example, are Vanni, *La struttura*, pp. 171-72; Lambrecht, "Structuration," pp. 78-79; Frederick D. Mazzaferri, *The Genre of the Book of Revelation from a Source-critical Perspective* (BZNW 54; Berlin: Walter de Gruyter, 1989), p. 334.

[8] E.g., 13:9-10 and 14:12. This phenomenon will be examined as the textual analysis proceeds in greater detail.

[9] Beale, *Revelation*, pp. 136-41, 152-61. Beale also argues that it is used to orient the reader to the theological outlook of the book (p. 141). See

The frequency of allusions to Daniel throughout the book is most satisfactorily explained by the assumption that Daniel forms an important and readily accessible part of the mutual cognitive environment. The author of the Apocalypse appears to assume that his text is heard against a prior knowledge of Daniel. Therefore the closure obtained by the use of the words at the beginning and end of our text is reinforced by the evocation of similar closure in Dan 2. The precise use of words in 1:3 presupposes a (proto-)Theodotion version of Daniel, and the fact that Dan 2:28 has spoken of θεὸς ἐν οὐρανῷ ἀποκαλύπτων μυστήρια is evoked by the title of the Apocalypse itself. The effect of the allusion and inclusio, then, is to identify the whole Apocalypse as the content of God's revelation regarding his sovereignty over the course of history and over human empires, however powerful they may appear.[10]

Second, Rev 1:1-3 is linked to the rest of the Apocalypse by the unusual degree of introspective interest, or meta-reference. No other New Testament document is so interested in itself as a document, or in the process of its own writing.[11] This interest begins with the title, 1:1-2, with no main verb to turn it into an action sentence. But it is then focused by the reference in 1:3 to τοὺς λόγους τῆς προφητείας and τὰ ἐν αὐτῇ γεγραμμένα. The command to write occurs twelve times in the visionary sections of the Apocalypse,[12] but it is in the closing section that the meta-reference to the book itself or its contents is again prominent. Here references to "this book" or "this prophecy" or the like occur at 22:7, 9, 10, 18, 19. Again, the fact that this time the introspective interest is on different

---

chapter 2, pp. 86-87 above. See also the treatment by Vanni, *La struttura*, pp. 116-19. J. Ramsey Michaels, "Revelation 1.19 and the Narrative Voices of the Apocalypse," *NTS* 37 (1991): 604-620, argues that 1:19 is not so much a structural key as a key to the narrative technique of the Apocalypse, a point to which we will return.

[10] The context of Dan 2, once opened, remains a fruitful source of interpretive clues as we shall see.

[11] In Revelation, 17 out of 29 occurrences of the forms of γράφειν are meta-referential, while the remainder refer to items within the visions themselves. None refer to the OT. By contrast in the rest of the NT, over 50% of its occurrences refer to the OT and less than a third are meta-referential. The other Johannine writings are the closest to Revelation in this regard.

[12] Γράψον occurs at Rev 1:11, 19; 2:1, 8, 12, 18; 3:1, 7, 14; 14:13; 19:9; 21:5; and only twice elsewhere in the entire NT (Luke 16:6-7).

communication levels, none of which are the same as that of 1:3, reinforces the integration of 1:1-3 with the whole, as each level shares this perspective. Most marked of the meta-references in Rev 22 are the warnings of 22:18-19, which explicitly guard the integrity and closure of the book. While formally they are imbedded speech within the letter of John to the churches, semantically and functionally they most closely correspond to the blessing of 1:3. They are strongly evocative of Deut 28–29, with its meta-referential focus.[13]

Finally, we can note that it is in 1:1-3, not in the formal letter opening at 1:4, that we find the characterization of the author of the letter which was normally part of the letter opening in other NT letters. More evidence could be adduced by way of detailed comparisons of the language, for the essential unity of the entire text, but sufficient contextual effects have been adduced to put the matter beyond reasonable doubt.

3.2 The two primary divisions of the text

Despite the unity argued above, the difference between the communication situation of the first three verses and that of the rest of the book, and in particular the shift from third person to first person reference to John, appears puzzling. And although the macarism in 1:3 is closely echoed by that of 22:7, there is also a significant difference. While those who hear and those who keep the words of the book are referred to on a number of occasions, only at 1:3 do we have a reference to the reading of the book, an event that objectifies the whole text. This reinforces the impression that 1:1-3 both stands outside and is closely integrated with the remainder of the Apocalypse. So is one or other of these communication levels a literary fiction? Is John both author of the letter and narrator of the apocalypse, and the audience precisely the members of the seven churches? In this case John has framed his letter so as to give the impression that the seven churches are part of a wider audience. Or is the letter from John a literary fiction, never intended for those particular churches? Both of these options result in a loss of relevance to some

---

[13] Note especially Deut 28:58, 61; 29:20-21. This feature of Deuteronomy has become a starting point for deconstruction of the authority structure of the book itself. See references and a response in Kevin J. Vanhoozer, *Is There a Meaning in This Text?: The Bible, the Reader and the Morality of Literary Knowledge* (Leicester: Apollos, 1998), pp. 174-77.

degree or another. There appears no logical reason to justify the first, and the second means that the high degree of local detail in the messages from the risen Christ diminishes rather than increases the relevance of the whole.[14]

But there is another explanation, which renders the dichotomy unnecessary. The apparent change in communication situation, where John is first referred to in the third person and then in the first, is in fact a generic feature of both prophetic and apocalyptic literature. Numerous examples can be adduced in both canonical and deuterocanonical books.[15] With such a strongly evidenced cognitive environment, we can affirm both that the entire text is intended as a communication from an individual (we will continue to call him John) to a particular group of people, and that it is intended to be seen in continuity with the prophetic and revelatory literature with which the audience would have been familiar. This assumption is productive for the most fruitful cognitive effects (both for the original audience and for the scholar).

Since it is the letter body, the bulk of the text, which will occupy most of our attention, it is worth noting briefly at this point that the introduction, 1:1-3, is itself a composite structure, consisting of a title statement

---

[14] A number of writers downplay the importance of the epistolary framework. Yarbro Collins, *Combat Myth*, pp. 6-7, dismisses it as "superficial" and of "secondary importance." Hellholm, "Problem," p. 47 does not give adequate attention to the standard components of the epistolary form. (See also chapter 2, p. 69 above, for a critique of his handling of 1:1-3). Lambrecht, "Structuration," p. 78-79, divides the book into three major parts, 1:1-3, 1:4–22:5 and 22:6-21, an analysis that ignores both the letter structure and (as we shall see) the plague angel sequences. Wendland, "7 X 7," p. 375, appears to ignore the overall letter form and treats 1:4-20 as introducing the 7 messages. By way of contrast, see Barbara W. Snyder, "Triple-Form and Space/Time Transitions: Literary Structuring Devices in the Apocalypse," *SBLSP* 30 (1991): 440-50, who gives the epistolary form an equal status with the apocalyptic and prophetic modes, saying that it functions to identify the intended audience of the book.

[15] Isa 1:1 (cf. 6:1); Jer 1:1-2 (cf. 1:4); Dan 7:1 (cf. 7:2); Hos 1:1-8 (cf. 3:1); Micah 1:1 (cf. 1:8); Hab 1:1 (cf. 1:2); Zech 1:7 (cf. 1:8); *1 Enoch* 1:1 (cf. 1:2); 12:1 (cf. 12:3); 13:1 (cf. 13:3); 37:1 (cf. 37:2).

(1:1-2), a complex noun clause with no main verb, and a macarism (1:3), typically as a participial clause.[16] It is interesting to note that on the two major levels of communication, which are the most involved with the "real world," there is no reference whatsoever to any member of what might be termed the "opposition"— human or spiritual forces of evil.[17] They are consigned to lower levels of the discourse. The significance of this will be explored later.

3.3 Untangling the endings of the major text levels

The Apocalypse is characterized by a series of discrete beginnings and a single, composite and convoluted ending.[18] It is relatively easy to identify where the major subdivisions of the text begin. The text begins at 1:1, the letter at 1:4, the letter body at 1:9, and the vision description at 1:10. But it is much more difficult to disentangle their endings. We have already seen that although the introduction has no corresponding communication situation at the end, it is strongly reflected in an embedded communication situation. Besides this, not only is the ending of the whole text identical with the ending of the letter, but the end of the vision description is intertwined with the end of the letter body. Although 1:4-6 is relatively well defined as the formal letter opening, corresponding to the formal closure in 22:21, the situation is less clear for 1:7-8 and 22:6-20, resulting in considerable divergence in scholarly opinion as to how to analyze the ending. As far as 22:5 everyone is agreed that we are still in

---

[16] For a more detailed analysis of the introduction, see David Hellholm, "The Visions He Saw or: To Encode the Future in Writing. An Analysis of the Prologue of John's Apocalyptic Letter," in *Text and Logos: The Humanistic Interpretation of the New Testament. Essays in Honor of Hendrikus W. Boers* (ed. Theodore W. Jennings; Atlanta: Scholars Press, 1990), pp. 109-146. Here Hellholm has overcome some of the difficulties I noted in his earlier presentation, but the result is exceedingly complex and hard to follow.

[17] By the two levels here, I intend the level of the narrator and audience of the Apocalypse, and the level of the sender and recipients of the letter.

[18] The open-ended nature of much of Revelation is noted by Schüssler Fiorenza, "Composition," p. 360; Lambrecht, "Structuration," p. 87.

the vision description. But of 22:6-20, how much constitutes the "epilogue"?[19] Some of the data needs to be reviewed briefly:

22:6 is closely linked to what precedes it (Καὶ εἶπέν μοι; cf. 22:1 Καὶ ἔδειξέν μοι), but the meta-reference, ἃ δεῖ γενέσθαι ἐν τάχει, is also a mark of closure with 1:1 on the highest communication level.

22:7, at least on the surface, appears to represent a change of speaker, but the macarism itself closely echoes 1:3.

22:8 is clearly defined as a break by the renominalization of John in the first person (cf. 1:4, 9) and the meta-reference of ταῦτα. Yet there is also a strong anaphoric link to the preceding sections in the mention of the angel.

22:10 appears to continue the same communication situation as 22:6-7, 9 but also contains a meta-reference to the whole book, with echoes of 1:3.

22:12 returns to the same communication situation as 22:7, but the whole section 22:12-20 reflects many features of 1:4-8. These include the direct speech of the deity (Jesus in 22:12, 16; cf. God in 1:8) through John to the audience, the use of Ναί and Ἀμήν in affirmation or response, the coming of Jesus, the alpha and omega statements, and the explicit reference to the churches and to the Spirit.

But probably the major cause of the confusion here is the variety of different voices that are heard through 22:6-21 and the consequent difficulty in assigning them to John, to the angel, or to Jesus.[20] Relevance considerations have potential to shed some light on the problem, especially the contention that the context within which an utterance is interpreted is a subset of the mutual cognitive environment of the author and

---

[19] The most common view is to take the epilogue as 22:6-21: Lambrecht, "Structuration," pp. 78-79; Vanni, *La struttura*, pp. 107-115; Wendland, "7 X 7," p. 386; Mazzaferri, *Genre*, p. 334; Yarbro Collins, *Combat Myth*, p. 19; Hellholm, "Problem," p. 52; Snyder, "Triple-Form," p. 443; Ugo Vanni, "Liturgical Dialogue as a Literary Form in the Book of Revelation," *NTS* 37 (1991): 348-72; Talbert, *Apocalypse*, p. 12. Others take the epilogue as beginning at 22:8, for example Ernst Lohmeyer, *Die Offenbarung des Johannes* (HNT 16; Tübingen: J. C. B. Mohr, 1953), p. 2; at 22:10, for example Aune, *Revelation 1–5*, p. c; Aune, *Revelation 17–22*, p. 1195; Michaels, *Interpreting*, p. 71; or at 22:12, for example Charles H. Giblin, *The Book of Revelation: The Open Book of Prophecy* (GNS 34; Collegeville, Minn.: Liturgical Press, 1991), pp. 16-17.

[20] See Boring, "The Voice of Jesus"; Vanni, "Liturgical Dialogue"; Michaels, "Revelation 1:19."

DISCOURSE STRUCTURE OF THE APOCALYPSE: LARGE-SCALE STRUCTURES

the audience. Let us consider the way the communication situations presented by the text contribute to the cognitive environment.

The communication situation that is established at the beginning of the letter is between John and the seven churches, with God and Jesus as external to the situation (e.g., 1:4-7). But the voice of God, complete with a messenger formula, breaks into the conversation (1:8) and this begins the process of disturbing the communication situation by forcing it open. This breaking open continues when Jesus directs John to write to the "angels" of the churches. Here, on the surface level, the communication situation of John => churches is preserved, since the whole account is a report of what John saw and heard. Yet the direct address of Jesus to each of the churches, the "I know"s, and the challenge to hear "what the Spirit is saying to the churches" blur the boundaries between a John => churches and a Jesus => churches communication axis. This is precisely what is happening in the ending, especially 22:12-20 but also anticipated in 22:7. Only 22:21 is unambiguously on the level of John => churches. The effect of this is to integrate the external communication situation, in which John's letter is being read to the assembled church, with the text-internal communication situation, where the angels, God and Jesus are communicating with John. The apparent confusion of voices is not the result of inept editing, but a deliberate shattering of the boundaries of the text, so that the vision account itself becomes not merely an account of what John saw, which the audience is called to consider objectively, but a story that involves the audience itself, in the course of which they hear the words of God and Jesus to them.

Does the audience have cognitive assumptions that form a context for understanding such a crossover of communication modes? Here again the concept of a cognitive environment, which includes both textual and situational presuppositions, can help. If the immediate context of hearing the letter is the church gathered for worship, then there is also the strong expectation that they are there to hear the voice of Jesus. Ἐκεῖ εἰμι ἐν μέσῳ αὐτῶν would be a promise that, in one form or another, was kept alive in the churches.[21] To hear the voice of Jesus in the gathered church was not at all unexpected and the mode through which this happened was Christian prophecy.[22] The voice of the prophet carries the message of

---

[21] As it is to this day. See Matt 18:20.

[22] See Boring, "The Voice of Jesus," and the discussion in David Hill, *New Testament Prophecy* (London: Marshall Morgan & Scott, 1979), pp. 160-85.

Jesus. Furthermore, there is the contextual concept of the Pauline letter, with its implications of *author-ity* and the textual mediation both of the authorial presence (cf. 1 Cor 5:3-5) and the voice of the Lord (cf. 1 Cor 7:10).[23] Both the letter form, and the frequent description of the text as prophecy, then, are not a confusion of generic categories, but again a deliberate communicative technique. In the words of the letter from John to the churches, God, Jesus and the Spirit are communicating directly to the gathered church. This is both appropriated and delegated speech, to use Wolterstorff's categories.[24]

Having addressed the problematic features of the ending of the text, we must still ask if it is possible to trace a meaningful structure. The variety of attempts that have been made is a warning against claiming unique or final status for a new proposal. However, an examination of the detailed lexical and semantic links evoked by Rev 22:6-21 shows not only that the passage is strongly linked to every major section of the Apocalypse, but also that it appears to parallel in reverse order several of the opening text sequences.

As we have already observed, 1:1-3 finds strong closure with 22:6-7. But equally clearly 22:6-9 is the final scene of the angelic revelation which begins at 21:9 and which closely parallels in form that of 17:1–19:10. Thus 22:6-9 corresponds closely to 19:6-10 and, despite the embedded voice of Jesus, rightly belongs with the vision section. But the formal letter opening, 1:4-6, is matched by a formal closing in 22:21.

On the surface 22:10-11 appears to be a continuation of the same communication situation as 22:6-9.[25] But on the other hand, the command in 22:10 not to seal the book forms a fitting semantic closure to 1:11, at the very beginning of the revelatory experience, where John is commanded to

---

[23] Yarbro Collins, *Combat Myth*, p. 7, notes that Günther Bornkamm, "On the Understanding of Worship," in *Early Christian Experience* (New York: Harper & Row, 1969), pp. 169-79, esp. 171-73, compares the ending of Revelation to liturgical formulae in 1 Cor 16:20-24, with the implication that the reading was a prelude to the celebration of the Eucharist. See also Lohmeyer, *Offenbarung*, p. 179.

[24] Wolterstorff, *Divine Discourse*, pp. 37-57. See chapter 1, pp. 38-45 above.

[25] Rev 22:6 Καὶ εἶπέν μοι . . . 9 καὶ λέγει μοι . . . 10 καὶ λέγει μοι. But note that UBS[4] capitalizes the last of these, indicating a more significant break.

write what he sees in a book.[26] This suggests that 22:10-11 may be on the same communication level as 1:9-11.

At 22:12 the voice of Jesus breaks in unannounced. It is possible to construe the whole of what follows in 22:12-20 as the voice of Jesus, with a few responses: Jesus speaks 12-16; response 17a; Jesus speaks 17b-20a; response 20b. Thus this passage corresponds most closely to 1:7-8, where the voice of God similarly alternated with responses.[27]

This analysis results in an outline structure for the epistolary part (1:4–22:21) which is broadly chiastic:

1:4–22:21 Letter
A 1:4-6 Formal letter opening
B 1:7-8 Prophetic messages and response
C 1:9–22:11 Letter body
    C1 1:9-11 Prologue to vision reports – audition of command to write
    C2 1:12–22:9 Vision reports
    C1' 22:10-11 Epilogue to vision reports – audition of command not to seal
B' 22:12-20 Prophetic messages and response
A' 22:21 Formal letter closing

But this chiasmus is rather more superficial than others that have been proposed.[28] Furthermore, there are features, some of which we have already noted, which tell against any attempt rigidly to divide up the closing section.[29]

---

[26] Compare also 1:19 and note the link to 1:3.

[27] But, as noted above, the voice of Jesus has already been heard at 22:7, embedded in the final vision report. This is one of the features which binds the whole ending together.

[28] See the references in chapter 2, p. 63, note 12.

[29] These include (1) the strong binding effect of meta-level focus on the book itself at 22:7, 9, 10, 18, 19; (2) references to the coming of Jesus at 22:7, 12, 17, 20; (3) the renominalization of John, which last occurred at 1:9 introducing the vision, occurring at 22:8, embedded in the end of the angelic revelation of 21:9–22:9; (4) the only two occurrences of κύριος Ἰησοῦς in the book, at 22:20b (directed to Jesus) and 22:21 (directed to the churches); (5) macarisms occurring at 22:7 and 22:14; and (6) the inclusion in the closing prophetic messages (in 22:14-20) of many features

3.4 Discourse Structure Diagram 1

At this point in our analysis we will begin to present a series of discourse structure diagrams showing progressively the results of our discussion of the issues. The diagrams display the text delimited into text sequences, whose boundaries and titles are in boldface type. Hierarchical subordination of text sequences is indicated in two ways. First, each new layer or grade is indented from the text sequence of which it is a subsequence. In addition a sequence label (in parentheses before the text reference) indicates precisely the position this text occupies in the overall structure. Thus the whole text is considered a zero-grade sequence, made up of two first-grade sequences, **(1) 1:1-3** and **(2) 1:4–22:21**.[30] The first of these is composed of two second-grade subsequences, **(1.1) 1:1-2** and **(1.2) 1:3**, and so on. To avoid these strings of number becoming unreadable, only Discourse Structure Diagram 1 shows the overall structure of the entire Apocalypse. Succeeding diagrams will each show the detailed structure of a part of the whole, and the sequence labels will be abbreviated. Generally the analysis only goes as far as paragraph level and reference is made to other works that provide a more detailed analysis. On a few occasions, where the outcome may be significant for the overall structure or argument, paragraphs are analyzed further.

The text delimitation has been done with respect to a number of features. In the diagrams the significant features that distinguish and mark out the text sequences are shown under the sequence label, and with the same indentation. The features that may be used are defined here.

Delimiters are textual signals that mark off the text sequence. These may be lexical, syntactic, semantic, or formal. Initial and final delimiters are separated by a semicolon. The final delimiters may be features of the end of the current text sequence, or of the beginning of the following one. In the latter case they will be enclosed in square brackets.

Communication axis refers to the source and target of the text sequence as a communication unit. A given communication axis automatically applies to all text sequences that are hierarchically subordinate to

---

that come from the final vision sequence (21:9–22:9), perhaps most notably the city and the tree of life.

[30] See Discourse Structure Diagram 1 in the following section. The grade of the sequence equals the length of the string of numbers in the label.

the given sequence. Only new embedded communication axes are listed for subordinate sequences.

Personal reference lists human, divine or spiritual beings named in the text sequence at the level being analyzed but not acting in it. Those that only occur at lower levels, are not listed.

Dramatis personae are participants who are described as performing some action within a text sequence. These are distinct from the poles of the communication axis, and from the persons only referred to in the text sequence.

Spatial signals are locations or directions of movement in space which characterize a text sequence.

Temporal signals are locations or directions of movement in time which characterize a text sequence.

Not all of these features will be significant for any particular text sequence. Features that only apply to a subsequence are not normally listed in the description of the major sequence to which the subsequence is subordinated. Question marks indicate uncertainties. Parentheses are explanatory notes.

Discourse Structure Diagram 1 (Rev 1:1–22:21)

(0) 1:1–22:21 APOCALYPSE
Delimiters: ᾽Αποκάλυψις . . . (= text opening); text ending (= letter closing)[31]
Communication axis: Author => audience
Personal reference: God, his servants, his angel, John, Jesus Christ, the reader, the listeners.

   (1) 1:1-3 Introduction
   Delimiters: ᾽Αποκάλυψις . . . , 3rd person reference to John; [᾽Ιωάννης (letter opening), 1st person reference]
   Communication axis: author => audience

      (1.1) 1:1-2 Title
      Delimiters: ᾽Αποκάλυψις . . . ; asyndeton
      Personal reference: Jesus Christ, God, his servants, his angel, John

---

[31] According to ℵ, the Byzantine tradition and a number of other witnesses, the text of Revelation ends with ἀμήν. However, UBS[4] rates the omission of ἀμήν as almost certain.

(1.2) 1:3 Macarism
Delimiters: asyndeton; ['Ιωάννης (letter opening)]
Personal reference: the one who reads, the ones who hear and keep
(2) 1:4–22:21 Letter
Delimiters: 'Ιωάννης (letter opening); letter closing
Communication axis: John => seven churches in Asia
Personal reference: John, seven churches, God, Jesus Christ, the seven spirits
   (2.1) 1:4-6 Formal letter opening
   Delimiters: 'Ιωάννης (letter opening); ἀμήν ['Ιδοὺ (prophetic message)]
   (2.2) 1:7-8 Prophetic messages and response
   Delimiters: 'Ιδοὺ; ['Εγὼ 'Ιωάννης (renominalization)]
   Communication axes: Deity (=> John) => churches, audience => deity[32]
   (2.3) 1:9–22:11 Letter body
   Delimiters: 'Εγὼ 'Ιωάννης; final delimiter ambiguous
   Communication axis: John => churches

      (2.3.1) 1:9-11 Prologue to vision reports – audition of command to write
      Delimiters: 'Εγὼ 'Ιωάννης; [Καὶ ἐπέστρεψα βλέπειν]
      Communication axes: John => churches, voice => John
      Personal reference: God, Jesus, seven churches (named)
      Dramatis personae: John, voice
      Spatial signals: Patmos
      Temporal signals: the Lord's day
      (2.3.2) 1:12–22:9 Vision reports
      Delimiters: Καὶ ἐπέστρεψα βλέπειν . . . καὶ . . . εἶδον; end of visual components
      Communication axes: John => churches, deity (=> John) => churches
      Dramatis personae: John, one like Son of Man, angels
      (2.3.3) 22:10-11 Epilogue to vision reports – audition of command not to seal
      Delimiters: καὶ λέγει μοι; ['Ιδοὺ (asyndeton)]

---

[32] Where multiple communication axes are listed, the text sequence should, strictly speaking, be further divided. However, for the sake of this broad-scale analysis, I have not separated the smaller text sequences.

Communication axes: John => churches, angel? => John
Personal reference: evildoers, the filthy, the righteous, the
holy
Dramatis personae: John, angel?
(2.4) 22:12-20 Prophetic messages and response
Delimiters: Ἰδοὺ (asyndeton); [Ἡ χάρις (letter closing formula)]
Communication axes: Jesus (=> John) => churches, churches =>
Jesus
Personal reference: those who wash their robes, list of outsiders,
angel, David, hypothetical person who adds or takes away
Dramatis personae: Jesus, Spirit, bride
(2.5) 22:21 Formal letter closing
Delimiters: Ἡ χάρις; text ending
Communication axis: John => churches
Personal reference: the Lord Jesus, the saints

3.5 Broad structure of the central visionary section (1:12–22:9)

Moving inwards, we will now examine the discourse structure of the
central section, 1:12–22:9, the report of John's visions. The essential
unity of the section is supported by a number of features. First, the section is bracketed by the command in 1:11, Ὃ βλέπεις γράψον εἰς βιβλίον,
and the prohibition in 22:10, Μὴ σφραγίσῃς τοὺς λόγους τῆς προφητείας
τοῦ βιβλίου τούτου. The only intervening meta-referential uses of βιβλίου
come in 22:7, 9, at the very end of the vision report, where the integration
of communication situations which we have noticed is taking place. Every
other occurrence within this section is a reference to something seen in
the vision. Although 1:11 also reports the instruction to send the book to
the seven named churches, and neither the names nor the churches are
mentioned after 3:22 (until 22:16), it is equally clear that the things that
John sees, which are to be the subject of his book, include the whole vision narrative. Not only is there no closure of the book following 3:22, but
there are close connections between the contents of the messages to the
churches and the remainder of the book.[33] Thus 1:9-11 is preparatory to

---

[33] See Austin Farrer, *The Revelation of St. John the Divine* (Oxford:
Clarendon, 1964), pp. 83-86; J. P. M. Sweet, *Revelation* (SCM Pelican
Commentaries; London: SCM, 1979), pp. 44-45. Note also Schüssler

the whole visionary experience, which is all therefore anchored in the "real" space-time world as taking place on the island of Patmos, on the Lord's day. Nevertheless, there are strong reasons for seeing a fundamental division within the visionary section, between 1:12–3:22 and 4:1–22:9.[34] First, there are a number of surface-level discourse markers that delimit the two subsections. The concept of what John *sees* has already been given meta-referential status in the title at 1:2 (ἐμαρτύρησεν ... ὅσα εἶδεν), and again in the instruction to write in 1:11, as we have seen. Now εἶδον is first used with structural significance at 1:12, and then not again until 4:1.[35] Furthermore, its use in 4:1 is as part of what will become an important cataphoric marker of new visionary material, εἶδον, καὶ ἰδοὺ .... Preceding this at 4:1 is the phrase Μετὰ ταῦτα, used here for the first time as a structural meta-referential marker. Similar usage, to locate a subsequent action or vision with respect to a preceding sequence, occurs in John's narrative at 7:9; 15:5; 18:1; and 19:1, while at 9:12 and 20:3 it is in embedded speech and operates at a somewhat different level, though still to relate elements within the world of the vision. Here at 4:1, the ταῦτα would most easily refer to the whole sequence of vision and audition stretching from the previous use of εἶδον in 1:12. But, in fact, μετὰ ταῦτα occurs twice in 4:1, the second time in the clause δείξω σοι ἃ δεῖ γενέσθαι μετὰ ταῦτα. This evokes contextual allusion to both 1:1 and 1:19.[36] Thus the double use of the formula here in 4:1 accomplishes at least two things. It links 4:1 back to the title in much the same way as the first vision sequence is linked. But it also integrates two time sequences, the sequence within the world of the visions, where μετὰ ταῦτα marks the relationship of the following material with what has preceded

---

Fiorenza's suggestion, "Composition," p. 364, of the relationship of chapters 1–3 with chapters 19–22.

[34] Wide support for this division comes from, among many others: Hellholm, "Problem," p. 48; Müller, *Microstructural Analysis*, pp. 200-202; Aune, *Revelation 1–5*, p. c; Lambrecht, "Structuration," p. 79; Wendland, "7 X 7," p. 376; Vanni, *La struttura*, pp. 171-72.

[35] Its use at 1:17 is anaphoric and subordinate to 1:12, serving merely to resume the narrative of action after the description of what John saw.

[36] 1:1 has δεῖξαι ... ἃ δεῖ γενέσθαι ἐν τάχει, and 1:19 ἃ μέλλει γενέσθαι μετὰ ταῦτα. As noted previously (see chapter 2, pp. 86-87, and chapter 3, pp. 91-92 above), Beale has persuasively argued that this pattern of usage sets up Dan 2 as a structural template for the whole book.

it, and the sequence in the world of the author and audience, where μετὰ ταῦτα marks the relationship of the events represented by the *whole* vision sequence to the author's present. Nothing in 1:12–3:22 has moved the temporal frame of reference from the author's present and hence 4:1 marks a significantly new stage in the revelation.

Spatial location is another major difference between the two subsections. John is on Patmos, in the spirit, when he hears a voice *behind him* and *turns* to see the owner of the voice (1:10, 12). Having seen the one like the Son of Man and fallen at his feet, the remainder of the section consists of what John heard. Nothing in all of this has moved him, in reality or "in the spirit" from his location on Patmos. But at 4:1 his attention is seized (εἶδον, καὶ ἰδοὺ) by the sight of a door *in heaven*, and he is invited to "come up." Although he does not relate a movement in response to this invitation, the location of subsequent visions is *in heaven*.[37]

Two semantic features underline the new start at 4:1-2 by linking directly to the prologue to the vision reports (specifically to 1:10). These are the references to John being ἐν πνεύματι (4:2) and to ἡ φωνὴ ἡ πρώτη ἣν ἤκουσα ὡς σάλπιγγος (4:1).[38] But there is a distinct *lack* of lexical and semantic linkage between the body of the first vision section and the beginning of the second. While the messages to the churches have many points of contact with subsequent parts of the second vision, very little of the throne-room scene of chapters 4–5 is anticipated in chapters 2–3.[39]

Last, but by no means least, of the features that compel us to analyze the central vision report in two related but distinct sections, is the change in communication situation which takes place. Although on one

---

[37] Οὐρανός occurs 51 times from 4:1 to the end, eighteen times in the phrase ἐν τῷ οὐρανῷ. The only prior occurrence was an anticipatory reference at 3:12.

[38] The latter is parallel to the similar anaphoric reference to the voice at the start of the first vision section, 1:12.

[39] The most significant parallels are: falling down in worship (2:5; cf. 4:10; 5:8); the seven spirits of God (3:1; cf. 4:5; 5:6); seven stars (2:1; 3:1; cf. 4:5; 5:6); Jesus conquers (3:21; cf. 5:5); crowns (2:10; 3:11; cf. 4:4, 10); throne of God/Christ (3:21; cf. 4–5 passim); clothed in white garments (3:4, 5; cf. 4:4); an open door (3:8, 20; cf. 4:1); holy (3:7; cf. 4:8; 5:8); David (3:7; cf. 5:5). The more numerous connections with later passages will be examined in due course. On the paucity of direct linkage between chapters 1–3 and 4–5, see also R. Dean Davis, *The Heavenly Court Judgment of Revelation 4–5* (Lanham: University Press of America, 1992), p. 19.

level John relates his vision continuously from 1:12 to 22:9, throughout the early part the seven churches, the real recipients of the document, are very strongly in focus.[40] John relates his vision of Christ, and this includes a report of what Christ instructed him to write to the seven churches. Yet although formally reporting, he is in fact obeying the instruction, communicating the message of Christ to the churches. Furthermore, the messages in chapters 2–3 are specifically directed to individual churches or, more correctly, to all the churches as exemplified by the seven specific churches. Thus the function of John's reporting, as has been noticed previously, is to shatter the "box" into which a vision report could easily be placed. By means of the vision report being read to the gathered assembly, not only the words of John, but in fact the words of Jesus are directed to the churches. Thus the surface-level communication situations could be displayed thus:

John => text (Jesus => John) => lector => churches

But in fact what is happening is more like:

Jesus => (John => text => lector) => churches

The communication situation is turned inside out. Nothing occurs on such a scale in 4:1–22:9. With the exception of a few verses where they may be directly addressed, the real audience does not feature at all.[41] John simply relates the sequence of visions that he sees "in heaven."[42] To

---

[40] Strictly by "real" I mean "implied."

[41] The verses concerned are 13:9-10, 18; 14:12; 16:15; 17:9a; 19:6b; 20:5b-6 and 22:7. See p. 147 below for further discussion.

[42] Mazzaferri, *Genre*, pp. 338-39, follows W. R. Kempson in claiming primary structural significance for the phrase ἐν πνεύματι (1:10; 4:2; 17:3; 21:10), resulting in "four principal literary divisions . . . 1:9–3:22, 4:1–16:21, 17:1–21:8 and 21:9–22:5." This had earlier been suggested by Merrill C. Tenney, *Interpreting Revelation* (Grand Rapids: Eerdmans, 1957), pp. 32-33. While none of the occurrences marks the beginning of a text sequence, they do indicate the commencement of narration of a new visionary experience. But notice should also be taken of the difference between the first two, which are initiatory (in each case John says ἐγενόμην ἐν πνεύματι) and the last two, where ἐν πνεύματι describes a state he is already in, and are therefore subordinated to the occurrence at 4:2. Further, to elevate this phrase as the primary marker is to ignore other very significant intervening markers. Snyder, "Triple-Form," pp.

elucidate the relationship between the real audience, so prominent in 1:12–3:22 (as well as in the outer envelope), and the elements of the visions John sees to which they might relate, is in fact one of the primary goals of this study.

3.6 Features of the first major vision report (1:12–3:22)

Discussion of the structure of the messages to the churches need only be brief as it is relatively uncontroversial and has been investigated by a number of scholars.[43]

The general communication situation has been discussed above. In addition it should be noted that the repeated phrase ὁ ἔχων οὖς ἀκουσάτω τί τὸ πνεῦμα λέγει ταῖς ἐκκλησίαις has two implications. First, although each message is addressed to an individual "angel," they are clearly intended to be heard by all, hence no distinction need be made in the communication situations of each message. Second, it creates a deliberate ambiguity where the words of Jesus to the churches are also the words of the Spirit.[44]

Two features regarding the personal references in this section are worthy of note. First, it is here, within the vision report and not in the outer

---

445-49, is somewhat more reserved, suggesting only that the phrase indicates important transitions in space and possibly time. Smith, "Structure," presents a more sophisticated version of this structuring plan. By exploring the nature of textual structure in other apocalyptic texts, he suggests that there is an expectation in the genre that everything will not be straightforward, at least in terms of the relationship of literary to narrative structures. His final outline (p. 392) is very useful in displaying what might be called "pneumatic locations" of the book. But the disjunctions between textual, literary and narrative sequences in the section labeled " 'In the Spirit' in Heaven" (essentially 4:1–16:21 + 19:11–21:8) are severe and must raise the question of whether such a structure can be consistent with the principle of relevance.

[43] For example, Wendland, "7 X 7," pp. 375-76; Aune, *Revelation 1–5*, pp. 119-24; Beale, *Revelation*, pp. 224-28; William H. Shea, "The Covenantal Form of the Letters to the Seven Churches," *AUSS* 21 (1983): 71-84; Vanni, *La struttura*, pp. 175-81.

[44] See Anne-Marit Enroth, "The Hearing Formula in the Book of Revelation," *NTS* 36 (1990): 598-608; Beale, *Revelation*, pp. 236-39.

epistolary layers, that we encounter *specific* reference to the people of God who constitute the "churches in Asia." The identification of the "angel" of each church has led to considerable discussion, but whatever the significance of the rhetorical device, the text in each case quickly moves to consider the behavior of the church members themselves.[45] They are reprimanded and applauded for their actions and attitudes, and in some cases encouraged to change or to maintain these attitudes and actions. Second, it is at this level that the first mention of human and spiritual opposition occurs. We have already noted their complete absence from the outer communication situations. Here we find reference to Satan as the power behind human opponents of the Christians both within and without the church, and the devil in his familiar role of tester and accuser. Human opposition would appear to come both from without and within the church. External opposition is focused on those described as "the synagogue of Satan" (2:9; 3:9).[46] Internal tension centers around the self-styled apostles, Jezebel and her followers, the Nicolaitans, and perhaps Balaam (though it is less clear whether the name refers to a contemporary individual or is merely used to characterize a teaching). These people are clearly part of the Christian community, but equally clearly are not addressed by the author, forming instead a foil of error over against which John calls the churches to faithfulness.[47] But in the case of

---

[45] On the angels, see for example, Aune, *Revelation 1–5*, pp. 108-112, and references there; see also Enroth, "Hearing Formula."

[46] It is sometimes suggested that these are Judaizing Christians. See, for example, Stephen Goranson, "Essene Polemic in the Apocalypse of John," in *Legal Texts and Legal Issues: Proceedings of the Second Meeting of the International Organization for Qumran Studies, Cambridge 1995* (ed. Moshe Bernstein, Florentino García Martínez and John Kampen; *STDJ* 23; Leiden: E. J. Brill, 1997), pp. 453-60. I am more interested at this point in the overt representations on the surface of the text.

[47] Some scholars suggest that this distinction is clearly polemic, and needs to be "read against." See, for example, Schüssler Fiorenza, *Revelation*, pp. 132-39; Paul B. Duff, " 'I Will Give To Each of You as Your Works Deserve': Witchcraft Accusations and the Fiery-Eyed Son of God in Rev 2.18-23," *NTS* 43 (1997): 116-33; Adela Yarbro Collins, "Vilification and Self-Definition in the Book of Revelation," *HTR* 79 (1986): 308-320. Without denying the polemic involved here, for the purposes of this study I will read with the text, which does not address these people directly.

Thyatira and Sardis there would appear to be a further distinction implied among those who receive the letter, between those who are caught up in error and those who are not (2:24; 3:4). Furthermore, there are the repeated challenges to the audience to hear, and the promises to those who conquer, which imply another potential distinction within the communities addressed, between those who will respond appropriately and those who will not. This is a complex picture and requires the attention of any serious student of the text.

3.7 Discourse Structure Diagram 2

We can now expand our presentation of the overall discourse structure, to include the detail of the first major vision sequence. Note that in this and all subsequent discourse structure diagrams only part of the text of Revelation is displayed, and the sequence labels are consequently abbreviated. Thus Discourse Structure Diagram 2 shows the structure of the third-grade sequence **(2.3.2) 1:12–22:9**. The text sequence labels are shown beginning with a full stop, which means that the sequence labeled **(.1)** is actually sequence **(2.3.2.1)**. In this way the relationship of text sequences within one part of the text are obvious without the string being too unwieldy.

<u>Discourse Structure Diagram 2 (Rev 1:12–22:9)</u>

This diagram concentrates on the vision reports proper, giving the detail of only the first one. Every section number is preceded by **2.3.2**. The whole diagram is a third-grade sequence.

1:12–22:9 Vision reports
Communication axis: John => churches
   (.1) 1:12–3:22 John's vision of Jesus on Patmos
   Delimiters: Καὶ ἐπέστρεψα . . . καὶ . . . εἶδον; [Μετὰ ταῦτα εἶδον, καὶ ἰδού]
   Personal reference: seven churches, angels of seven churches
   Dramatis personae: John, one like the Son of Man
   Spatial signals: ἐπέστρεψα
      (.1.1) 1:12-16 John sees Jesus
      Delimiters: εἶδον; [Καὶ ὅτε εἶδον]

109

(.1.2) 1:17ab Reaction and response
Delimiters: Καὶ ὅτε εἶδον; λέγων
(.1.2.1) 1:17a John falls down
(.1.2.2) 1:17b Jesus places his hand on John
(.1.3) 1:17c-3:22 The words of Jesus[48]
Delimiters: [λέγων]; [Μετὰ ταῦτα εἶδον, καὶ ἰδοὺ]
(.1.3.1) 1:17c–20 The words of Jesus to John
Delimiters: [λέγων]; [Τῷ ἀγγέλῳ . . .]
Communication axis: Jesus => John
Personal reference: seven churches, angels of seven churches
(.1.3.2) 2:1–3:22 The words of Jesus to the churches through John
Delimiters: Τῷ ἀγγέλῳ . . . ; [Μετὰ ταῦτα εἶδον, καὶ ἰδοὺ]
Communication axis: Jesus => (John) => churches, Spirit => churches
  (.1.3.2.1) 2:1-7 Message to Ephesus
  Delimiters: Τῷ ἀγγέλῳ . . . (and the same for each message)
  Personal reference: angel of church in Ephesus, self-styled apostles, Nicolaitans, God
  (.1.3.2.2) 2:8-11 Message to Smyrna
  Personal reference: angel of church at Smyrna, so-called Jews (= synagogue of Satan), the devil
  (.1.3.2.3) 2:12-17 Message to Pergamum
  Personal reference: angel of church at Pergamum, Satan, Antipas, Balaam, Balak, children of Israel, Nicolaitans
  (.1.3.2.4) 2:18-29 Message to Thyatira
  Personal reference: angel of church at Thyatira, Son of God, Jezebel, those who commit adultery with her, her children, the rest in Thyatira, Satan, the nations, my Father
  (.1.3.2.5) 3:1-6 Message to Sardis
  Personal reference: angel of church at Sardis, my God, a few names not blemished, my Father, his angels
  (.1.3.2.6) 3:7-13 Message to Philadelphia

---

[48] Hellholm, "Problem," p. 48, does not place the messages to the churches hierarchically under the vision, but in fact they are subordinate to the vision sequence.

Personal reference: angel of church at Philadelphia, David, synagogue of Satan (= self-styled Jews), earth-dwellers, my God, holy city (= New Jerusalem)

(.1.3.2.7) 3:14-22 Message to Laodicea
Personal reference: angel of church at Laodicea, God, my Father

(.2) 4:1–22:9 John's vision of "things which must happen after this" in heaven[49]
Delimiters: Μετὰ ταῦτα εἶδον, καὶ ἰδού; end of vision reports
Communication axis: John => churches (occasionally author => audience or Jesus => ?)
Dramatis personae: John, angels
Spatial signals: in heaven
Temporal signals: Μετὰ ταῦτα

---

[49] Hellholm, "Problem," pp. 48-49, presents essentially the same analysis, except that his main division ends at 22:5.

Chapter 4

Discourse Structure of the Apocalypse
Part 2: The second major vision

In this chapter we will investigate in more detail the broad structure of the second major vision report, 4:1–22:9, and then the detail of the first half of this report.

4.1 Broad structure of the second major vision report (4:1–22:9)

4.1.1 Integrity and major subdivisions

The integrity of 4:1–22:9 as a unit of relevance is established both externally and internally. Externally it is delimited from the preceding and following text sequences in ways that have already been discussed. Internally two features are prominent throughout. First, there is the mode of narration of the vision and/or audition, which is characterized by the first person aorist forms εἶδον and ἤκουσα. Only two out of forty-five occurrences of the former (1:12, 17), and one out of twenty-seven of the latter (1:10) are outside the bounds of this major text sequence. Second, there is a single perspective, evident in nearly every subsection, which could best be described as a relationship to heaven and to the earth. Οὐρανός occurs in each of chapters 4–21 except chapter 7, and the only occurrence outside these limits is an anticipatory reference in 3:12. Most characteristically, action is seen and heard to take place ἐν τῷ οὐρανῷ or something comes ἐκ τοῦ οὐρανοῦ.[1] Not only does this whole text sequence

---

[1] The difference between the perspectives expressed by these two prepositional phrases is interesting in itself and will be commented on below, p. 124. There is one occurrence of εἰς τὸν οὐρανὸν (10:5). Interestingly, the location of action in or coming from heaven is not a feature of

share this perspective, but the other sequences lack it completely. Connected to the "heavenly" perspective is a view of the whole earth, as if from outer space, which also permeates the text sequence. References to the earth outside of this section are rare and anticipatory, and point to groups of people rather than to the earth itself.[2] Here the earth is frequently the object of some action or something moves εἰς τὴν γῆν.[3] Only rarely is action said to take place explicitly ἐπὶ τῆς γῆς.[4] But a perspective closely tied to the earth is implicit in many other locative expressions. There is also a significant interest throughout on the peoples of the earth.[5] The cosmic perspective is enhanced by the frequent linking of heaven and earth.[6]

While the unity of this major text sequence, comprising the greater part of the book, is apparent, its complex internal structure is both easy to observe and difficult to delineate with precision. Some scenes are clearly demarcated by their content or form; for example, the vision of two witnesses (11:1-13), the vision of the woman and the dragon (12:1-18), the vision of the two beasts (13:1-18), and the two visions with angel guides (17:1–19:10 and 21:9–22:9). While others, such as the numbered sequences of seals, trumpets and vials, appear to be straightforward, their precise limits are notoriously controversial. And the hierarchical relationship of different visionary text sequences is most problematical.[7]

---

the Greek book of Daniel. There heaven either occurs in the phrase "the God of heaven" (especially in chapter 4) or is a spatial marker internal to the description of the visions (again most common in chapter 4).

[2] Kings of the earth (1:5); tribes of the earth (1:7); inhabitants of the earth (3:10).

[3] 5:6; 6:13; 8:5, 7; 9:1, 3; 12:4, 9, 13; 13:13; 14:19; 16:1, 2. There are single occurrences only of ἐκ τῆς γῆς (13:11) and ἀπὸ τῆς γῆς (14:3).

[4] 7:1; 10:2, 5, 8. But note also 20:8, 9.

[5] Kings of the earth (6:15; 17:2, 18; 18:3, 9; 19:19; 21:24); inhabitants of the earth (6:10; 8:13; 11:10; 13:8, 14; 14:6; 17:2, 8); merchants of the earth (18:3, 11); magnates of the earth (18:23); metonymy for peoples of the earth (6:8; 11:6; 13:3; 14:3).

[6] 5:3, 13; 10:6; 14:7; 20:11; 21:1 (twice).

[7] Note, for example, Hellholm, "Problem," p. 49, who in 5:1 reads ἔσωθεν καὶ ἔξωθεν, with 025, 046, fam 1006, 1611, 1854, 2050 and the majority of Byzantine texts, in place of ἔσωθεν καὶ ὄπισθεν (see Aune, *Revelation 1–5*, p. 322, for details). Hellholm then assigns 6:1–22:5 to the

Several words or phrases offer themselves as surface-level discourse markers.[8] There are nine occurrences of μετὰ ταῦτα, but closer examination shows that these perform several different functions. Twice the phrase relates the events described in the totality of the visions to the real time of John's present (1:19 and 4:1, second occurrence). This is the usage that is strongly evocative of the phrase in Dan 2:29, 45 (Th).[9] Twice it is internal to a vision, relating events in the sequence of vision time, not with respect to John's time (9:12; 20:3). Twice it is a relatively low-level marker within the first angelic vision sequence (18:1; 19:1). This leaves three occurrences where it is potentially of major significance within the time frame of John's visionary experience (4:1; 7:9; 15:5) and of these the last is possibly downgraded by a paratactic καὶ. At both 4:1 and 7:9, the phrase combines with other discourse markers to form the sequence Μετὰ ταῦτα εἶδον, καὶ ἰδού. Only once (7:1) there is Μετὰ τοῦτο εἶδον, where the singular τοῦτο appears to have less scope than the

---

contents of the heavenly scroll, a fourth-grade sequence, and divides it into two fifth-grade sequences, the *scriptura exterior* (6:1–7:17), and the *scriptura interior* (8:1–22:5). By contrast, Schüssler Fiorenza, "Composition," p. 363, assigns 4:1–9:21; 11:15-19; 15:1; 15:5–16:21; 17:1–19:10 to the "seven-sealed scroll," 10:1–15:4 (without 11:15-19) to the "little scroll" of chapter 10, and 19:11–22:9 to a final distinct section. Vanni, *La struttura*, p. 249 and Lambrecht, "Structuration," pp. 85-86, nest the three plague sequences within each other, a structure that Aune, *Revelation 1–5*, pp. c-cv, appears to follow. Wendland, "7 X 7," divides the text into seven scenes, which requires incorporating 22:10-21 into the text also. (His sevenfold structures internal to the scenes are often equally forced.) Other types of division will be seen as we proceed.

[8] Schüssler Fiorenza, "Composition," p. 362, points out that "these 'dividing marks' do not occupy such a clear position in the outline of Revelation that the author could have intended to indicate the structure of his work with them. The author does not divide the text into separate sections or parts, but *joins* units together by interweaving them with each other . . ." (italics hers). The second point is well made, and we shall have occasion to return to it. But "divisions" of the book certainly exist and I will argue here that some of the markers *are* intended to indicate transition from one to another.

[9] The only other occurrences in the Greek of Daniel are a single use in the real-world time sequence (1:5, Th) and a similar use but within the vision-world time sequence (7:6, OG).

plural ταῦτα. I have already noted the frequency of εἶδον, which, along with ἤκουσα, creates continuity through the whole of 4:1–22:9.[10] Both draw attention to a new feature of a vision or audition, shifting the focus, or the breadth or depth of the vision, from the previous segment but still within the same perspective. Both most commonly are immediately preceded by καὶ in clause-initial position.[11] The preponderance of the conjunctive καὶ in Revelation as a whole is enormous, and by itself it is the default conjunction for linking elements of the same vision segment.[12] This gives a primarily paratactic flavor to the narrative, similar to Hebrew narrative style. It combines with εἶδον or ἤκουσα to form a somewhat higher level discourse connective as already described. Ἰδού most often occurs in direct speech as a marker of semantic emphasis or attention. In narrative, however, combined with εἶδον, it draws emphatic attention to a new visual component.[13] Εἶδον, καὶ ἰδού thus marks a stronger shift in focus than εἶδον by itself. On three occasions (4:2; 12:3;

---

[10] Εἶδον and ἤκουσα also appear to have another narrative function. The continuity of perception represents the visionary's perspective and this keeps the visionary himself within the audience's view. This feature was pointed out to me by my supervisor, Dr. Tim Meadowcroft, and parallels the situation he noted in Dan 7. See Tim J. Meadowcroft, *Aramaic Daniel and Greek Daniel: A Literary Comparison* (JSOTSup 198; Sheffield: Sheffield Academic Press, 1995), pp. 208-209.

[11] Εἶδον in 32 out of 45 occurrences; ἤκουσα in 17 out of 27 occurrences. Occasionally they are separated from the καὶ by an intervening phrase. Not uncommonly they occur in anaphoric relative clauses, referring back to an earlier vision or audition.

[12] Καὶ occurs 1123 times in Revelation, on average nearly three times per verse. This contrasts with other common conjunctions: δέ (7 times), οὖν (6 times, only once outside of chapters 2–3), ἀλλὰ (8 times, once outside of chapters 2–3). There are no occurrences of μέν, but γὰρ is slightly more common with 16 widely spread occurrences.

[13] This may also be true of the first occurrence, at 1:7, in a prophetic speech. Both usages of ἰδού are common in the Old Greek text of Daniel, but in Theodotion the use in direct speech as a marker of semantic emphasis is rare (3:92; 8:19; 11:2). Much more common is its use to draw attention to a new visual stimulus. On the discourse functions of ἰδού, see Roger Van Otterloo, "Towards an Understanding of 'Lo' and 'Behold': Functions of ἰδού and ἴδε in the Greek New Testament," *OPTAT* 2 (1988): 34-64.

19:11) καὶ ἰδού heads the second clause of a sentence, as part of a high-level complex shift to a new discourse segment. We can thus suggest an approximate hierarchy of discourse connectives:

μετὰ ταῦτα εἶδον, καὶ ἰδού
(καὶ) εἶδον, καὶ ἰδού; (clause) καὶ ἰδού; μετὰ ταῦτα (εἶδον or ἤκουσα)
καὶ . . . εἶδον; καὶ . . . ἤκουσα; μετὰ τοῦτο εἶδον
καὶ

Based on these markers alone, we would expect to find major new segments or subsegments beginning at 4:1; 7:1, 9; 12:1; 14:1, 14; 19:11. However, the picture is much more complicated than this. The numbered sequence of seals imposes a structure that overrides the breaks at 7:1 and 7:9. But when the seals are considered together with the trumpets, the break at 12:1 is reinforced. 12:1 also introduces another discourse delimiter, the appearance of σημεῖον . . . ἐν τῷ οὐρανῷ, which occurs again in 12:3 and 15:1.[14] For the time being, therefore, I will consider 4:1–11:19 as a single text sequence, with a question mark hanging over the status of chapter 7 and the two major discourse breaks in it.[15] The decision to close this sequence at 11:19, however, needs some defense.

---

[14] Korner, "Apocalyptic Literary Convention," has recently attempted to outline a discourse structure based on a hierarchy of discourse markers, which are, in descending order of significance (p. 162), the "space/time referent," μετὰ ταῦτα εἶδον, and καὶ εἶδον, (καὶ ἰδού). This approach is commendable in noticing the significance of these surface-level markers, but has a tendency to oversimplify the distinctions between variants. Furthermore, he takes no account of the many other markers of discourse structure, such as the epistolary envelope, the angelic journeys, the variety of communication situations in the epilogue and the symmetry and closure it produces, and the role of σημεῖον μέγα mentioned above. Thus the set of six vision blocks he ends up with (p. 174) is suspect. The outline I arrive at can be seen on pp. 123-24 below.

[15] This basic division is supported, to quote two widely separated examples, by Swete, *Apocalypse*, pp. xxxix-xli, and Yarbro Collins, *Combat Myth*, pp. 28-31. Strand, "Chiastic Structure," pp. 401-408, argues that the main turning point in the book comes between chapters 14 and 15, rather than between chapters 11 and 12. However, the evidence he adduces, in particular the way in which the "Evil Hierarchy" is introduced from 12:3 and then punished in the reverse order, only serves to emphasize the essential unity of the sequence. Jan A. du Rand, "A 'Basso

4.1.2 Revelation 11:19 as a hinge verse

Müller argues that the use of ἐν τῷ οὐρανῷ and ὤφθη in 11:19 links it closely to 12:1, and that it is in some ways comparable to the throne scene of chapters 4–5, providing an introductory worship scene for the bowl series, as those chapters did for the seals. [16] The first point may be granted, but could equally be explained as part of John's interlocking technique.[17] The second is most unlikely, as this single verse is both too short and too far distant from the bowls to be in any way comparable to chapters 4–5, where the throne scene led straight into the opening of the seals. Chapter 15 itself provides a suitable and immediate introduction to the bowl series. Aune supports the linking of 11:19 to chapter 12 with a number of arguments of varying degrees of cogency.[18] Whether the thunder opens or closes scenes is admittedly ambiguous.[19] The suggestion that at 8:5; 11:19 and 16:18-21 it closes the seals, trumpets and bowls, corresponding to its opening appearance in the throne-room scene, is at least as likely as any other. The further argument that the opening of the heavenly temple functions to open a scene, corresponding to the open door in heaven (4:1) and the opened heaven (19:11), is more weighty. But in both those cases a perfect participle is used to describe an existing state of affairs. In 11:19 an aorist indicative suggests an action seen by

---

Ostinato' in the Structuring of the Apocalypse of John?" *Neot* 27 (1993): 299-311, finds that references to "the Christ-event" bind three major subdivisions, chapters 1–3, 4–11, and 12–22, into a unity. On the other hand, the schemes proposed by Hellholm and Schüssler Fiorenza (see note 7, pp. 114-15 above) both fail by the principle of relevance. At least from our admittedly distant perspective in time, there are no elements in the text or its context that would lead to these particular structures presenting themselves to the hearer as optimally relevant. The use of ἐν πνεύματι to obtain a different division has been mentioned above (note 42, pp. 106-107).

[16] Müller, *Microstructural Analysis*, pp. 325-31. See also Kenneth A. Strand, "The 'Victorious Introduction' Scenes in the Visions in the Book of Revelation," *AUSS* 25 (1987): 267-88.

[17] See chapter 2, p. 80 (especially note 72) and pp. 121-22 below.

[18] David E. Aune, *Revelation 6–16* (WBC 52B; Dallas: Word, 1998), pp. 661-62.

[19] See also Vanni, *La struttura*, pp. 141-48; Lambrecht, "Structuration," pp. 93-95; Bauckham, *Climax*, pp. 199-209.

John in the vision.[20] In fact, the closest link to 11:19 comes not in chapters 12–14 but in 15:5.[21]

The most interesting argument, from a relevance perspective, in favor of linking 11:19 to chapter 12, is Aune's suggestion (without using relevance-theoretic terminology) that Isa 66:6-7 is the cognitive environment which provides the structural clues.[22] However, if Relevance Theory allows this argument to be heard, it also disposes of it. There is nothing in 11:19 which, in itself, would lead to the opening of Isa 66:6 as a possible context of interpretation. Revelation does, of course, have a "voice from the temple," but in 16:1, 17, not 11:19. And if the context of Isaiah is suggested retrospectively when the audience hears 12:5 (or 16:1), then it must be said that it requires far more processing effort than other more accessible contexts, built from the text of Revelation itself. The temple is completely absent from 12:1–14:13.

Conversely, the feature of 11:19 that is totally new and unexpected is ἡ κιβωτὸς τῆς διαθήκης. This is one of only two references to this focal cultic object in the entire NT and raises a significant problem for the relevance of this verse. What co-text or context is accessible within which to make sense of this reference?[23] Or, more to the point in our current structural study, are there cognitive environments that give it structural significance?

First, it is closely linked with all the other furnishings of the tabernacle.[24] Among these is the θυσιαστήριον, which is prominent in Rev 6–11, but disappears from sight along with the temple, before two final

---

[20] 11:19 has ἠνοίγη; cf. 4:1 with ἠνεῳγμένη; 19:11 with ἠνεῳγμένον.

[21] Aune treats 11:19 as introducing 12:1-17. If it is introductory, it should be to 12:1–16:21 or even 12:1–22:9.

[22] Isa 66:6 with φωνὴ ἐκ ναοῦ (cf. Rev 11:19); Isa 66:7 with ἔτεκεν ἄρσεν (cf. Rev 12:5).

[23] Bauckham's suggestion, *Climax*, p. 203, that it "must be the throne of God which chapter 4 describes," offers an interesting possibility, but the associations cannot be said to be very strong. Rev 7:15 has made the connection between the throne and the sanctuary, but the ark of the covenant is never explicitly described as a throne in the OT and the ναός is not mentioned in the throne-room vision at all.

[24] Note especially Exodus chapters 25–26, 31, 37–40, and the only other NT occurrence, Heb 9:4. The tabernacle is called a σκηνή τοῦ μαρτυρίου in Exo 40:34-35; cf. Rev 15:5.

occurrences in chapters 14 and 16.[25] Second, when the tabernacle is set up, the ark is screened from sight by a κατακάλυμμα τοῦ καταπετάσματος.[26] And in one of the most fascinating references, 2 Macc 2:4-8, Jeremiah is said to have hidden the ark, with the tent and the altar of incense, in a cave and sealed (ἐνέφραξεν) the entrance, declaring that the place would remain unknown until God gathered his people and the glory of the Lord and the cloud would appear (ὀφθήσεται). The ark, covered, hidden or sealed, linked to the appearance of the glory of God and the cloud (recalling both the initial installation of the tabernacle and the dedication of Solomon's temple) are all motifs quite coherent with the text sequences preceding 11:19 and not at all with those immediately following it. Third, when the ark is established in its tent outside Jerusalem in 1 Chr 16, Benaiah and Jahaziel were appointed "to blow trumpets regularly" before it (1 Chr 16:6), providing a further link back to the trumpet sequence of Rev 8:2–11:18.[27] It must be acknowledged that these possible contexts for understanding the significance of the ark are somewhat distant. Nevertheless, the principle of relevance suggests that such a prominent feature will prompt the audience to investigate possible contexts until adequate contextual effects are found. One of these contextual effects, I suggest, is the association of 11:19 primarily with what precedes it.

Finally, with regard to 11:19, it must be stressed that although there is little connection to 12:1–14:13, thereafter the links begin to be formed again, until 15:5-8 brings us strongly back to the same context. But in addition to this, the end of the bowl septet, 16:17-21, not only repeats the thunder and lightning, but expands on both the earthquake and the hail. It is almost as though the entire bowl sequence is an expansion on 11:19. It seems likely that John uses it as a joint or hinge, to close the temple scene opened in 11:1, and the whole trumpet series, and to provide a link forward to chapter 15, where the main narrative will resume and the temple becomes the dominant spatial marker.

---

[25] The references are Rev 6:9; 8:3, 5; 9:13; 11:1; 14:18; 16:7.

[26] Exo 40:21. In our text the ark is part of the ἀποκάλυψις.

[27] This is part of the close association of the ark with David, pointed out by Sa-Moon Kang, *Divine War in the Old Testament and in the Ancient Near East* (BZAW 177; Berlin: Walter de Gruyter, 1989), pp. 208-212, an association which strengthens the conclusion that 11:19 closes the section which explicitly names its main protagonist "the Lion of the tribe of Judah, the Root of David" (5:5).

4.1.3 Broad outline of 12:1–22:9

The audience hearing the reading of the Apocalypse will almost certainly have perceived a major new section beginning at 12:1, a section whose structure of "great signs" will go on to include the bowl sequence. Yet at the same time, the return to the temple and all its associated phenomena will have had the effect of bracketing chapters 12–14 and linking the bowls closely with the earlier septets, though not as closely as the trumpets are linked to the seals.[28]

The occurrences of σημεῖον μέγα . . . ἐν τῷ οὐρανῷ are an obvious structuring device. But 12:3 clearly does not introduce a new sequence since the story of the woman and the story of the dragon are inextricably linked. If 15:1 can be seen as parallel to 12:1, it can also stand as a title over the whole of 15:1–22:9, since, with the exception of the interlude in 19:11–21:8, the plague-bearing angels are significant actors throughout. In 15:1–16:21 they are the principal actors, but one of their number is the angelic guide in each of the vision journeys, 17:1–19:10 and 21:9–22:9, which define the main outlines of the remainder of the central vision section.[29] On this analysis, the status of chapter 14 is difficult to determine. With its pairing of significant discourse markers (Καὶ εἶδον, καὶ ἰδού in 14:1, 14) introducing two quite different sections, one largely retrospective in its linkages, the other largely, though not entirely, prospective, it stands as something of a bridge between the text sequences 12:1–13:18 and 15:1–22:9.

4.1.4 Overlaps and interlockings

Despite the degree of coherence evidenced by these subsections, there are a number of features that cross the boundaries. In fact, John appears at times deliberately to introduce an anticipatory reference to something

---

[28] Giblin, *Revelation*, p. 15, considers the seventh trumpet to include 11:15–15:8 and to be composed of a sevenfold chiasmus, focused on 14:1-5. This is intriguing but I suggest that it is a pattern which would be imperceptible to the hearer and overrides significant structural discontinuities.

[29] Mazzaferri, *Genre*, pp. 338-39, argues, against W. R. Kempson, that σημεῖον connects 12:1–15:1, not 12:1–16:21, but fails to notice that 15:1 itself is connected, not only to the whole of chapters 15–16, but with the rest of the Apocalypse, as far as 22:9, by the device of the plague-bearing angels.

that will become the focus of a later vision, so that the vision sequences are more like the links of a chain than a discrete linear sequence.[30] For example, the beast receives an anticipatory mention at 11:7 and is then focal in the next major sequence (12:1–14:13). After this it links to the subsequent one at 15:2, becomes focal again in chapter 17, and links again to the penultimate sequence at 19:19; 20:4, 10. The first and second sequences are also linked by the songs of victory at 11:15-18 and 12:10-12. Babylon is mentioned at 14:8, and again in the next section at 16:19, before it becomes focal in chapters 17–19. The connection of wine and wrath is made (in two different ways) at 14:8, 10 and is picked up again in the next section at 14:19 and 16:19. The blood of saints is first explicit at 16:6, then again at 17:6 and 18:24. The bride links 19:6-9 with 21:2, 9. Thus the theme of the marriage of the Lamb spans the penultimate section of visions of the opened heaven. Jerusalem, the holy city, strongly connects the final two sections (21:2 and 21:10). The throne of God, which is the center of all action in chapters 4–11, moves somewhat to the background until 19:4, and the heavenly temple is the point of reference in the section 14:14–16:21. The elders and the living creatures, prominent in the throne scene, also recede into the background and after 7:13 are only mentioned at a couple of significant junctures.[31] Many more examples could be adduced of lexical and semantic strands woven through the whole section of 4:1–22:9, but these are the main chaining motifs, and they are sufficient to indicate that the integrity of the sections which I have proposed needs to be further investigated. They are also a warning not to expect to find a watertight, logical structure within this major section of the text.[32]

---

[30] Schüssler Fiorenza makes a similar point (see note 8, p. 115 above).

[31] Living creatures (14:3; 15:7; 19:4); elders (14:3; 19:4). Note that the throne of God also becomes focal again at 19:4, having had only two occurrences (12:5 and 16:17) since the end of chapter 11.

[32] Schüssler Fiorenza, "Composition," p. 360, notes that the "technique of *intercalation* . . . makes a diagramming of the successive sections of Revelation almost impossible" (see chapter 2, note 10, pp. 62-63, for a definition of intercalation). This feature certainly means that the linear displays of structure, such as the ones we have given in chapters 3–5, give a far from comprehensive idea of the interconnectedness of Revelation.

4.1.5 Discourse Structure Diagram 3

At this point we can view the overall structure of the second major vision section, the individual subsections of which we will examine in more detail shortly.

Discourse Structure Diagram 3 (Rev 4:1–22:9)

This diagram gives the broad outline of the second vision narrative. Every section number is preceded by **2.3.2.2**. The whole diagram represents a fourth-grade sequence. The highest level subtexts will each be diagrammed separately.

4:1–22:9 John's vision of "things which must happen after this" in heaven
(.1) 4:1–11:19 Vision of throne room, leading on to the 7 seals and 7 trumpets
Delimiters: Μετὰ ταῦτα εἶδον, καὶ ἰδού; thunder, etc. [Καὶ σημεῖον μέγα ὤφθη . . .]
Spatial signals: in heaven, from heaven, around/before/beside the throne
    (.1.1) 4:1–7:8 Heavenly worship and the first six seals
    Delimiters: Μετὰ ταῦτα εἶδον, καὶ ἰδού; [Μετὰ ταῦτα εἶδον, καὶ ἰδού]
    Spatial signals: in heaven, around/before the throne
    (.1.2) 7:9–11:19 Heavenly worship and the seventh seal
    Delimiters: Μετὰ ταῦτα εἶδον, καὶ ἰδού; [Καὶ σημεῖον μέγα ὤφθη ἐν τῷ οὐρανῷ]
    Dramatis personae: great crowd, angels, living creatures, elders, bowl angels, strong angel
    Spatial signals: in heaven, from heaven
    Temporal signals: Μετὰ ταῦτα
(.2) 12:1–22:9 Signs and visions in heaven
Delimiters: Καὶ σημεῖον μέγα; end of vision reports
Communication axis: vision narration broken by author => audience asides
Dramatis personae: Lamb, beast
Spatial signals: πόλις
    (.2.1) 12:1–14:20 Signs and visions of conflict
    Delimiters: Καὶ σημεῖον μέγα ὤφθη ἐν τῷ οὐρανῷ; [Καὶ εἶδον ἄλλο σημεῖον]

Dramatis personae: dragon, beast, people of God, Lamb
Spatial signals: in heaven, on earth

(.2.2) 15:1–22:9 Signs and visions of judgment and victory, involving plague angels
Delimiters: Καὶ εἶδον ἄλλο σημεῖον; end of vision narration
Dramatis personae: plague angels

(.2.2.1) 15:1–16:21 Seven plague angels pour out their bowls
Delimiters: Καὶ εἶδον ἄλλο σημεῖον; [Καὶ ἦλθεν εἷς ἐκ τῶν ἑπτὰ ἀγγέλων]
Spatial signals: out of the temple

(.2.2.2) 17:1–19:10 First vision sequence with angel-guided journey – Babylon
Delimiters: Καὶ ἦλθεν εἷς ἐκ τῶν ἑπτὰ ἀγγέλων; final interaction with angel
Spatial signals: into the wilderness, the throne (chapter 19)

(.2.2.3) 19:11–21:8 Visions of the opened heaven
Delimiters: end of first angelic journey; beginning of second
Spatial signals: in heaven, on earth, the throne (20:11; 21:3)

(.2.2.4) 21:9–22:9 Second vision sequence with angel-guided journey – New Jerusalem
Delimiters: Καὶ ἦλθεν εἷς ἐκ τῶν ἑπτὰ ἀγγέλων; end of vision sequence
Spatial signals: a great, high mountain, out of heaven

4.2 Detailed structure of the first sequence (4:1–11:19)

4.2.1 Heaven and worship

This text sequence is defined by its spatial references to heaven and the throne of God, and by the prominence of the worship that takes place there. Although the earth is often the object of action, it is rarely set as the scene. Prepositional phrases with respect to heaven show an interesting distribution between action *in* heaven and action originating *from* heaven:

ἐν τῷ οὐρανῷ	4:1, 2; 5:3, 13; 8:1	11:15, 19
ἐκ τοῦ οὐρανοῦ	8:10; 9:1; 10:1, 4, 8; 11:12	

The first series covers the throne scene (chapters 4–5) and spans the breaking of the seven seals, which also takes place, though implicitly, in heaven. The second series covers the first six trumpets, but links them with the scroll vision of chapter 10 and its sequel in the story of the witnesses in chapter 11. The importance of the two series of seven (seals and trumpets) for the structure of this whole section is both obvious and controversial. It highlights the major question challenging the unity of this whole text sequence. Does the series of seals end with 8:1, and a completely new section begin with the introduction of the trumpets in 8:2, or are the trumpets a part of the vision of the seventh seal?[33] Alternatively, is chapter 7 a bridge between two subsections, the first of which comprises the first six seals and the second includes both the seventh seal and the seven trumpets? The pattern of spatial signals displayed above, with a return to "in heaven" for the last of the trumpets and the final scene of 11:19, underlines the essential unity of perspective of this whole section, and supports the subordination of the trumpets to the seventh seal, as will be argued further below. But before turning to some detail, note also that worship in heaven is another feature that adds to the symmetry and coherence of this sequence, being prominent in the opening scene (chapters 4–5), towards the end of the seals (7:9-17), and at the beginning and end of the trumpets (8:3-5; 11:15-19).

4.2.2 Vision and audition in 4:1–8:1

Following the opening of the major new text sequence in 4:1-2, the rest of chapter 4 is John's description of the scene in heaven using present participles and present or future indicatives to indicate the repeated or continuous state of affairs, strung together with 23 paratactic καὶs at phrase level or higher (plus 11 at word level). Having taken in the whole scene, John's attention is then seized several times by new features of the vision and by developmental action (as opposed to the earlier stative or repetitive action) that takes place. Καὶ εἶδον at 5:1, 2, 6, 11; 6:1, and καὶ ἤκουσα at 5:11, 13; 6:1, and a number of other aorist verbs, help this forward movement. The frequency of markers of both visionary and auditory perception increases in chapter 6 with the series of seal openings, but the first is the most marked and would appear therefore to subordinate the others to it:

6:1-2   Καὶ εἶδον . . . καὶ ἤκουσα . . . καὶ εἶδον, καὶ ἰδού

---

[33] See especially Müller, *Microstructural Analysis*, pp. 233-44, and the references there.

6:3   Καὶ . . . ἤκουσα[34]
6:5   Καὶ . . . ἤκουσα . . . καὶ εἶδον, καὶ ἰδού
6:7-8   Καὶ . . . ἤκουσα . . . καὶ εἶδον, καὶ ἰδού
6:9   Καὶ . . . εἶδον
6:12   Καὶ εἶδον

In between these the action is carried forward by καὶ parataxis. As is often noted, the first four seals have additional structural components in the voice of the living creatures, and the riders on the horses. But each of these seals has both auditory and visual components. The first four explicitly have the living creatures calling forth the horses, but the fifth and sixth seals include the voices of the souls under the altar and the people calling out in terror respectively. This pattern creates the expectation that the seventh seal will comprise both auditory and visual components. When, at last, the seventh seal is opened in 8:1, in place of voices there is silence. Max Wilcox, drawing on Qumran and Targumic literature, suggests that this may reflect the result of a midrashic exegesis linking Exo 19:16 with 1 Kgs 19:11-12, and that the silence can be understood as the voice of God.[35] But the visual dimension is also present in 8:2 with immediate relevance—the seven trumpet angels are the visual component of the seventh seal.[36] There is no textual indication that would require the audience to access any other cognitive assumption. Thus the following is added to the series above:

8:1-2   Καὶ . . . (silence) . . . καὶ εἶδον

---

[34] Note that ℵ increases the symmetry by including a visual component. Following the ἔρχου, in place of the simple καὶ found in A, C, etc., ℵ has ἔρχου καὶ ἴδε, καὶ εἶδον, καὶ ἰδού. (The ἴδε features in each of the first four seal openings in ℵ and functions to redirect the command to "Come" toward John rather than the horsemen.)

[35] Max Wilcox, "'Silence in Heaven' (Rev 8:1) and Early Jewish Thought," in *Mogilany 1989: Papers on the Dead Sea Scrolls offered in memory of Jean Carmignac. Part II: The Teacher of Righteousness / Literary Studies* (ed. Zdzislaw J. Kapera; Qumranica Mogilanensia 3; Kraków: Enigma Press, 1991), pp. 241-44.

[36] As noted previously, Vanni, *La struttura*, p. 249, Lambrecht, "Structuration," pp. 85-86; and Aune, *Revelation 1–5*, pp. c-cv, nest the trumpet series within the seventh seal. See also Jan Lambrecht, "The Opening of the Seals (Rev 6,1–8,6)," *Bib* 79 (1998): 212-16.

This, however, is one of the pivotal issues for the structure of Revelation, so we will examine it in some further detail.

4.2.3 Revelation 8:1 – closure or open-endedness?

Müller has argued that the seal septet closes definitively with 8:1, and that 8:2 marks the beginning of a completely new section of Revelation, thus separating the trumpets from the seals.[37] His motivation for this is at least partly to ensure that the trumpets recapitulate the seals, rather than being a subsequent series of events (a motivation that directly contradicts his professed interest only in the surface structure of the text). He appears to ignore the fact that the literary device of embedment does not *necessarily* imply chronological sequence.[38] Two of Müller's arguments, namely that 8:2-6 forms an introduction to the trumpet series, and that it has a chiastic structure, may be true in themselves but say nothing whatsoever about the relationship of the trumpet series to the seventh seal.[39] He further argues that καὶ εἶδον in 8:2 opens a new section. Yet the same phrase occurs internally to the first, third and fourth seals, so there appears no reason why it might not also be internal to the seventh. I have already pointed out that the status of the thunder is somewhat ambiguous, but 16:17-21 suggests it may function to close scenes as well as to open them.[40] Finally, Müller is concerned that if the trumpets issue out of the seventh seal, the effect is anticlimactic. But is this doubling back not a recurring feature of Revelation, whose overall

---

[37] Müller, *Microstructural Analysis*, pp. 233-44.

[38] Note the comment by Adela Yarbro Collins, *The Apocalypse* (NTM 22; Wilmington, Del.: Michael Glazier, 1979), p 55: "...the whole cycle of the trumpets is, in a sense, a series of events set in motion by the opening of the seventh seal. But this relationship should not be understood chronologically . . . the interlocking of the two cycles is a literary device. It provides an opportunity for beginning again and telling the story from another perspective." On the other hand, Aune, *Revelation 1–5*, p. xciii, attributes this recapitulation only to the hypothetical sources of the material, and asserts that the author of the book intends "a single chronological narrative."

[39] Note, however, that Beale, *Revelation*, pp. 460-64, sees 8:1, 3-5 as the conclusion to the seals, with an anticipatory reference to the trumpets in 8:2, which interlocks the two series. For Biguzzi, *I settenari*, p. 226, 8:1 is a vertex or point of intersection between the first cycle and what follows.

[40] See section 4.1.2, pp. 118-20 above.

progress is rather more like a spiral staircase than a straight ladder? Again, structure and chronology, though clearly associated, do not travel on parallel lines. It must be said, then, that none of Müller's arguments are sufficient to outweigh the clear gains in relevance by considering the trumpets as the visual part of the seventh seal.[41]

4.2.4 Revelation 7 – interlude or hinge?

The status of chapter 7 now requires closer examination. The sixth seal (6:12-17) has unfolded as a single cataclysmic event, described with extensive καὶ parataxis.[42] In fact each of the preceding seals unveiled a single scene. Since the total number of seals was given at 5:1, 5, there is a structural expectation of a seventh to come. 7:1 appears therefore as something of a break in the pattern. However, the unique Μετὰ τοῦτο appears to have local reference, not only because of the singular τοῦτο, but also because there is no change in scene.[43] Although the overall perspective of this whole section is "in heaven" and this is where the seal opening takes place, the action following from opening each seal inevitably involves the earth. The falling of the stars at 6:13 indicates that the perspective internal to the scene itself is centered on the earth. Thus the four angels standing at the four corners of the earth do not represent a departure from this, but rather a shift in focus within the one scene, in much the same way as 5:1, following a single description using καὶ parataxis, focuses on a new feature noticed in the same scene. But here at 7:1 there is a difference. The image of the stars falling like figs from a fig tree shaken in the *wind* (6:13) is surely recalled in 7:1-3 by the reference to the holding back of the four *winds*, lest they harm earth or sea or *any tree*.[44] This suggests that the new element in the vision introduced at 7:1

---

[41] Giblin, *Revelation*, pp. 13-14, extends the seventh seal to 8:5 (and in "Recapitulation," p. 85, pushes it further to include 8:6), but still has a complete break before the beginning of the trumpets. This overlooks the deliberate interlocking of the two sequences.

[42] 13 occur at phrase level or higher, plus 7 at word level.

[43] Aune, *Revelation 1–5*, p. 276, gives too much prominence to this marker, which is manifestly different from μετὰ ταῦτα, and too little to Μετὰ ταῦτα in 7:9.

[44] Beale, *Revelation*, p. 396, correctly points to the primary source of the image of stars falling from heaven in Isa 34:4, where they are compared with *leaves* falling from a fig tree. John, as usual, is creative with his sources.

is retrospective. The cataclysmic events described in the sixth seal, using standard apocalyptic motifs, and the plight of the whole population of earth in the face of the "day of wrath" have raised the question of the status of God's elect in this catastrophe. 7:1-8 answers this by its vision of the preparatory sealing of the slaves of God, *before* the catastrophe. The unity of this passage with the sixth seal is further supported by the probability that it assumes as a mutual cognitive environment the same traditions as underlie the Synoptic Apocalypse.[45] Restricting our attention to issues of structure rather than interpretation, the fact that in Matt 24 the gathering of the elect from the four winds follows the cosmic disasters

---

[45] We are assuming that the Synoptic Apocalypse (Matt 24; Mark 13; Luke 17; 21) forms part of the mutual cognitive environment. See Lars Hartman, *Prophecy Interpreted: The Formation of Some Jewish Apocalyptic Texts and of the Eschatological Discourse, Mark 13 Par.* (trans. Neil Tomkinson, with the assistance of Jean Gray; ConBNT 1; Lund, Sweden: CWK Gleerup, 1966); Louis A. Vos, *The Synoptic Traditions in the Apocalypse* (Kampen: J. H. Kok, 1965); Beale, "Use of Daniel"; and especially Eugenio Corsini, *The Apocalypse: The Perennial Revelation of Jesus Christ* (ed. and trans. Francis J. Moloney; GNS 5; Dublin: Veritas, 1983). See also the discussion in Beale, *Revelation*, pp. 396-97, on the OT sources behind this material. While we cannot assume that the audience had Matthew's or any other Gospel in its present form, there is a reasonable presumption that such material, significant enough for the early church to be included in all three Synoptic Gospels, was part of the received traditions. For a comparison between chapter 6 and the Synoptic material, see Davis, *Heavenly Court*, pp. 176-81; and M. D. Goulder, "The Phasing of the Future," in *Texts and Contexts: Biblical Texts in Their Textual and Situational Contexts, Essays in Honor of Lars Hartman* (ed. Tord Fornberg and David Hellholm; Oslo: Scandinavian University Press, 1995), pp. 391-408. Note the points of contact with the book of Revelation, underlined in the following extracts from Matt 24:29-32:

[29]Εὐθέως δὲ μετὰ τὴν θλῖψιν τῶν ἡμερῶν ἐκείνων ὁ ἥλιος σκοτισθήσεται, καὶ ἡ σελήνη οὐ δώσει τὸ φέγγος αὐτῆς, καὶ οἱ ἀστέρες πεσοῦνται ἀπὸ τοῦ οὐρανοῦ, καὶ αἱ δυνάμεις τῶν οὐρανῶν σαλευθήσονται.
[30]. . . καὶ τότε κόψονται πᾶσαι αἱ φυλαὶ τῆς γῆς καὶ ὄψονται τὸν υἱὸν τοῦ ἀνθρώπου ἐρχόμενον ἐπὶ τῶν νεφελῶν . . .
[31]καὶ ἀποστελεῖ τοὺς ἀγγέλους αὐτοῦ μετὰ σάλπιγγος μεγάλης, καὶ ἐπισυνάξουσιν τοὺς ἐκλεκτοὺς αὐτοῦ ἐκ τῶν τεσσάρων ἀνέμων . . .
[32]Ἀπὸ δὲ τῆς συκῆς μάθετε τὴν παραβολήν.

raises the presumption that 7:1-8 will be heard as one scene with 6:12-17.[46]

The break at 7:9 is of a different order altogether. The high order discourse marker Μετὰ ταῦτα εἶδον, καὶ ἰδοὺ recalls 4:1, and the scene shifts back from the catastrophe on earth to the worship of heaven before the throne. The similarities between 7:9-17 and 4:1–5:14 are numerous: the centrality of the one sitting on the throne and the Lamb, the content of the worship, the prominence of the elders and the living creatures, the interaction between John and one of the elders, and the theme of salvation of peoples of all tribes, nations and tongues through the blood of the Lamb. This combination of features strongly suggests that the passage is intended to be seen as a new beginning, almost on a par with that of chapter 4. Yet the structural tension, created by anticipation of the opening of the seventh seal, is still unresolved. It would seem, then, that two structures are being superimposed. On one scheme seven seals follow one another with a close parallel structure. On the other scheme a new beginning is made at 7:9 with the seventh seal, comprising the silence and the seven trumpets, given similar status to the first six seals together.

4.2.5 Discourse Structure Diagram 4

At this point we can display in some detail the discourse structure of Rev 4:1–7:8. A number of scholars emphasize the links between the early and latter parts of chapter 7, and this close relationship, which is not apparent in my diagram at this point, should not be underestimated.[47]

---

[46] There is, in fact, an even greater concentration of symbols which this section of Revelation shares with the Synoptic passage, including tribulation, the trumpet, and the fig tree. See the references mentioned in the previous note. Müller, *Microstructural Analysis*, pp. 254-69, and Ferdinand Hahn, "Zum Aufbau der Johannesoffenbarung," in *Kirche und Bibel: Festgabe für Bischof Eduard Schick* (ed. O. Böcher et al.; Paderborn, Germany: Ferdinand Schöningh, 1979), pp. 150, 153, are among many writers who see a degree of relationship between the sixth seal and chapter 7. Mazzaferri, *Genre*, pp. 335-36, rejects this association, because it upsets the eschatological timetable and chronology. This is the same kind of confusion between literary form and chronology against which Yarbro Collins has warned. See note 38, p. 127 above.

[47] Thus Hellholm ("Problem," p.49) puts 7:1-14 (by which he presumably means 17) on the same level as the first six seals taken together. See

Discourse Structure Diagram 4 (Rev 4:1–7:8)

This diagram shows detail of the text sequence encompassing the first six seals.[48] Each section number is preceded by **2.3.2.2.1.1**. The whole diagram represents a sixth-grade sequence.

4:1–7:8 Heavenly worship and the first six seals
Delimiters: Μετὰ ταῦτα εἶδον, καὶ ἰδού; [Μετὰ ταῦτα εἶδον, καὶ ἰδού]
Spatial signals: in heaven, around/before the throne
> **(.1) 4:1-2a Vision of door in heaven and John's journey**
> *Delimiters*: Μετὰ ταῦτα εἶδον, καὶ ἰδού; [καὶ ἰδού]
> *Dramatis personae*: John, voice like a trumpet
> *Spatial signals*: in heaven, "Come up here"
> **(.2) 4:2b-11 God on his throne is worshiped in heaven**
> *Delimiters*: καὶ ἰδού; [Καὶ εἶδον]
> *Personal reference*: all creation
> *Dramatis personae*: one sitting on throne, 24 elders, four living creatures
> *Spatial signals*: the throne—on, from, in front of, in the middle of, around it
> *Temporal signals*: verbal aspect continuous
> **(.3) 5:1-14 The scroll and the Lamb[49]**
> *Delimiters*: Καὶ εἶδον; [Καὶ εἶδον ὅτε ἤνοιξεν]

---

also Müller, *Microstructural Analysis*, pp. 266-69. The relationship is such that Andrew Steinmann, "The Tripartite Structure of the Sixth Seal, the Sixth Trumpet, and the Sixth Bowl of John's Apocalypse (Rev 6:12–7:17; 9:13–11:14; 16:12-16)," *JETS* 35 (1992): 69-79, and Biguzzi, *I settenari*, pp. 134-49, treat the whole of chapter 7 as integral to the sixth seal, which they both see falling into three parts. See also Aune, *Revelation 6–16*, p. 434. Lambrecht, "Structuration," pp. 95-96; Lambrecht, "Opening," pp. 210-12, treats all of chapter 7 as an intercalation in the sixth seal (similarly Vanni, *La struttura*, pp. 182-205).

[48] No *Dramatis personae* are listed for the sequence as a whole unit. See Scott C. Berthiaume, "Participant Tracking in Revelation 4–7: Toward a Theory of Markedness," *JOTT* 7 (1996): 87-108, for a rather complex analysis of participants in this sequence of text.

[49] See Hellholm, "Problem," pp. 48-49, for an analysis of this sequence into three equal status subsequences.

Personal reference: Lion of tribe of Judah = root of David; the redeemed from all nations
Dramatis personae: one sitting on throne, mighty angel, John, one of the elders, Lamb, 24 elders and 4 living creatures, many angels, all creation
Spatial signals: on, around and in middle of throne, in heaven, on earth, under earth
Temporal signals: verbal aspect progressive, aorist tenses

(.4) 6:1–7:8 Opening the first six seals
Delimiters: Καὶ εἶδον ὅτε ἤνοιξεν; [Μετὰ ταῦτα εἶδον, καὶ ἰδού]
Dramatis personae: Lamb (implicit), 4 living creatures, four horsemen
Temporal signals: sequential opening of seals

(.4.1) 6:1-2 Seal 1[50]
Delimiters: Καὶ εἶδον ὅτε ἤνοιξεν; [Καὶ ὅτε ἤνοιξεν] (similarly for seals 2-5 below)
Dramatis personae: Lamb, 1st living creature, rider on white horse

(.4.2) 6:3-4 Seal 2
Personal reference: earth-dwellers
Dramatis personae: Lamb, 2nd living creature, rider on red horse

(.4.3) 6:5-6 Seal 3
Dramatis personae: Lamb, 3rd living creature, rider on black horse, voice

(.4.4) 6:7-8 Seal 4
Personal reference: a quarter of the earth
Dramatis personae: Lamb, 4th living creature, rider on pale horse

(.4.5) 6:9-11 Seal 5
Personal reference: God, their fellow slaves and brethren
Dramatis personae: Lamb, souls under the altar

(.4.6) 6:12–7:8 Seal 6
Delimiters: Καὶ εἶδον ὅτε ἤνοιξεν; [Μετὰ ταῦτα εἶδον, καὶ ἰδού]

(.4.6.1) 6:12-17 First part of sixth seal
Delimiters: Καὶ εἶδον ὅτε ἤνοιξεν; [Μετὰ τοῦτο εἶδον]
Personal reference: Lamb, one sitting on throne
Dramatis personae: Lamb, kings, great ones, generals, rich, poor, slave, free

---

[50] See Müller, *Microstructural Analysis*, pp. 244-54, 272-73, for the detailed structure of the first six seals.

(.4.6.2) 7:1-8 Second part of sixth seal

Delimiters: Μετὰ τοῦτο εἶδον; [Μετὰ ταῦτα εἶδον, καὶ ἰδοὺ]
Personal reference: servants of God, sons of Israel (by tribes)
Dramatis personae: four angels, another angel

4.2.6 Detail of the text sequence 7:9–11:19

The scene of heavenly worship in 7:9-17 is constructed largely by para-taxis.[51] Only the speech of the elder, 7:14-17, shows a more complex syntactic structure. Throughout this scene the tension created by the expectation of the seventh seal is maintained until its final resolution at 8:1.[52] I have already noted the double structure of the seal which parallels that of the previous seals. The vision of the seven angels being given the seven trumpets then stands as a summary and title over the whole section through to 11:19. This is supported by the fact that neither in 8:3-5, which intervenes before the trumpets are sounded, nor in any of the first four trumpet scenes, is there a further mention of John seeing or hearing anything. This contrasts strongly with the density of such references in the seal sequence.[53] The trumpet sequence is broken after the fourth by the vision and audition of the eagle (8:13), whose voice is probably to be heard again at 9:12 and 11:14 and provides a second level

---

[51] A total of 29 occurrences of καὶ (16 at phrase level or above).

[52] Hellholm, "Problem," p. 49, by introducing a major (fifth-grade) text sequence at 8:1, entirely cuts off not only the trumpets, but also the seventh seal, from the seal sequence, resulting in a significant failure of relevance. Seven seals are expected but only six revealed in the *scriptura exterior*. Aune, *Revelation 1–5*, p. ci, appears to divide the text similarly, but not with such a high-level division (taking 8:1–11:19 as a unit). Mazzaferri, *Genre*, p. 336, argues that chapter 7 is an intrusion by saying, "It asks too much of the verb in 8:1 to look back to so distant an antecedent" (as the Lamb in 6:1). But this is not a particularly difficult task. The precisely parallel form of each of the seal openings preserves the subject in active memory, and the last occurrence at 6:12 is only about five minutes old. Furthermore there have been two mentions of the Lamb since (6:16; 7:17).

[53] There are only 6 occurrences of εἶδον (8:2, 13; 9:1, 17; 10:1, 5) and 5 of ἤκουσα (8:13; 9:13, 16; 10:4, 8) in this whole section. Leaving aside the eagle vision, only those at 8:2; 9:1, 13; 10:1, 4 perform a significant structural role.

of enumeration alongside the numbering of the trumpets.[54] As with the seals there is tension created by delay both at the beginning and the end of the sequence.

While each of the first four trumpets presents a relatively simple picture, the fifth is complex and extended, and the sixth even more so.[55] In fact, with the sixth trumpet there are indications of other structures superimposed on the one we are following. First, chapter 10 intrudes what can fairly be described as a kind of prophetic call narrative, with strong evocations of Ezek 2–3. So marked is this resemblance that it has led some to suggest the beginning of a new text sequence here, and to assert that the contents of the scroll which John eats are displayed in some or all of the ensuing chapters.[56] This is unlikely for a number of reasons. First, within the cognitive context of prophetic call narratives which the audience can be expected to share with the author, there are some that occur at or near the beginning of the written record of the prophet's message and some that are embedded within the message.[57] In all cases the

---

[54] If these verses are not the voice of the eagle himself, they are a very close reference to his initial call. Müller, *Microstructural Analysis*, pp. 381, 399, presents an analysis very similar to mine. I will return to the identity of the third woe later.

[55] See Aune, *Revelation 6–16*, p. 497, for parallels between trumpets five and six.

[56] See, for example, Yarbro Collins, *Combat Myth*, pp. 26-28; Schüssler Fiorenza, "Composition," pp. 361-63; Edith M. Humphrey, "The Sweet and the Sour: Epics of Wrath and Return in the Apocalypse," *SBLSP* (1991): 451-60. Aune, *Revelation 6–16*, pp. 571-72, discusses several alternative views for the identity and contents of the scroll, but appears to find none of them convincing. C. van der Waal, "The last book of the Bible and the Jewish Apocalypses," *Neot* 12 (1978): 121-22, suggests that chapters 1–16 can be divided into two parallel parts, 1:9–9:21 and 10:1–16:21, each with a call narrative heading it. This results, interestingly, in chapters 7 and 14 being placed in parallel, and the trumpets and the bowls similarly. Apart from that, there is little to support the suggestion.

[57] Examples of the former include Jer 1:4-10; Ezek 1:1–3:11. Examples of the latter include Isa 6:1-13; Amos 7:14-17 (on which see James L. Mays, *Amos* [OTL; London: SCM Press, 1969], pp. 137-40). I am referring here to the literary form in which the prophet's works are extant, not to any critical assessment of the order of composition of the books, or to any historical-critical reconstruction of the life of the prophets.

message that the prophet is told to prophesy is implicitly meta-referential, taking in his whole recorded text and including the call narrative. So here, the charge given to John to prophesy has retrospective as well as prospective extent. If the contents of the scroll are to be identified in any way, the most accessible clue in the cognitive environment is probably the "words of lamentation and mourning and woe" of Ezek 2:10. Second, notice that John describes himself as actively involved in the task he was first assigned—writing down his experiences (10:4). The prohibition from recording the voice of the thunders only serves to emphasize that everything else *was* recorded. Hence there is no new task in view here which requires us to override the surface structure.[58] The episode is firmly anchored in its present environment. It is introduced simply by καὶ εἶδον as are many previous episodes (e.g., 9:1). Just as prior to the seventh seal there was a scene that recalled the opening throne scene, so here there are a number of similarities, in particular the scroll in the right hand of a heavenly being and John's personal involvement in what takes place. Again, the explicit reference to the seventh trumpet yet to come (10:7) locates it precisely within the scope of the sixth trumpet and would appear to be a way of ensuring that the hearers locate the scene within the structure of the seven trumpets.[59]

---

[58] I am not so much interested in the interpretation of the scene at this point, as in its role in the structure of the book.

[59] Hellholm, "Problem," p. 50, has wrongly labeled the whole section 10:1–11:14 a sixth-grade sequence, since on p. 49 he has already delimited a sixth-grade sequence stretching from 8:1 to 11:14. He considers that 11:1-13 is the contents of the little scroll, as does Lambrecht, "Structuration," pp. 85-86, who, however, integrates all of chapters 10–11 into the sixth trumpet (similarly Hahn, "Aufbau," p. 154). Mazzaferri, *Genre*, pp. 336-38, finds that the section interrupts the trumpet sequence, just as chapter 7 did to the seals. Aune, *Revelation 6–16*, p. 555, treats 10:1-11 and 11:1-13 as two independent insertions. Schüssler Fiorenza, "Composition," p. 361, considers that 10:1–11:14 introduces chapters 12–14 and together they form the content of the "small prophetic scroll" since they refer "to the same time period as well as to the prophetic Christian's persecution by the beast." (Cf. Yarbro Collins, *Combat Myth*, p. 26, who considers the content of the scroll to commence only at chapter 12.) Against this it must be argued that the connections between 10:1–11:14 and chapters 12–14 are no more significant than those between any two sections of the Apocalypse, that there is a major loss of relevance in splitting

135

The scene then merges into the story of the two witnesses by means of the speech in which John is commanded to measure the temple. John himself is the only point of contact between the two and there is considerable ambiguity in the origin of the various voices heard, in particular the voice from heaven in 10:8, the plural speakers of 10:11, and the voice of command in 11:1. The story of the two witnesses presents its own problems. There is no indication that the voice which was speaking to John stops speaking at the end of verse 3. In fact, there is more of a break between verses 2 and 3, with the only point of contact being the referential equivalence of 42 months and 1260 days.[60] The story of the witnesses continues to be carried forward with the main verbs in the present or future until verse 11, when there is a sudden switch to aorist until verse 13. In terms of content this story appears to have little in common with other parts of Revelation and it has often been considered to represent an earlier narrative incorporated by John at this point.[61] Certainly John himself, having been closely involved in the action in 10:1–11:2, is almost totally absent.[62] Yet on closer examination there is surprisingly little vocabulary that is unique to this story. Verse 8 is a marked exception, where a collection of significant words occurs uniquely here in Revelation.[63] The role of the witnesses and their testimony is, of course, central to the whole Apocalypse and has already been

---

the seventh trumpet from its predecessors, and that if John had intended his audience to understand the content of the scroll as a portion of his text, he provided no clues to the construction of a context within which this is an accessible cognitive implication. Further, Schüssler Fiorenza's disjointed identification of the content of the two scrolls ("Composition," p. 363) appears not only to beg the question of relevance, but also to ignore her earlier comment that "If one changes the order of a text one changes its meaning" (p. 344).

[60] So also Müller, *Microstructural Analysis*, pp. 352-53; Aune, *Revelation 6–16*, p. 585.

[61] See Aune, *Revelation 6–16*, pp. 590-93; Yarbro Collins, *Combat Myth*, p. 27; and Pattemore, "The People of God," chapter 6, pp. 276-80.

[62] This is also true of chapter 12.

[63] Πτῶμα, πνευματικῶς, Σόδομα, Αἴγυπτος, and σταυρόω are all unique to verse 8. Other words occurring only in chapter 11 are ἐλαία (verse 4), ἐχθρός (verse 5), ὑετὸς βρέχῃ (verse 6), μνῆμα (verse 9), and δῶρον (verse 10).

prominent.[64] Prophets and prophecy are likewise frequently in focus, especially within the immediate context of chapter 10.[65] Particularly interesting is the way in which the language of chapter 9 is reused, not always with the same sense, but nevertheless clearly intended as an echo in counterpoint.[66] A number of these motifs, along with some others prominent in chapter 11, become even more important in subsequent chapters.[67] Finally, the woe cry of 11:14 links backward to the cry of the eagle in 8:13 and 9:12, and forward to the completion of the trumpet sequence, thus binding the whole tightly together.[68]

---

[64] Words in the μάρτυς/μαρτυρία/μαρτυρέω family occur unambiguously of Jesus at 1:5; 3:14; 22:18, 20, of the witness of Christians at 2:13; 6:9; 11:3, 7; 12:11; 17:6, of the heavenly sanctuary at 15:5, of an angel at 22:16, and in the phrase μαρτυρία Ἰησοῦ (Χριστοῦ) at 1:2, 9; 12:17; 19:10; 20:4.

[65] 11:3, 6, 10, 18; cf. 10:7, 11 and many other references.

[66] Ἀδικέω 11:5; cf. 9:4, 10, 19; πῦρ . . . ἐκ τοῦ στόματος 11:5; cf. 9:17, 18; ἀποκτείνω 11:5, 7, 13; cf. 9:5, 15, 18, 20; ἐξουσία 11:6; cf. 9:3, 10, 19; πληγή 11:6; cf. 9:18, 20; ἄβυσσος 11:7; cf. 9:1, 2, 11; πόλεμος 11:7; cf. 9:7, 9; βασανίζω 11:10; cf. 9:5. See Müller, *Microstructural Analysis*, pp. 381-82, for further examples.

[67] In particular, plagues, war, the beast and the city.

[68] Not all scholars give adequate weight to the structuring role of this third woe cry in delineating the trumpet sequence. Among those who do are Mazzaferri, *Genre*, p. 337, and Müller, *Microstructural Analysis*, pp. 383-85. Schüssler Fiorenza, "Composition," p. 363; Hellholm, "Problem," p. 50 (where it is wrongly labeled as 11:16); and Aune, *Revelation 6–16*, pp. 495, 584, 587-88, all link it too closely with either 11:1-13 or the whole of chapters 10–11 and hence obscure the immediate connection to 11:15. Similarly Vanni, *La struttura*, pp. 182-205, although he groups it with all of 8:1–11:14, does not appear to notice the link between 11:14 and 11:15. Aune, *Revelation 1–5*, p. ci, does not include the second woe cry as part of the surface structure. His identity of the woe and the connections forward also cause considerable confusion. Hellholm's analysis suffers a major failure of relevance by claiming that the bowl sequence begins at 11:15, where there is nothing whatever to indicate this in the context. Sweet, *Revelation*, pp. 46, 175, 190, identifies the woe not with what follows the blowing of the seventh trumpet but with the woe in 12:12 (and hence with all of chapters 12–13). Aune, *Revelation 6–16*, p. 495, is similar. Lambrecht, "Structuration," p. 93, says the third woe may

4.2.7 Discourse Structure Diagram 5

Discourse Structure Diagram 5 (Rev 7:9–11:19)

This diagram shows the detail of the text sequence comprising the seventh seal and the trumpets. Each section number is preceded by 2.3.2.2.1.2. The whole diagram represents a sixth-grade sequence.

7:9–11:19 Heavenly worship and the seventh seal
  (.1) 7:9-17 Vision of a great crowd worshiping God and the Lamb
  Delimiters: Μετὰ ταῦτα εἶδον, καὶ ἰδοὺ; [Καὶ ὅταν ἤνοιξεν τὴν σφραγῖδα τὴν ἑβδόμην]
  Personal reference: God, Lamb, those who have come through the great ordeal
  Dramatis personae: great crowd, Lamb, throne, angels, elders, living creatures, John
  Spatial signals: before the throne
  Temporal signals: aorist action => present description
  (.2) 8:1–11:19 Opening the seventh seal
  Delimiters: Καὶ ὅταν ἤνοιξεν . . . ; disjuncture => [Καὶ σημεῖον μέγα ὤφθη]
    (.2.1) 8:1 Auditory part: silence
    Delimiters: ἐγένετο; [καὶ εἶδον]
    Spatial signals: in heaven
    Temporal signals: about half an hour
    (.2.2) 8:2–11:19 Visual part: seven trumpets
    Delimiters: καὶ εἶδον; lightning, voices, thunder, hail
    Dramatis personae: seven angels who stand before God
      (.2.2.1) 8:2-6 Preparation for blowing the trumpets
      Delimiters: καὶ εἶδον; [Καὶ ὁ πρῶτος ἐσάλπισεν]
        (.2.2.1.1) 8:2 Seven angels given trumpets
        Dramatis personae: seven angels
        Spatial signal: before God
        (.2.2.1.2) 8:3-5 Another angel offers the prayers of the saints and throws fire to earth
        Personal reference: the saints, God

---

be open-ended and include all that follows. Müller, *Microstructural Analysis*, pp. 383-85, compares a number of views and decides that the third woe is identical to the seventh trumpet in 11:15-18.

Dramatis personae: another angel
Spatial markers: on the altar of incense, before God, onto earth

(.2.2.1.3) 8:6 Preparation to blow trumpets
Dramatis personae: seven angels with trumpets

(.2.2.2) 8:7-12 First four trumpets
Delimiters: Καὶ ὁ πρῶτος ἐσάλπισεν; [Καὶ εἶδον, καὶ ἤκουσα]

(.2.2.2.1) 8:7 First trumpet[69]
Delimiters: Καὶ ὁ πρῶτος . . . (similarly for second, third and fourth trumpets)
Dramatis personae: first angel
Spatial marker: into earth

(.2.2.2.2) 8:8-9 Second trumpet
Dramatis personae: second angel, sea creatures
Spatial signals: into the sea, in the sea

(.2.2.2.3) 8:10-11 Third trumpet
Dramatis personae: third angel, human beings
Spatial signals: out of heaven, onto the rivers and springs

(.2.2.2.4) 8:12 Fourth trumpet
Dramatis personae: fourth angel

(.2.2.3) 8:13–11:19 The last three trumpets
Delimiters: Καὶ εἶδον, καὶ ἤκουσα ἑνὸς ἀετου; thunder lightning, etc.

(.2.2.3.1) 8:13 The woe-crying eagle
Delimiters: Καὶ εἶδον, καὶ ἤκουσα ἑνὸς ἀετου;
[Καὶ ὁ πέμπτος . . .]
Personal reference: the inhabitants of earth, the remaining three angels
Dramatis personae: eagle
Spatial marker: in midheaven

(.2.2.3.2) 9:1-11 Fifth trumpet
Delimiters: Καὶ ὁ πέμπτος . . . ; [Ἡ οὐαὶ ἡ μία ἀπῆλθεν]
Dramatis personae: fallen star, locust army, human beings, Apollyon
Spatial signals: from heaven, into earth, from the abyss

---

[69] Müller, *Microstructural Analysis*, pp. 331-52, gives a detailed analysis of the structure of each trumpet sequence.

Temporal signals: for five months, in those days, tense shifts perfect => aorist => future => imperfect and present

(.2.2.3.3) 9:12 Woe cry
Delimiters: Ἡ οὐαὶ ἡ μία ἀπῆλθεν; [Καὶ ὁ ἕκτος . . .]
Dramatis personae: eagle?

(.2.2.3.4) 9:13 –11:13 Sixth trumpet
Delimiters: Καὶ ὁ ἕκτος . . . ; ['Η οὐαὶ ἡ δευτέρα ἀπῆλθεν]

(.2.2.3.4.1) 9:13-21 Sixth angel blows trumpet
Delimiters: Καὶ ὁ ἕκτος . . . ; [Καὶ εἶδον ἄλλον ἄγγελον]
Dramatis personae: sixth angel, voice, four bound angels, army on horseback, humankind
Spatial signals: from the altar of incense before God, on the Euphrates
Temporal signals: this hour and day and month and year

(.2.2.3.4.2) 10:1–11:13 Major interlude
Delimiters: Καὶ εἶδον ἄλλον ἄγγελον; ['Η οὐαὶ ἡ δευτέρα . . .]
Dramatis personae: John

(.2.2.3.4.2.1) 10:1-11 The strong angel and the little scroll
Delimiters: Καὶ εἶδον . . . ; [Καὶ ἐδόθη μοι]
Personal reference: God, seventh angel, slaves of God, peoples, nations, languages and kings
Dramatis personae: another strong angel, seven thunders, John, a voice from heaven
Spatial signals: out of heaven, on the sea, on earth, toward heaven

(.2.2.3.4.2.2) 11:1-13 The temple and the witnesses
Delimiters: Καὶ ἐδόθη μοι; ['Η οὐαὶ ἡ δευτέρα . . .]
Dramatis personae: John

(.2.2.3.4.2.2.1) 11:1a John given rod
Delimiters: Καὶ ἐδόθη . . . ; λέγων
Dramatis personae: John, unidentified giver

(.2.2.3.4.2.2.2) 11:1b-13 Command to measure and story of the two witnesses[70]
Delimiters: [λέγων]; ['H οὐαὶ ἡ δευτέρα]
Communication axis: unidentified speaker => John
Dramatis personae: unidentified speaker
(.2.2.3.5) 11:14 Woe cry
Delimiters: 'H οὐαὶ ἡ δευτέρα; [Καὶ ὁ ἕβδομος . . .]
Dramatis personae: eagle?
(.2.2.3.6) 11:15-19 Seventh trumpet
Delimiters: Καὶ ὁ ἕβδομος . . . ; thunder, lightning, etc.
Dramatis personae: seventh angel
(.2.2.3.6.1) 11:15 Seventh trumpet blown
Delimiters: Καὶ ὁ ἕβδομος . . . ; [καὶ οἱ . . .
πρεσβύτεροι]
Personal reference: our Lord and his Christ
Dramatis personae: seventh angel, voices in heaven
Spatial signals: in heaven
(.2.2.3.6.2) 11:16-18 Worship of the 24 elders
Delimiters: καὶ οἱ . . . πρεσβύτεροι; [καὶ ἠνοίγη ὁ ναὸς]
Personal reference: God, the nations, God's slaves the prophets and saints and those who fear him
Dramatis personae: 24 elders
Spatial signals: before God, on their thrones
(.2.2.3.6.3) 11:19 Opening of the temple
Delimiters: καὶ ἠνοίγη ὁ ναὸς; lightning, thunder, etc.
Dramatis personae: unidentified temple-opener
Spatial signals: in heaven, in the temple

4.3 Role of the people of God in 4:1–11:19

At this point we may pause to consider in what ways the people of God feature in the two major text sequences that comprise 4:1–11:19.[71]

---

[70] This sequence can be further analyzed into two subsequences, **(.2.2.3.4.2.2.2.1) 11:1b-2 Command to measure the temple** and **(.2.2.3.4.2.2.2.2) 11:3-13 The story of the two witnesses.**

Whether the 24 elders can be taken in some sense as a representation of the people of God, or as an angelic counterpart of the 12 patriarchs and 12 apostles, is an issue of interpretation which must be dealt with separately. We simply note here their function in heavenly worship in chapters 4–5; 7:11-12; 11:17-18, and as interacting with John at 5:5 and 7:13-17, both of which have been helpful structural features.[72]

There are remarkably few direct mentions of God's people in the first major text sequence (4:1–7:8). They are implicitly included in references to creation (4:11; 5:13), among those "on earth" not able to open the seals (5:3), and in the references to the tribe of Judah and to David. They are referred to as those who have been redeemed by the blood of the Lamb and made kings and priests (5:9-10) and as the slaves of God who are sealed (7:1-8). Their prayers are visualized as the incense in the golden bowls (5:8). But only in 6:9-11 are the people of God themselves directly in focus. Here John sees the souls of those who had been killed "for the word of God and for the testimony they had given" (cf. 1:9b). They cry to God for vengeance and are given white garments and told to rest until the number of their σύνδουλοι and ἀδελφοὶ who are to be killed is complete. In contrast to the people of God, the "inhabitants of the earth" are strongly implicit or explicit in the whole of chapter 6, especially through to their plaintive and poignant speech at 6:16-17.

In the second major sequence, 7:9–11:19, there are two passages in which the people of God are focused. First, there is a general representation in the scene of the innumerable crowd worshiping God in heaven (7:9-17). Then there is a pair of more specific and structurally related scenes (10:1-11; 11:1-13), where first John's interaction with the angel and then the two witnesses focus attention on the prophets and the prophetic ministry. Apart from these passages there are only brief references to the prayers of the saints (8:3) and to the time for rewarding the people of God (11:18).

---

[71] Of particular interest are the indicators of *Personal reference* and *Dramatis personae* listed under the various text sequences in the previous section.

[72] See also Joseph M. Baumgarten, "The Duodecimal Courts of Qumran, Revelation, and the Sanhedrin," *JBL* 95 (1976): 59-78, who suggests a judging role for them as well.

Chapter 5

Discourse Structure of the Apocalypse
Part 3: The final vision sequence of the second major vision

In this chapter we will focus on the detailed structure of the second part of the second vision sequence, the part that extends from 12:1 to 22:9

5.1 Integrity of 12:1–22:9

The latter half of John's second vision report is less tightly structured than the former, which was entirely encompassed by the two embedded series of sevens, the seals and the trumpets. There is a further numbered series of seven, but it is more compact in scope (15:1–16:21) and does not draw into itself, in quite such a marked way, the other material around it. Nevertheless, there are indications of some unity of outlook for this latter half which crystallizes around a number of motifs or symbols. The most unifying motif is the Lamb, found in each of the clearly marked subsections. The Lamb had been prominent in chapters 5–7 but then is not mentioned again until 12:11. Thus he serves not only to unify the second half of the visions but also to link it back to the first half. In the opposite corner, the motifs representing the forces in opposition to God and the Lamb are either (in the case of the beast in its various guises) common to all sections but the last, or bracket all but the last section.[1] These relationships might best be viewed in tabular form:

---

[1] Occurrences in the first half of the main vision sequence are rare: ὄφις at 9:19 (but in a simile) and θηρίον at 11:7 (and a literal usage at

Table 5.1 – Distribution of key participants in Revelation 12–22

	ἀρνίου	Σατανᾶς/Διάβολος/ὄφις	δράκων	θηρίον
12–13	12:11; 13:8	12:9, 12, 14, 15	11 times	16 times
14	14:1, 4, 10			14:9, 11
15–16	15:3		16:13	15:2; 16:2, 10, 13
17:1–19:10	17:14; 19:7, 9			9 times
19:11–21:8		20:2, 7, 10	20:2	19:19, 20; 20:4, 10
21:9–22:9	21:9, 14, 22, 23			
	21:27; 22:1, 3			

This defines a virtual space, a combat field, and all of 12:1–22:9 is seen in relation to this conflict between the forces of good (represented by the Lamb and those with him) and the forces of evil (represented by Satan and the beast). The outcome of the conflict is clear, not only from the explicit description of the fate of the forces of evil in the penultimate section, but by their total absence from the description of the New Jerusalem. Undoubtedly the best contextual effects are obtained by reading this as one story with the sustained conflict leading to a climax and resolution.

One further piece of evidence for the unity of this large text sequence is the role of the πόλις. Previously mentioned in anticipatory fashion in 3:12 and 11:2, 8, 13, the second half of the book becomes, as well as a combat story, a tale of two cities. Babylon holds the early parts together (14:20; 16:19; 18 passim) and the New Jerusalem the latter parts (20:9; 21:2 and passim).

On the highest level of text sequences, the clearest discourse structure is given by the use of "great signs in heaven" (12:1; 15:1).[2] The first of these leads into a double story, whose integrity we will need to examine, and the second introduces the seven plague angels who will dominate the remainder of the book. As I have already mentioned, chapter 14 occupies a bridge position between these two segments.

6:8). There are also some references to the devil and Satan in the messages to the churches.

[2] See section 4.1.3 above.

5.2 Visions seen in heaven (12:1–14:20)

5.2.1 Structural features

With 12:1 the text appears to take off in a new direction.[3] The trumpets are completed, with their sequence rounded out by the opening of the temple, the appearance of the ark, and the most complete set of physical accompaniments to theophany yet encountered.[4] The temple becomes an important focal point from 14:14 on, but until then it plays no further part. The bowl angels have not yet appeared to introduce a further seven-sequence, and the scene that begins here runs continuously, at least on one level, until 13:18, or perhaps even until 14:13. On another level there is a significant difference between chapters 12 and 13–14. We have already noted the absence of markers for John's visionary or auditory perspective in the latter part of chapter 10 and in chapter 11. This continues through chapter 12, with the exception of the voice that he hears from heaven in 12:10-12. Starting at 13:1, however, the repetition of Καὶ εἶδον recommences.[5] This strengthens the presumption that in 12:1-9, 13-17 John has incorporated pre-existing material into his account.[6] Nevertheless the story has been firmly anchored in its present location. The dragon's destruction of a third of the stars recalls the fourth trumpet (8:12) and the destiny of the child to rule the nations with an iron rod opens not only the Messianic context of Psa 2:9 but, more immediately, the promise to the church at Thyatira (2:27). The 1260 days of the woman's desert sojourn corresponds to the period of ministry of the two

---

[3] Müller, *Microstructural Analysis*, pp. 594-607, presents a preliminary analysis of this which is essentially similar to mine. Note also the display of common terminology (pp. 590-93). Lambrecht, "Structuration," pp. 98-99, regards chapters 12–14 as an intercalation within the bowl sequence, unusually placed very early in the sequence (11:15–22:5). Previous septets have had an intercalation toward the end, and his explanations of this difference are unconvincing, raising significant doubts about his hypothesis that the bowls are contained within the seventh trumpet.

[4] ἀστραπαὶ καὶ φωναὶ καὶ βρονταὶ καὶ σεισμὸς καὶ χάλαζα μεγάλη in 11:19; cf. 4:5; 8:5; 16:18.

[5] Note the gap: Καὶ εἶδον appears at 10:1, then 13:1, 11; 14:1, 6, 14; 15:1, 2, etc.

[6] See Yarbro Collins, *Combat Myth*, pp. 57-100; Aune, *Revelation 6–16*, pp. 664-74.

witnesses (11:3). The story is closely integrated with the following visions of the beasts in a number of ways. The dragon ends up standing beside the sea (12:18) from which the first beast immediately emerges (13:1). Like the dragon, this beast has seven heads and ten horns, and it is immediately endowed with the dragon's authority (13:2).[7] This results in worship of the dragon as well as the beast (13:4).[8] The second beast speaks like a dragon (13:11).[9] The loud victory call from heaven in 12:10-12 recalls themes from 7:10 (the salvation of God), 5:9 (the blood of the Lamb), and 6:9 (the testimony of the people of God leading to their martyrdom).

Though the signs of the woman and the dragon both appear in heaven, most of the action takes place on earth. It is as if heaven is the screen for the projection of a film set on earth. The dragon, however, moves between heaven and earth. His being cast down from heaven to earth provides the counterpoint to the male child's enrapture to the throne of God. The internal structure of the story of the dragon and the woman is a movement from a description of a state of affairs (12:1-4) to progressive action from the birth of the child onward.[10] The line of action continues directly from 12:9 to 12:13. The cry of victory in 12:10-12 is linked to its occasion by the reference to the casting down of the enemy from heaven to earth (and sea) but nowhere refers explicitly to the *dragon*. Instead the speech leaves the symbolic world and identifies the enemy as ὁ κατήγωρ τῶν ἀδελφῶν ἡμῶν and the devil (an association already made in 12:9). The cognitive environment within which this vision is to be understood, as well as its internal structure, has been investigated in detail by Yarbro Collins and will not detain us further here.[11]

---

[7] Note also the similar description of the scarlet beast in 17:3.

[8] The two are closely associated again in 16:13.

[9] Thus Lambrecht, "Structuration," p. 98, argues that chapters 12 and 13 belong together. Aune, *Revelation 6–16*, p. 725, treats all such points of contact as redactional, but this does not diminish their importance to our present text.

[10] Nearly all the verb forms in 12:1-4 are perfect or present, and most are participles. The only aorists are the casting down of the stars and the anticipatory aorist subjunctive καταφάγῃ. From ἔτεκεν (12:5) onward the story is carried forward entirely in the aorist.

[11] See the references in note 6, p. 145 above. Relevance Theory adds a note of caution here, however. The context within which the story of the dragon and the woman will be understood will be the one most readily

146

The internal coherence of the narrative of the vision of the two beasts is too strong to require much comment. The opening scene is dramatically linked to the final scene of chapter 12, by its seaside location and the interaction between the first beast and the dragon. The vision of the first beast is largely told in the aorist, while that of the second is almost entirely present, the exception being the repeated ἐδόθη (13:14, 15; cf. 13:5, 7), which appears to place all of the hubristic actions of the two beasts under the sovereignty of God. The most significant structural complexity of this chapter occurs when spatial, temporal and communicative coherence is broken in verses 9-10 and again in verse 18. Neither makes any sense as part of the vision description. They cannot be interpreted as the words of any actor to any other actor. Both include imperatives, extremely rare outside of the letters to the churches, and the imperative of 13:9 is almost identical to the repeated challenge in those letters to hear. Both stand outside the framework of the narrative and point to it with Ὧδέ (. . .) ἐστιν. What cognitive assumptions allow the audience to maximize relevance at these points? It must be a change in communication situation. John is still (through the lector) speaking to the audience, but it would seem that at these points he ceases to narrate and turns to address the audience directly. He is no longer recounting a vision he had at some point in the past, but referring to that vision as a challenge to the present action of his audience. These verses stand on the same communication level, not as the preceding or following vision narratives, but as the entire vision narrative taken together. This is John the preacher, rather than John the storyteller.

The relationship of chapter 14 with what precedes and follows it is ambiguous, to say the least. In itself it is composed of two quite distinct

---

accessible to the audience, in other words the most immediate context to which the author knows his audience will turn. Long before the advent of RT, Farrer, *Revelation*, pp. 53-54 had made this clear: "It is true, in a sense, that St. John's beast is Tiamat. The chaos-monster of Old Sumerian tradition did undergo a whole series of rehandlings in successive biblical strata and make its last scriptural appearance in Revelation. But the long history of the image, however interesting in itself, is largely irrelevant to the interpretation of St. John . . . We have to appreciate in any given case how deep and how shallow that background is. He goes back to Daniel, and to the other Old Testament texts, as they appeared to primitive Christian eyes. It is fantastic to suggest that he goes back to Babylonian epic."

scenes, each of which has two parts.[12] With the opening of the first of these scenes, we would appear to have left the vision of the two beasts behind. The setting is itself somewhat ambiguous. The 144,000 followers of the Lamb are described first as being on Mount Zion and then as standing before the throne with all the throne attendants who had appeared in the early heavenly throne-room passages of chapters 4–5. The second half of the scene involves three angels flying in midheaven. In both halves, visionary and auditory elements are followed by explanatory comments on the people of God—their behavior, their relationship to God, and their salvation. The most readily accessible context that this scene opens is that of chapter 7. The 144,000 followers, the Lamb, worship of both redeemed people and heavenly throne attendants, and salvation after suffering are the principal common themes.[13] Yet the more immediate connections to the visions of chapters 12–13 should not be ignored. The Lamb is seen standing on (ἑστὸς ἐπὶ in 14:1) Mount Zion just as the dragon was on the seashore (ἐστάθη ἐπὶ in 12:18). The Lamb has been parodied by the second beast (13:11), but he has already been celebrated as the source of his people's victory (12:11) and his followers have by implication not worshiped the beast (13:8).[14] Under the beast's regime they could not buy (ἀγοράσαι in 13:17) but they themselves are bought (ἠγορασμένοι in 14:3). Instead of the name of the beast, they have the name of the Lamb and his Father on their foreheads (14:1; cf. 13:16-17). The various groupings depicting all humankind over which the beast had authority are the very ones to whom the angel brings the eternal gospel (14:6; cf. 13:7). But those who worship the beast or receive his mark are destined for eternal punishment (14:9-11; cf. 13:4, 8, 15, 16). Finally, 14:12-13 breaks the communication situation in the same way as 13:9-10 and 13:18. Ὧδε . . . ἐστιν of 14:12 echoes 13:10 very closely, but this time it is followed by a voice from heaven (back in the narrative report framework) and the voice of the Spirit for the first time (though it has been implicit in chapters 2–3), affirming the outcome of the

---

[12] Scene 1: 14:1 Καὶ εἶδον, καὶ ἰδοὺ . . . 14:6 Καὶ εἶδον . . . ; Scene 2: 14:14 Καὶ εἶδον, καὶ ἰδοὺ . . . 14:17 Καὶ ἄλλος ἄγγελος . . . .

[13] It is not coincidental then that both chapters are interludes or bridges. There are obvious connections behind chapter 7 back to the throne scene of chapters 4–5.

[14] Note also that although chapter 14 does not directly mention the blood of the Lamb, it is supplied by the context in 5:9, which is opened by the reference to his followers as redeemed.

endurance of God's people. This evidence shows convincingly that 14:1-13 is intended to be understood in the context of chapters 12–13.[15] On the other hand, there are a number of features that anticipate later visions. The references to Babylon (14:8; cf. chapter 18), the wine of fornication (14:8; cf. 17:2; 18:3) and of God's wrath (14:10; cf. 16:19; 19:15), the fire and sulfur (14:10; cf. 19:20; 20:10), the smoke (14:11; cf. 15:8; 18:9, 18; 19:3), and the torment (14:11; cf. 18:7, 10, 15) are all anticipatory cataphorae, which for the most part are held suspended through the sequence of the bowls.

The situation with 14:14-20 is quite different. On the surface, very little directly links it to chapters 12–13.[16] The features that link it to the following passages will be explored later, but two points need to be made here. First, 14:14-20 is connected to the first half of the chapter both formally and as the fulfilment of the judgment promised in the future by the angels of 14:6-11.[17] But there is a more important anaphoric connection than this, one that is dependent for its force on the kind of intertextual linkage which I have elsewhere interpreted by means of Relevance Theory.[18] The beast from the sea combines features found in the four beasts of Dan 7:1-7.[19] The beast of Rev 13, just as the final beast of Dan 7,

---

[15] See Aune, *Revelation 6–16*, pp. 794-96, for further links between the passages.

[16] Again see Aune, *Revelation 6–16*, pp. 794-96.

[17] For the formal links, see note 12, p. 148. For the relationship between the angels, see Aune, *Revelation 6–16*, pp. 794-96.

[18] See Pattemore, "The People of God," pp. 59-73, and Stephen W. Pattemore, "Relevance Theory, Intertextuality, and the Book of Revelation," in *Current Trends in Scripture Translation* (ed. Philip Noss; UBS Bulletin 194/195; Reading, England: UBS, 2003), pp. 43-60. The linkage, called "metalepsis" or "transumption," following John Hollander, *The Figure of an Echo: A Mode of Allusion in Milton and After* (Berkeley: University of California Press, 1981), is described in the following way by Hays, *Echoes*, p. 20: "When a literary echo links the text in which it occurs to an earlier text, the figurative effect of the echo can lie in the unstated or suppressed (transumed) points of resonance between the two texts." This requires that the wider context of a quote or allusion is formative for its interpretation in its new setting.

[19] They too emerge from the sea (Dan 7:3; cf. Rev 13:1). The features of a lion, a bear and a leopard (Dan 7:4-7) are combined in Rev 13:2. Other points of similarity are the ten horns (Dan 7:7; cf. Rev 13:1), the

makes war on the saints.[20] The period of the sea-beast's authority (Rev 13:5) corresponds to the time for which Daniel's beast holds power over the saints (Dan 7:25). This connection has wider implications than we can investigate here, but what is of significance at this point is its implications for the structure. With the contents of Dan 7 opened for the hearers as an accessible cognitive environment, Rev 13 finishes in tension. There has been no resolution of the fate of God's people and one "like a son of man" has not yet appeared. The hearers, knowing Dan 7, anticipate the outcome, but knowing from what they have heard so far, that John rarely adopts OT material without modifying it for his own purposes, they cannot yet see how the outcome will be depicted. The resolution comes in Rev 14. Not only does 14:1-12 depict the vindication of God's people, but it predicts the final judgment of their opponents, a judgment carried out by the "Son of Man" figure in 14:14-16, appearing, as expected, in association with clouds.[21] Thus it would seem that maximum cognitive effects are achieved by hearing the whole of chapter 14 together with chapters 12–13. Furthermore this means that the next occurrence of a "great sign in heaven" is confirmed as the marker of a new stage of the vision narrative. But this does not exhaust the influence of Dan 7 on the structure of Revelation. It may be recalled that Rev 7 opened with a scene of four angels restraining the four winds from blowing on earth or sea or trees. The vision of Dan 7 opens with the four winds of heaven "stirring up the great sea." It is not possible to show so

---

authority of one of the beasts (Dan 7:6; cf. Rev 13:5), and the στόμα λαλοῦν μεγάλα (Dan 7:8; cf. Rev 13:5).

[20] Note Dan 7:8 (OG) ἐποίει πόλεμον πρὸς τοὺς ἁγίους; Dan 7:21 (Th) ἐποίει πόλεμον μετὰ τῶν ἁγίων καὶ ἴσχυσεν πρὸς αὐτούς; Rev 13:7 ποιῆσαι πόλεμον μετὰ τῶν ἁγίων καὶ νικῆσαι αὐτούς.

[21] So Lohmeyer, *Offenbarung*, p. 1, and Hanns Lilje, *Das letzte Buch der Bibel: Eine Einführung in die Offenbarung Johannes* (Hamburg: Furche-Verlag, 1955), p. 11, take the whole of chapter 14 as a separate septet, "Die sieben Visionen vom (Kommen des) Meschensohnes." On the other hand, A. Feuillet, "La moisson et la vendange de l'Apocalypse (14, 14-20): La signification chrétienne de la révélation johannique," *NRTh* 94 (1972): 113-32, 225-50, following Anthony T. Hanson, *The Wrath of the Lamb* (London: SPCK, 1957), pp. 173-77, argues for a positive interpretation of the harvest and vintage. See also Bauckham, *Climax*, pp. 290-96. Aune, *Revelation 6–16*, pp. 801-803, argues for the more common view that final judgment is represented.

distant a connection in the kind of outline I have been producing, but the relationship is one with great significance for the interpretation of these chapters.[22]

5.2.2 Discourse Structure Diagram 6

The discourse structure of 12:1–14:20 can now be displayed in some detail.[23]

Discourse Structure Diagram 6 (Rev 12:1–14:20)

This diagram shows the detailed structure of the "visions of conflict." Each section number is preceded by **2.3.2.2.2.1**. The whole diagram represents a sixth grade sequence.

12:1–14:20 Signs and visions of conflict
Delimiters: Καὶ σημεῖον μέγα ὤφθη ἐν τῷ οὐρανῷ; [Καὶ εἶδον ἄλλο σημεῖον]
Dramatis personae: dragon, beast, people of God, Lamb
Spatial signals: in heaven, on earth
   (.1) 12:1–13:18 Visions of the dragon and the beasts
   Delimiters: Καὶ σημεῖον μέγα ὤφθη; [Καὶ εἶδον, καὶ ἰδού]
   Dramatis personae: dragon (appears in all subscenes)
      (.1.1) 12:1-18 The woman and the dragon
      Delimiters: as above; [Καὶ εἶδον]
      Dramatis personae: dragon, woman clothed with the sun

---

[22] A table summarizing the literary connections can be found in Appendix B, pp. 206-207. For further details see Pattemore, "The People of God," pp. 227-35.

[23] A number of alternative structures may be noted. Yarbro Collins, *Combat Myth*, pp. 37-38, finds a series of seven unnumbered visions, differing slightly from those proposed by Farrer, *Rebirth of Images*, p. 45, for 11:15–14:20. Others find quite a different septet stretching over 11:19–15:4; for example, Wendland, "7 X 7," pp. 380-81; John E. Hurtgen, *Anti-Language in the Apocalypse of John* (Lewiston, N.Y.: Mellen Biblical Press, 1993), pp. 91-95. Such differences illustrate the subjectivity of looking for sevens when John has not chosen to draw his audience's attention to them. On quite a different approach, the chiasmi proposed by Lund, *Chiasmus*, pp. 395, 398-401, 403-404, are much more convincing when they deal with a short stretch of text (e.g., 13:1-5, p. 403) than over a longer stretch.

(.1.1.1) 12:1-2 The woman – opening situation
Delimiters: as above; [καὶ ὤφθη ἄλλο σημεῖον]
Dramatis personae: woman clothed with the sun
Spatial signals: in heaven, moon under her feet
Temporal signals: in the pain of childbirth
(.1.1.2) 12:3-4 The dragon – opening situation
Delimiters: καὶ ὤφθη ἄλλο σημεῖον; [καὶ ἔτεκεν]
Personal reference: woman, her child
Dramatis personae: dragon
Spatial signals: in heaven, onto earth, in front of the woman
Temporal signals: when she should give birth
(.1.1.3) 12:5-9 Action on two planes
Delimiters: καὶ ἔτεκεν; [καὶ ἤκουσα]
Dramatis personae: (see below)
    (.1.1.3.1) 12:5-6 Pursuit on earth
    Delimiters: καὶ ἔτεκεν; [Καὶ ἐγένετο]
    Personal reference: the nations, God
    Dramatis personae: woman, her son, dragon
    Spatial signals: (up) to God and his throne, into the
    desert
    Temporal signals: (future rule of male child), 1260 days
    (.1.1.3.2) 12:7-9 War in heaven
    Delimiters: Καὶ ἐγένετο; [καὶ ἤκουσα]
    Personal reference: dragon = serpent/Devil/Satan, whole
    world
    Dramatis personae: Michael and his angels, dragon and
    his angels
    Spatial signals: in heaven
**(.1.1.4) 12:10-12 Interlude – audition of a voice in heaven –
triumph song**
Delimiters: καὶ ἤκουσα; [Καὶ ὅτε εἶδεν] (resumptive aorist)
Communication axis: voice => heaven and its inhabitants
(overheard by John?)
Personal reference: God, Christ, the accuser, our brethren,
Lamb, heavens and their inhabitants, earth and sea, devil
Dramatis personae: voice
Spatial signals: in heaven
Temporal signals: Ἄρτι, aorists
(.1.1.5) 12:13-17 Action resumes
Delimiters: Καὶ ὅτε εἶδεν (resumptive aorist)

Personal reference: woman's son
Dramatis personae: dragon = serpent, woman, earth, rest of
the woman's seed
Spatial signals: onto earth, into the desert
Temporal signals: a time and times and half a time
(.1.1.6) 12:18 Final state – dragon on seashore
Dramatis personae: dragon
Spatial signals: on the shore of the sea
(.1.2) 13:1-18 The two beasts
Delimiters: Καὶ εἶδον; [Καὶ εἶδον, καὶ ἰδοὺ]
  (.1.2.1) 13:1-8 The beast from the sea
  Delimiters: Καὶ εἶδον; asyndeton
    (.1.2.1.1) 13:1-3a Emergence of beast
    Delimiters: as above; [καὶ ἐθαυμάσθη]
    Dramatis personae: beast, dragon
    Spatial signals: out of the sea
    (.1.2.1.2) 13:3b-4 Response of earth to beast
    Delimiters: καὶ ἐθαυμάσθη; [Καὶ ἐδόθη]
    Personal reference: beast, dragon
    Dramatis personae: whole earth, beast, dragon
    (.1.2.1.3) 13:5-8 Empowering of beast and its results
    Delimiters: Καὶ ἐδόθη; [Εἴ τις . . .] (asyndeton and
    communication shift)
    Personal reference: God, heaven-dwellers, Lamb
    Dramatis personae: beast, saints, all peoples, nations,
    etc., all earth-dwellers
    Spatial signals: (indirect: on the earth)
    Temporal signals: aorist => future
  (.1.2.2) 13:9-10 Direct address to audience
  Delimiters: asyndeton and shift in communication situation
    (.1.2.2.1) 13:9-10a Prophetic word
    Delimiters: Εἴ τις; [Ὧδέ ἐστίν]
    Communication axis: Spirit? => (John) => audience
    Personal reference: anyone with ears, those destined for
    captivity and the sword
    (.1.2.2.2) 13:10b Challenge to endurance
    Delimiters: Ὧδέ ἐστίν; [Καὶ εἶδον]
    Communication axis: John => audience (outside vision
    narration)
    Personal reference: saints

(.1.2.3) 13:11-17 The beast from the earth
Delimiters: Καὶ εἶδον ἄλλο θηρίον; ['Ὧδε . . . ἐστίν]
(.1.2.3.1) 13:11 Physical description
Delimiters: . . . ἄλλο θηρίον; [καὶ . . . ποιεῖ]
Dramatis personae: another beast
Spatial signals: from the earth
(.1.2.3.2) 13:12-17 Actions of the earth-beast
Delimiters: καὶ . . . ποιεῖ; ['Ὧδε . . . ἐστίν]
Personal reference: first beast, those without the mark
(implicit)
Dramatis personae: earth-beast, earth-dwellers—small
and great, rich and poor, free and slave
Temporal signals: present tense
(.1.2.4) 13:18 Direct address to audience
Delimiters: 'Ὧδε . . . ἐστίν; [Καὶ εἶδον, καὶ ἰδοὺ]
Communication axis: John => audience (outside vision
narration)
Personal reference: beast, anyone with wisdom
(.2) 14:1-13 Visions of the Lamb and his followers
Delimiters: Καὶ εἶδον, καὶ ἰδοὺ; [Καὶ εἶδον, καὶ ἰδοὺ]
(.2.1) 14:1-5 The Lamb and his followers
Delimiters: Καὶ εἶδον, καὶ ἰδοὺ; [Καὶ εἶδον]
(.2.1.1) 14:1 Vision of the Lamb and the 144,000
Delimiters: . . . καὶ ἰδοὺ; [καὶ ἤκουσα]
Personal reference: father of the Lamb
Dramatis personae: Lamb, the 144,000
Spatial signals: on Mount Zion
(.2.1.2) 14:2-3 Audition of a voice
Delimiters: καὶ ἤκουσα; [οὗτοι εἰσιν (aside?)]
Personal reference: the "throne," the 24 elders and 4 living
creatures
Dramatis personae: the 144,000
Spatial signals: from heaven, before the throne, from earth
(.2.1.3) 14:4-5 Comment on the 144,000
Delimiters: οὗτοι εἰσιν; [Καὶ εἶδον]
Personal reference: the 144,000, women, Lamb, God,
humanity
Temporal signals: present tense
(.2.2) 14:6-11 Vision of three angels
Delimiters: Καὶ εἶδον; ['Ὧδε . . . ἐστίν]

154

(.2.2.1) 14:6-7 First angel – with gospel proclamation
Delimiters: Καὶ εἶδον ἄλλον ἄγγελον; [Καὶ ἄλλος ἄγγελος]
Personal reference: God
Dramatis personae: another angel, inhabitants of earth—all nations, etc.
Spatial signals: in midheaven, on the earth
(.2.2.2) 14:8 Second angel – with message of fall of Babylon
Delimiters: Καὶ ἄλλος ἄγγελος; [Καὶ ἄλλος ἄγγελος]
Personal reference: Babylon, all the nations
Dramatis personae: another angel (second one)
Spatial signals: following (the above)
(.2.2.3) 14:9-11 Third angel – with description of fate of beast-worshipers
Delimiters: Καὶ ἄλλος ἄγγελος; [῟Ωδε . . . ἐστίν]
Personal reference: worshipers of the beast, beast, God, his holy angels, Lamb
Dramatis personae: another angel (third one)
Temporal signals: forever and ever
(.2.3) 14:12 Direct address to audience
Delimiters: ῟Ωδε . . . ἐστίν; [Καὶ ἤκουσα]
Communication axis: John => audience (outside vision narration)
Personal reference: saints
(.2.4) 14:13 Audition of a voice from heaven
Delimiters: Καὶ ἤκουσα; [Καὶ εἶδον, καὶ ἰδοὺ]
Communication axis: Spirit => (John) => audience
Personal reference: those that die in the Lord
Dramatis personae: voice from heaven, Spirit
(.3) 14:14-20 Vision of the Son of Man bringing final judgment
Delimiters: Καὶ εἶδον, καὶ ἰδοὺ; [Καὶ εἶδον ἄλλο σημεῖον]
Dramatis personae: one like the Son of Man, three angels
Spatial signals: on the cloud
(.3.1) 14:14 Description of scene
Delimiters: . . . καὶ ἰδοὺ; [καὶ ἄλλος ἄγγελος]
Dramatis personae: one like the Son of Man
Spatial signals: on the cloud
(.3.2) 14:15-20 Two descriptions of harvest involving the cloud-sitter and three angels
(.3.2.1) 14:15-16 First description
Delimiters: καὶ ἄλλος ἄγγελος; [Καὶ ἄλλος ἄγγελος]
Dramatis personae: another angel, cloud-sitter

155

Spatial signals: from the temple, onto earth
(.3.2.2) 14:17-20 Second description
Delimiters: Καὶ ἄλλος ἄγγελος;[Καὶ εἶδον ἄλλο σημεῖον]
Dramatis personae: another angel, yet another angel,
unnamed vintage-treader, horses?
Spatial signals: from the temple, from the altar of incense,
onto earth, outside the city, for 1600 stadia

5.2.3 The people of God in 12:1–14:20

The role of the people of God in these central chapters is remarkable in a number of ways. On the surface of the story of the woman and the dragon (12:1-9, 13-18), they hardly appear at all until the end where they clearly become the focus of the dragon's attention.[24] But already in the hymn section (12:10-12), the result of this second campaign of the dragon is anticipated by the victory of Michael and his angels, which is reinterpreted as a victory of "our brethren." The connections, both explicit and implicit, between the earthly struggle of the people of God and the conflict on a cosmic level, make this a centrally important passage.

But no less important is the story of the two beasts. In this story the people of God are largely in focus as objects of action rather than as actors: the first beast is empowered to make war on them and conquer them (13:7), and the second beast is empowered to kill them (13:15). They are implicitly described in contrast to others, as those whose names *are* in the Lamb's book of life (13:8) who do *not* worship the image (13:15), and as those unable to trade because of *not* having the mark of the beast (13:17). But in both parts of the vision the author seems to leave aside the narrative and turn to the actual audience, bringing them directly into relationship with these shadowy figures in the vision (13:9-10, 18). Here again, as in chapter 12, the connections between the "real world" of the audience and the world of the visions are both explicit and implicit, and deserve close scrutiny.

In the first few verses of chapter 14, the people of God are explicitly in focus for the first time in the whole sequence—in fact for the first time since chapter 7 and directly linking to that chapter. The 144,000

---

[24] The reference in 12:17 to the dragon going off to make war μετὰ τῶν λοιπῶν τοῦ σπέρματος αὐτῆς τῶν τηρούντων τὰς ἐντολὰς τοῦ θεοῦ καὶ ἐχόντων τὴν μαρτυρίαν ᾿Ιησοῦ, has clear connections both internal to chapter 12 and external to it and is part of the means of anchoring or contextualizing the story.

followers of the Lamb are presented here in contrast to those who have worshiped the beast and accepted its mark. These worship God and the Lamb, in company with the heavenly throne attendants whose role of eternal worship before the throne was emphasized in chapters 4–5. In place of the mark of the beast, they have the name of the Lamb and his Father on their foreheads. The additional descriptions of them (14:4) are both explicit and puzzling.[25]

In the second part of chapter 14, the people of God return somewhat to the background, present again by contrast, especially in the cry of the third angel (14:9). And again, following a "negative" image of the people of God, the author turns directly to the audience with a challenge to endurance (14:12).[26] What follows is formally part of the vision/audition, beginning with Καὶ ἤκουσα. But, within itself, it breaks the communication situation by introducing the voice of the Spirit. The mixed communication context that results is similar to those we have already encountered in 1:7-8 and 22:12-21, which we have linked to the operation of prophecy within the gathered assembly.

The outline of Dan 7, which we have traced from 7:1 to chapter 13, and then to 14:14, links together the passages that, so far, have proved most significant for understanding the message of Revelation with regard to the present and future of the people of God. It is as though there is a structure of Daniel *below* the overt surface-level structure of Revelation with its numerical coherence. Furthermore, it is in these same passages, in particular chapters 12–14, where the "real" audience is brought into closest contact with its visionary representations.

5.3 Visions involving the plague angels (15:1–22:9): Structural integrity

Already in 14:14-20, and increasingly from 15:5, the heavenly temple, last seen opened at the end of chapter 11, has become the central spatial indicator of the text. This in itself would have argued for the inclusion of

---

[25] For further details, see Pattemore, "The People of God," pp. 70-73, 303-310.

[26] The third angel's cry is clearly delimited by an inclusio: Εἴ τις προσκυνεῖ τὸ θηρίον . . . οἱ προσκυνοῦντες τὸ θηρίον . . . . This makes it clear that Ὧδε ἡ ὑπομονὴ τῶν ἁγίων ἐστίν stands apart as a separate statement. The similar remarks at 13:10 and 18 have both followed similar "negative image" descriptions of the people of God.

14:14-20 with what follows, had not other factors, and in particular the relationship with Dan 7, more certainly tied it to what precedes. With respect to the principle of relevance, the context created by the preceding material has a priority over that created by what follows, since it is easily accessed whereas what follows requires a suspension of judgment until the new material is processed. Nevertheless, the temple and the altar of incense function to link the two major text sequences together, and in this 14:14-20 does perform a bridging role.

The unity of the sequence 15:1–16:21 with the remaining sequences, 17:1–19:10, 19:11–21:8 and 21:9–22:9, is perhaps more tenuous than the links we have observed so far. The series of seven bowls in 15:1–16:21 is relatively discrete, as compared with the previous septets that drew other material into their structure. Nevertheless, we are justified in regarding 15:1–22:9 as a single sequence because of the structural significance of the plague-bearing angels.[27] They are first introduced in 15:1 as the anarthrous ἀγγέλους ἑπτὰ ἔχοντας πληγὰς ἑπτὰ τὰς ἐσχάτας, and after a short interlude (15:2-4) they become the central figures in what follows, referenced anaphorically as οἱ ἑπτὰ ἄγγελοι. The two vision sequences that focus on Babylon and the New Jerusalem are then each introduced to John by one angel from this group. The first is described as εἷς ἐκ τῶν ἑπτὰ ἀγγέλων τῶν ἐχόντων τὰς ἑπτὰ φιάλας (17:1) and the second, yet more specifically, as εἷς ἐκ τῶν ἑπτὰ ἀγγέλων τῶν ἐχόντων τὰς ἑπτὰ φιάλας τῶν γεμόντων τῶν ἑπτὰ πληγῶν τῶν ἐσχάτων (21:9).[28] The increase in detail would seem to be required by the greater distance from the original statement, and at the same time allows 21:9–22:9 to close the vision sequence begun with 15:1.[29]

---

[27] Lund, *Chiasmus*, pp. 342-43, finds in 17:1–22:5 a "great chiastic structure of seven sections," which he labels "The Last Series of Seven Angels." While the significance of angelic appearances is undoubted, the whole chiasmus is less than convincing. It has in fact only six angels, and the parallels on which the chiasmus is based are rather tenuous.

[28] The bowls and the plagues have previously been identified by their mutual association with the wrath of God (15:1,7; 16:1).

[29] Despite the very marked nature of these two introductions (the second is almost labored in its determination that the reader make the correct connection to the bowl sequence), a large number of commentators appear to ignore the structuring role of the plague angels in the latter part of the book. See, for example, J. Comblin, "La liturgie de la nouvelle Jérusalem (Apoc., XXI, 1–XXII, 5)," *ETL* 29 (1953): 5-40; Hellholm,

5.4 Seven plague angels pour out their bowls (15:1–16:21)

5.4.1 Structural features

Formally, this scene is tightly structured, with the introduction of the seven plague-bearing angels and instructions to them (chapter 15) followed by their sequential and complete action in pouring out the bowls. The location with respect to heaven is only lightly marked (John sees a sign in heaven, 15:1; the temple in heaven is opened, 15:5; hail comes from heaven, 16:21). It is the ναός that becomes the principal spatial marker throughout the scene (15:5, 6, 8; 16:1, 17), a factor that contributes strongly to the scene's coherence. We have already noted the angels appearing from the ναός at 14:15, 17. But the strongest echo of the opening of the heavenly temple in 15:5 is from further back at 11:19, which is in fact the first time that the ναός actually appears in the vision descriptions.[30]

"Problem," p. 51; Schüssler Fiorenza, "Composition," pp. 363-64; Lambrecht, "Structuration," pp. 85-86; Müller, *Microstructural Analysis*, pp. 608-698; Corsini, *Apocalypse*, pp. 62-63. Hahn, "Aufbau," p. 154, links 17:1–19:10 with the plague bowls, but then misses the equally clear association of 21:9–22:9. Kevin E. Miller, "The Nuptial Eschatology of Revelation 19–22," *CBQ* 60 (1998): 301-318, similarly ignores the obvious and argues for a unity of 19:5–22:9, based on the link of the bride. See Pattemore, "The People of God," pp. 316-32. Most surprisingly, Aune, *Revelation 1–5*, pp. cii-cv, does not use the link, which John is overtly supplying, to build his structure, despite the fact that he most clearly recognizes the parallels in the two angelic revelations, delineating them identically three times in his commentary (*Revelation 1–5*, pp. xcv-xcvii; *Revelation 17–22*, pp. 1020-21 and pp. 1202-203, following Giblin, "Structural and Thematic Correlations"). This is because he treats 17:1 as an "analeptic gloss" (*Revelation 17–22*, p. 928), allowing his source criticism to interfere with the surface structure of the finished document. Yarbro Collins, *Combat Myth*, p. 32, following Farrer, *Rebirth of Images*, pp. 55-58, correctly marks the two angelic revelations, but attaches only the first to the bowl sequence, with the second treated as an appendix to the somewhat doubtfully enumerated "Seven unnumbered visions." (See below, pp. 173-79, on 19:11–21:8.)

[30] Previously it has been referred to in 3:12 and 7:15 as a desirable location for God's people. Even when the angel tells John to measure the temple in 11:1-2, the fulfillment of the instruction is not mentioned and

The link to 11:19 is strengthened at the end of the scene by the occurrence of lightning, voices, thunder and earthquake (16:18) followed by hail (16:21). Thus, as I have already pointed out, the whole scene could in some ways be thought of as an expansion of 11:19.[31] However, the relationship to chapters 12–14 should not be overlooked. In the interlude, 15:2-4, which immediately follows the first mention of the seven angels, John sees and hears the worship of those who have conquered the beast, its image and the number of its name, motifs that all strongly echo chapter 13. Yet the content of the hymn of praise is reechoed by the angel of the waters (16:5-6) and the altar (16:7). The relationship of the seven plagues to the previous septets has often been analyzed, but we should note also that the first, fifth and sixth plagues explicitly involve the beast or the dragon or both.[32] On the other hand, cataphoric linking is most notably achieved by the focus in 16:19 on Babylon's destruction as part of the wrath of God. Thus this section is both well defined and yet strongly linked backwards and forwards.

Of the seven plagues that result from the pouring out of the bowls, the first, second, fourth and fifth have similarly simple structures, while the

---

the temple itself is not part of John's description of the scene. The only use of the word subsequent to this scene is in 21:22, where it is noted that there is no ναός but God himself in the New Jerusalem. The altar of incense featured more prominently in the earlier visions (6:9; 8:3, 5; 9:13) and was associated with the temple at 11:1 and 14:17-18. It appears in this scene only at 16:7.

[31] As previously noted, these associations have led some to suggest that 11:19 is the introduction to what follows, rather than the conclusion of the previous section. However, the role of the lightning, voices and thunder is more likely to signal the end of each of the three septets (seals 8:5; trumpets 11:19; bowls 16:18), in each case matching and intensifying the initial occurrence in the opening scene of the visionary section (4:5). See Mazzaferri, *Genre*, pp. 340-42; Bauckham, *Climax*, pp. 202-204; and the detailed discussion on pp. 118-20 above.

[32] For analyses of the relationship of the bowls to the earlier septets, see, for example, Beale, *Revelation*, pp. 127-29, 808-812; G. R. Beasley-Murray, *The Book of Revelation* (NCB; London: Marshall, Morgan & Scott, 1974), pp. 238-39; M. Eugene Boring, *Revelation* (Interpretation; Louisville: John Knox Press, 1989), pp. 120-21.

third, sixth and seventh have relatively complex structures.[33] Although the angels appear from the heavenly temple, and the voice of command also issues from there, most of the action is geocentrically oriented, and humanity as a whole appears to be the sufferer. In contrast to the previous two septets, the seventh bowl follows immediately after the sixth.[34] Its description is notable for the piling up of spatial markers, and for a time span encompassing the whole of human history, from the time humanity first appeared to the "It is done" of the voice from the temple.

5.4.2 Discourse Structure Diagram 7

Discourse Structure Diagram 7 (Rev 15:1–16:21)

This diagram shows the detail of structure of the bowl sequence with its introduction. Each section heading begins with **2.3.2.2.2.2.1**. The whole diagram is a seventh-grade sequence.

15:1–16:21 Seven plague angels pour out their bowls
Delimiters: Καὶ εἶδον ἄλλο σημεῖον; μεγάλη ἐστὶν ἡ πληγὴ αὐτῆς σφόδρα
Personal reference: God
Dramatis personae: seven angels
Spatial signals: temple (in heaven)
Temporal signals: aorists

(.1) 15:1-8 Seven angels given seven bowls
Delimiters: ἀγγέλους ἑπτὰ ἔχοντας πληγὰς ἑπτά; ἑπτὰ πληγαὶ τῶν ἑπτὰ ἀγγέλων

(.1.1) 15:1 Introduction to seven plague angels scene
Delimiters: Καὶ εἶδον; [Καὶ εἶδον]
Spatial signals: in heaven
Temporal signals: last plagues . . . wrath of God completed

(.1.2) 15:2-4 Hymn interlude (vision + audition)
Delimiters: Καὶ εἶδον; [Καὶ μετὰ ταῦτα εἶδον]
Personal reference: beast, its image and number, God, Moses, the nations
Dramatis personae: conquerors of the beast

---

[33] See the diagram in the following section. For a more detailed structure of the bowls, see Aune, *Revelation 6–16*, pp. 860-69.

[34] Attempts by Vanni, *La struttura*, pp. 182-205, and Lambrecht, "Structuration," pp. 85-86, to insinuate a gap here are entirely fanciful.

Spatial signals: crystal sea
Temporal signals: perfect and present participles, present indicative main verb

(.1.3) 15:5-8 Seven angels given seven bowls
Delimiters: Καὶ μετὰ ταῦτα εἶδον (resumptive after verses 2-4); [Καὶ ἤκουσα]
Personal reference: God
Dramatis personae: seven angels, one of the four living creatures
Spatial signals: temple . . . in heaven
Temporal signals: μετὰ ταῦτα

(.2) 16:1-21 Seven angels pour out their bowls
Delimiters: Και ἤκουσα; Καὶ ὁ ἔβδομος . . . [Καὶ ἦλθεν εἰς ἐκ τῶν ἑπτὰ]
Personal reference: God
Dramatis personae: a great voice, seven angels
Spatial signals: from the temple, onto earth

(.2.1) 16:1 Angels commanded to pour
Personal reference: angels, God
Dramatis personae: great voice

(.2.2) 16:2-21 Angels fulfill the command
Delimiters: Καὶ ἀπῆλθεν ὁ πρῶτος . . . .
Dramatis personae: seven angels (individually)

(.2.2.1) 16:2 Angel 1 pours[35]
Delimiters: ὁ πρῶτος . . . ἐξέχεεν . . . καὶ ἐγένετο
Dramatis personae: first angel, people with the mark of the beast
Spatial signals: the earth

(.2.2.2) 16:3 Angel 2 pours
Delimiters: Καὶ ὁ δεύτερος ἐξέχεεν . . . καὶ ἐγένετο
Dramatis personae: second angel, all living things in the sea
Spatial signals: sea

(.2.2.3) 16:4-7 Angel 3 pours
Delimiters: Καὶ ὁ τρίτος ἐξέχεεν . . . καὶ ἐγένετο
Dramatis personae: third angel
Spatial signals: rivers and springs

(.2.2.3.1) 16:4 Pouring of bowl turns water to blood
Delimiters: καὶ ἐγένετο; [καὶ ἤκουσα]

---

[35] For a detailed structure of the bowls, see Aune, *Revelation 6–16*, pp. 860-69.

(.2.2.3.2) 16:5-6 Audition of angel of waters
Delimiters: καὶ ἤκουσα; [καὶ ἤκουσα]
Personal reference: God, saints, prophets
Dramatis personae: angel of waters
(.2.2.3.3) 16:7 Audition of altar
Delimiters: καὶ ἤκουσα; [Καὶ ὁ τέταρτος]
Personal reference: God
Dramatis personae: altar of incense (or souls under it?)
(.2.2.4) 16:8-9 Angel 4 pours
Delimiters: Καὶ ὁ τέταρτος ἐξέχεεν
Personal reference: God
Dramatis personae: fourth angel, humankind
Spatial signals: sun
(.2.2.5) 16:10-11 Angel 5 pours
Delimiters: Καὶ ὁ πέμπτος ἐξέχεεν . . . καὶ ἐγένετο
Personal reference: beast, God
Dramatis personae: fifth angel, (unnamed) citizens of beast's kingdom
Spatial signals: throne of the beast
(.2.2.6) 16:12-16 Angel 6 pours
Delimiters: Καὶ ὁ ἕκτος ἐξέχεεν
Personal reference: God
Dramatis personae: sixth angel, kings
Spatial signals: Euphrates River, the east
> **(.2.2.6.1) 16:12 Pouring of bowl prepares a path for the kings**
> *Delimiters*: Καὶ . . . ἐξέχεεν . . . καὶ ἐξηράνθη; [Καὶ εἶδον]
> **(.2.2.6.2) 16:13-14 Assembling of kings by the demons**
> *Delimiters*: Καὶ εἶδον; ['Ιδοὺ (asyndeton)]
> *Dramatis personae*: dragon, beast, false prophet, 3 frog-spirits, kings of the whole earth
> *Temporal signals*: great day of God Almighty
> **(.2.2.6.3) 16:15 Prophetic word and macarism**
> *Delimiters*: 'Ιδοὺ (asyndeton); [καὶ]
> *Communication axis*: Jesus => audience
> *Personal reference*: those who watch and keep their garments
> **(.2.2.6.4) 16:16 Assembly of kings of the earth at Harmagedon**
> *Delimiters*: καὶ (resumptive)

Dramatis personae: kings (presumably)
Spatial signals: place called Harmagedon
(.2.2.7) 16:17-21 Angel 7 pours
Delimiters: Καὶ ὁ ἕβδομος ἐξέχεεν . . . καὶ ἐγένοντο . . .
καὶ ἐγένετο
Personal reference: God
Dramatis personae: seventh angel, great voice, humankind
Spatial signals: the air, out of the temple, on earth, city,
islands, mountains, from heaven
Temporal signals: "It is done," since humanity came

5.4.3 The people of God in 15:1–16:21

The people of God feature in this vision sequence in a number of ways—as actors, in personal reference, and as the objects of direct address. In the opening interlude (15:2-4), which links so strongly to chapter 13, John sees the conquerors of the beast and hears their song of worship. Although they are most notable by their absence from the remainder of the scene, and in particular the pouring out of the bowls, it may be more accurate to say they are present as an implicit contrast. They do not have the mark of the beast, nor do they blaspheme the name of God; they are not citizens of the beast's kingdom. They come into focus again in the speech of the angel of the waters, where the martyrdom of the saints and prophets is given as just cause for God's judgment (16:5-6). This is followed by the altar of incense speaking (16:7). The inference that it is the voice of the martyrs under the altar, previously encountered in 6:9-11, is strongly supported. First, the immediate previous context referred to the shedding of the blood of the saints and prophets. Second, the cry strongly echoes part of the song of the conquerors of the beast (15:3b).[36] Third, the cry of the souls under the altar was a call for judgment. Here it is a thanksgiving for judgment given.[37]

---

[36] Note also 12:11, where those who conquered the accuser "did not cling to life even in the face of death."

[37] The relevant phrases are 6:10 with Ἕως πότε, ὁ δεσπότης ὁ ἅγιος καὶ ἀληθινός, οὐ κρίνεις καὶ ἐκδικεῖς τὸ αἷμα ἡμῶν; 15:3b with δίκαιαι καὶ ἀληθιναὶ αἱ ὁδοί σου; 16:7 with ἀληθιναὶ καὶ δίκαιαι αἱ κρίσεις σου. In fact much of the vocabulary is repeated or echoed, including the reference to truth and justice and their blood; cf. 16:5b-6a: Δίκαιος εἶ, ὁ ὢν καὶ ὁ ἦν, ὁ ὅσιος, ὅτι ταῦτα ἔκρινας, ⁶ὅτι αἷμα ἁγίων καὶ προφητῶν ἐξέχεαν . . . . This

Finally, and very importantly, 16:15 appears to be another example of John breaking the communication situation to bring a direct word to his audience, this time a prophetic word from Jesus himself. As with some of the previous examples, there are no participants in the immediate vision sequence who could be imagined to speak or to receive this message. Here again is an important integration point, where the real audience is brought into close identification with the actors and action of the visions.[38]

5.5 A tale of two cities (17:1–22:9)

While there is an obvious increase in relevance achieved by associating 17:1–22:9 with the sequence of seven bowls (see section 5.3 above), it is not nearly so clear that these chapters form a coherent unit in themselves. In favor of this view is the parallel between the two angelic revelations of 17:1–19:10 and 21:9–22:9.[39] As a consequence of this, the larger section is a division of the visionary section of the book in which John himself has an active role. In chapter 10 and the beginning of chapter 11, John was an active participant in the heavenly drama, as previously at 4:1–5:5. But since then he has been a passive witness. Even the verbs of seeing and hearing have decreased in frequency through chapters 11–16.[40] But in chapter 17 and 19:9-10, John is directly involved and spoken to. He is drawn up into the heavenly drama again, which has not happened since 11:2. The same pattern is then repeated in 21:9-10 and 22:1, 6-9. On the other hand, between these two sequences is the vision of the opened heaven, 19:11–21:8, where verbs of seeing and hearing increase, but John is again a passive observer. Furthermore, there are no formal

---

relationship is explored in detail in Pattemore, "The People of God," pp. 173-225.

[38] Contrast Mazzaferri, *Genre*, pp. 337-38, who says that this verse is not an interlude because "it does not really disrupt the sequence." While it is entirely within the sixth bowl, it clearly does disrupt the communication situation and therefore must stand apart.

[39] See the parallels listed by Aune, in the references given in note 29, pp. 158-59 above.

[40] They will never be as frequent again as in chapters 5–6, but there is a small peak around chapter 14 and a larger one around chapters 19–21.

features of the language which create a block of text around 17:1–22:9.[41] In fact, when the angel invites John to go with him at 21:9, his description has more of the details of the plague angels of chapters 15–16 than does the description at 17:1. Further, he is not introduced either as *the* plague-bearing angel, or even as *another* of the plague-bearing angels, but simply as "one of the seven" in the same way as at 17:1. These facts suggest that both angelic journeys occupy the same structural relationship to the bowl sequence, which is the background to both, rather than a direct structural relationship to each other.

5.6 First vision sequence with angel-guided journey (17:1–19:10)

5.6.1 Structural features

No high-level formal markers set 17:1 off as a new section. The simple καὶ parataxis and the mention of the seven angels with their seven bowls, echoing 15:1, 7; 16:1, suggest that the same scene is in view and that this sequence either follows from the previous one or is a part of it.[42] A number of features of the first vision (chapter 17) recall the visions of chapters 12–13.[43] The final vision (19:1-8) similarly links *over* the immediately subsequent visions to the appearance of the bride of the Lamb in 21:2, 9. But the text sequence 17:1–19:10 itself is tightly bound both by the formal envelope of John's interaction with the angel

---

[41] Snyder, "Triple-Form," p. 448, suggests a concentric structure for 17:1–22:5 which has a degree of plausibility, but ignores John's own overt structuring in terms of the two angel-guided tours.

[42] Although Müller, *Microstructural Analysis*, p. 654, mistakenly begins a new sequence at 19:1, ignoring the outlines of the angelic revelation, he lists many significant links in vocabulary between chapters 17–18 and chapters 15–16 (pp. 612-13, 633-37). These are more than sufficient to establish a high degree of relevance for the combination. Thus Aune's claim (see note 29 above) that 17:1a is merely "an analeptic gloss" intended to create a secondary linkage, does not do justice to the evidence.

[43] Blasphemous names (17:3; cf. 13:1), a beast with seven heads and ten horns (17:3; cf. 12:3; 13:1), the death-resurrection motif (17:8; cf. 13:3), and the attitude toward the beast of those whose names are not written in the book of life (17:8; cf. 13:8).

166

(especially 17:1-3; 19:9-10) and by the predominant subject matter of the revelation, namely Babylon and its fall.[44]

However, while the outer limits of the sequence are clear, its internal structure is complex and potentially indeterminate at a number of points. Three main divisions are apparent, the second and third set off by Μετὰ ταῦτα: 17:3-18 with the vision of the scarlet woman on the beast and its explanation; 18:1-24 with the woe song for the fall of Babylon; and 19:1-8 with worship in heaven.

The first of these divisions involves John being taken off ἐν πνεύματι into the wilderness (17:3), a brief and static description of what he sees there (17:4-6a), his reaction (17:6b) and the angel's explanation (17:7-18), the most detailed explanation yet given of any of John's visions.[45]

Chapter 18 introduces another angel (18:1), another voice (18:4), and one strong angel (18:21). A large part of the chapter would appear to be a record of their speeches. But how much? Does the "other voice" continue

---

[44] Dagoberto R. Fernández, "The Judgment of God on the Multinationals: Revelation 18," in *Subversive Scriptures: Revolutionary Readings of the Christian Bible in Latin America* (ed. Leif E. Vaage; Valley Forge, Pa.: Trinity Press International, 1997), pp. 75-100, completely omits the final two verses from his structure, and is an example of someone whose hermeneutical interest appears to blind him to the obvious structural function of John's interaction with the angel. As already noted, Aune, *Revelation 17–22*, p. 915, suggests the unity of the section is an editorial feature rather than a substantive one. Whether or not this is so makes little difference for the analysis of the text as it stands.

[45] The two parts of the angel's explanation have a fairly regular structure, with each subsection referring back to an element of John's vision (17:8, 9, 12, 15, 18), giving a present tense meaning of the symbol, and going on to make predictions in the future tense. See Aune, *Revelation 17–22*, pp. 912-15. Aune, *Revelation 17–22*, pp. 919-28, also has a detailed discussion of the nature of 17:1-18, viewed as an *ekphrasis*, a "detailed description of a work of art." This certainly accounts for the fact that nothing *happens* in this vision, and the points of contact with the Dea Roma coin, depicted on p. 920, are indeed fascinating. Relevance Theory certainly requires that attention be given to allusions to nonliterary elements in the common cognitive environment. Yet the differences between Rev 17 and the scene depicted on the coin are also significant. To give only one example, there is no beast on the coin, but the seven hills are directly represented.

speaking after 18:8? There is a further complication due to a change in the verb tenses used. The second voice makes future predictions (18:8), which may or may not continue through the description of the mourning of the kings and merchants (18:9-17a—all essentially in the future). Then 18:17b-20 shifts to narrative past to describe the action of the seafarers. Yet there is strong parallelism between 18:17b-19 and the subsections 18:9-10, 11-14, and 15-17a.[46] Further, 18:20 does not appear to continue directly from 18:19. It does not fit well in the context of 18:9-19 at all. But it does potentially form an inclusion with 18:4-8, both being calls to the people of God to act with respect to Babylon, the aorist imperative recalling the string of aorist imperatives in 18:4-6. Therefore it seems likely that the whole of 18:4-20 is the angel's speech.[47] If this is the case, then this chapter has a broad chiastic structure, with an audition, or a series of auditions, bracketed by John's vision of the actions of the angels (18:1, 21).[48] But he does not actually see the various peoples or merchandise described.

The final subsection, 19:1-8, is again a series of auditions (note the voices at 19:1, 5, 6 and other auditory components at 19:3, 4) with a small

---

[46] Each of the subsections here has a parallel microstructure: a new group is introduced, some history of their association with Babylon described, and their song of woe recorded (Οὐαὶ οὐαὶ in 18:10, 16, 19). See Aune, *Revelation 17–22*, pp. 973-75, for a similar analysis.

[47] So Aune, *Revelation 17–22*, pp. 973-74, 976, following Adela Yarbro Collins, "Revelation 18: Taunt-Song or Dirge?" in *L'Apocalypse johannique et l'Apocalyptique dans le Nouveau Testament* (ed. J. Lambrecht; BETL 53; Gembloux, Belgium: J. Duculot, 1980), p. 193, and Bauckham, *Climax*, p. 340.

[48] William H. Shea, "Chiasm in Theme and by Form in Revelation 18," *AUSS* 20 (1982): 249-56, presents a chiastic structure for 18:2-24, the most attractive feature of which is that it makes some sense of the double introduction of the merchants, as compared to the single introductions of the kings and seafarers. However, by dividing 18:4-20 on the basis of semantic content, he overlooks the more obvious surface-level structuring in terms of the angelic speeches. The broad chiasmus in my structure (see p. 99 above) is more akin to that proposed by Kenneth A. Strand, "Two Aspects of Babylon's Judgment Portrayed in Revelation 18," *AUSS* 20 (1982): 53-60. See also Christopher R. Smith, "Reclaiming the Social Justice Message of Revelation: Materialism, Imperialism and Divine Judgement in Revelation 18," *Transformation* 7 (1990): 29.

visual component (19:4), which has strong links back to the opening scene of worship in heaven (chapter 4).[49]

5.6.2 Discourse Structure Diagram 8

Discourse Structure Diagram 8 (Rev 17:1–19:10)

This diagram shows the detailed structure of the first angel-guided journey, the vision of Babylon. Each section number begins with **2.3.2.2.2.2.2**. The entire diagram is a seventh-grade sequence.

17:1–19:10 First vision sequence with angel-guided journey – Babylon
Delimiters: Καὶ ἦλθεν εἰς ἐκ τῶν ἑπτὰ ἀγγέλων . . . ; [Καὶ εἶδον τὸν οὐρανὸν ἠνεῳγμένον]
Dramatis personae: one of the seven angels, John
> **(.1) 17:1-3a Initial interaction between John and the angel – John raptured to the desert**
> *Delimiters*: Καὶ ἦλθεν . . . ; [καὶ εἶδον]
> *Personal reference*: great prostitute, kings of the earth, dwellers on the earth
> *Spatial signals*: into the desert
> *Temporal signals*: aorist verbs, present participles
> **(.2) 17:3b–19:8 Content of the revelation**
> *Delimiters*: καὶ εἶδον; [Καὶ λέγει μοι, Γράψον·]
>> **(.2.1) 17:3b-18 The woman on the beast and the angel's explanation**
>> *Delimiters*: καὶ εἶδον; [Μετὰ ταῦτα εἶδον]
>> *Dramatis personae*: John, woman, beast, angel
>>> **(.2.1.1) 17:3b-6a John's vision – the woman on the beast**
>>> *Delimiters*: καὶ εἶδον . . . καὶ εἶδον . . . ; [Καὶ ἐθαύμασα]
>>> *Personal reference*: saints and witnesses of Jesus
>>> *Temporal signals*: aorist verbs for John, present and perfect participles

---

[49] See also William H. Shea, "Revelation 5 and 19 as Literary Reciprocals," *AUSS* 22 (1984): 249-57, whose highlighting of similarities in the contributions to the heavenly worship is more convincing than his attempts to find parallel or inverted structures. Wendland, "7 X 7," p. 383, divides this section into seven sayings, ignoring some of these more obvious structuring features, which do not result in quite such a neat result!

(.2.1.2) 17:6b John's response – amazement
Delimiters: Καὶ ἐθαύμασα; [καὶ εἶπεν μοι ὁ ἄγγελος]
(.2.1.3) 17:7-18 Angel's explanation of the vision
Delimiters: καὶ εἶπεν μοι ὁ ἄγγελος; [Μετὰ ταῦτα εἶδον]
Dramatis personae: angel, John

   (.2.1.3.1) 17:7 Angel offers to explain the vision
   Delimiters: καὶ εἶπεν μοι . . . ; [τὸ θηρίον ὅ εἶδες]
   Personal reference: woman and beast
   (.2.1.3.2) 17:8-14 First part of explanation – the beast and its horns
   Delimiters: τὸ θηρίον ὅ εἶδες; [Καὶ λέγει μοι]
   Personal reference: beast, inhabitants of the earth, seven kings, ten kings, Lamb, those with him
   Temporal signals: past => present => future movement
   (.2.1.3.3) 17:15-18 Second part of explanation – waters and the woman
   Delimiters: Καὶ λέγει μοι; [Μετὰ ταῦτα εἶδον]
   Personal reference: peoples, nations and tongues, ten horns, prostitute, God, beast, kings of the earth
   Temporal signals: past => present => future

(.2.2) 18:1-24 Woe songs over Babylon
Delimiters: Μετὰ ταῦτα εἶδον; [Μετὰ ταῦτα ἤκουσα]
Temporal signals: presumably follows 17:3b-18 in vision time

   (.2.2.1) 18:1-3 Another angel descends from heaven with a message
   Delimiters: . . . εἶδον ἄλλον ἄγγελον . . . ; [Καὶ ἤκουσα ἄλλην φωνὴν]
   Personal reference: Babylon, demons, etc., all nations, kings of the earth, merchants of the earth
   Dramatis personae: John, angel
   Spatial signals: from heaven, earth
   Temporal signals: aorist and perfect verbs throughout
   (.2.2.2) 18:4-20 Another voice speaks from heaven
   Delimiters: Καὶ ἤκουσα ἄλλην φωνὴν; [Καὶ ἦρεν εἷς ἄγγελος ἰσχυρὸς]
   Dramatis personae: John, voice (God's?)

      (.2.2.2.1) 18:4-8 Commands to God's people and prediction of Babylon's fate
      Delimiters: direct address to God's people

Communication axis: God => his people (embedded)[50]
Personal reference: Babylon, God
Dramatis personae: voice (God's?), "my people" (implicit)
Temporal signals: aorist imperatives, aorist and present reasons, future prediction

(.2.2.2.2) 18:9-19 Mourning by kings, merchants, and seafarers
Delimiters: preceded and followed by imperatives
Spatial signals: from afar
Temporal signals: in one hour

(.2.2.2.2.1) 18:9-10 The kings will mourn[51]
Delimiters: Καὶ (verb phrase) οἱ βασιλεῖς τῆς γῆς
Personal reference: kings of the earth, Babylon
Temporal signals: main verbs future

(.2.2.2.2.2) 18:11-17a The merchants will mourn
Delimiters: Καὶ οἱ ἔμποροι τῆς γῆς (verb phrase)
Personal reference: merchants of the earth, Babylon
Temporal signals: main verbs present and future, no longer

(.2.2.2.2.3) 18:17b-19 The seafarers mourned
Delimiters: Καὶ πᾶς κυβερνήτης (verb phrase)
Personal reference: captains and seafarers, Babylon
Temporal signals: main verbs aorist

(.2.2.2.3) 18:20 Call to God's people to rejoice for the judgment against Babylon
Delimiters: resumption of imperative; [Καὶ ἦρεν εἷς ἄγγελος ἰσχυρὸς]
Communication axis: angel => heaven, saints, etc. (embedded)[52]
Personal reference: God, Babylon
Dramatis personae: voice

---

[50] Note that on the surface this whole section is still formally John => churches. The embedded quote brings a new communication situation, as happens again in this sequence at 18:20 and 19:5.

[51] See Aune, *Revelation 17–22*, pp. 973-75, for an analysis of this section and the following two. See also Smith, "Reclaiming the Social Justice Message."

[52] See note 50 above.

(.2.2.3) 18:21-24 Strong angel throws millstone, and his message
Delimiters: Καὶ ἦρεν εἷς ἄγγελος ἰσχυρὸς; [Μετὰ ταῦτα ἤκουσα]
Personal reference: Babylon, merchants, nations, prophets, saints, the slain
Dramatis personae: one strong angel
Spatial signals: into the sea
Temporal signals: future predictions, for past reasons
(.2.3) 19:1-8 Worship in heaven
Delimiters: Μετὰ ταῦτα ἤκουσα; [Καὶ λέγει μοι]
Dramatis personae: John
Temporal signals: after the events of chapters 17–18
(.2.3.1) 19:1-4 Audition (and vision) of worship of the multitude
Delimiters: . . . ἤκουσα ὡς φωνὴν; [Καὶ φωνὴ]
Personal reference: God, prostitute, God's servants
Dramatis personae: John, (great crowd), 24 elders, 4 living beings, God
Spatial signals: in heaven, on the throne
(.2.3.2) 19:5 Voice from the throne
Delimiters: Καὶ φωνὴ; [καὶ ἤκουσα ὡς φωνὴν]
Communication axis: God => his slaves (embedded)[53]
Personal reference: God's slaves and those who fear him
Dramatis personae: voice from throne, God's slaves (implicit as addressees)
Spatial signals: from the throne
(.2.3.3) 19:6-8 Further audition of worship of the multitude
Delimiters: καὶ ἤκουσα ὡς φωνὴν; [Καὶ λέγει μοι]
Personal reference: God, Lamb, bride of the Lamb
Dramatis personae: John, (great crowd)
(.3) 19:9-10 Concluding interaction between John and the angel – John forbidden to worship
Delimiters: Καὶ λέγει μοι, Γράψον·; [Καὶ εἶδον τὸν οὐρανὸν ἠνεῳγμένον]
Personal reference: those invited to the marriage, God, brethren who have the witness of Jesus
Dramatis personae: angel, John

[53] See note 50 above.

172

5.6.3 The people of God in 17:1–19:10

The first significant thing to note about the people of God in this text sequence is that they never appear on the scene. John never sees them in any form, nor is their voice heard. The last time they actually appeared was in 15:2-4. Nevertheless, they are the ground against which much of the description is set and feature on a number of different levels of the text. The violent death of saints and martyrs is behind the condemnation of the prostitute/Babylon (17:6; 18:24) and their vindication is cause for celebration in heaven (19:2). They are associated with the Lamb in victory (17:14) and referred to both as his bride (19:7-8) and as invitees to his marriage feast (19:9).

But God's people are the addressees of two significant passages: 18:4-20 and 19:5. In both cases the speaker is presumably God himself. In the first case they are addressed as ὁ λαός μου, and called to come out from Babylon (18:4), perhaps to participate in her punishment (18:6-7); and as saints, apostles and prophets they are called to rejoice over their vindication (18:20).[54] In the second case οἱ δοῦλοι αὐτοῦ are urged to praise God (19:5).

On two occasions it is possible that John himself makes direct asides to the audience (17:9a; 19:8b), although these are less obviously so than those we have encountered previously.

5.7 Visions of the opened heaven (19:11–21:8)

5.7.1 Structural features

Between the first and second journeys ἐν πνεύματι are an unnumbered series of visions. Apart from being bounded by these two clearly parallel text sequences, there are further reasons to believe that they form a cohesive unit, rather than being a disjointed series. First, there is a hierarchy of discourse connectives that tie the unit together. The opening scene begins with Καὶ εἶδον τὸν οὐρανὸν ἠνεῳγμένον, καὶ ἰδοὺ . . . , which appears to be a relatively high-level marker, recalling both the earlier use of Καὶ εἶδον (. . .) καὶ ἰδού and the initial vision of the open door in heaven

---

[54] See also Smith, "Reclaiming the Social Justice Message," pp. 32-33. The question of who is addressed in 18:6-7 is discussed further in Pattemore, "The People of God," pp. 212-13.

(4:1).[55] Subsequent to this there are 7 further sentence-initial occurrences of Καὶ εἶδον, each of which could potentially be seen as introducing a new vision.[56] In between these markers, the text is for the most part strung together paratactically. The other lines of evidence for treating 19:11–21:8 as a cohesive sequence arise from lexical and semantic considerations that will become apparent when we have examined the internal structure more closely.

The eight possible visions delimited by Καὶ εἶδον reduce to seven when we consider that those at 20:11 and 20:12 are so closely linked by the scene of the throne that they must be taken as two aspects of the same vision, the first taking in the throne and its occupant and the second the scene around the throne. Seven is a seductively appropriate number of visions to find.[57] However, things are not quite so straightforward. Recall that we are working with the assumption that a unit of text is a sequence over which relevance is optimized. We can therefore explore text sequence boundaries by examining the degree of lexical and semantic unity within and between sequences. Let us number the seven visions we have so far obtained as visions 1 (19:11-16), 2 (19:17-18), 3 (19:19-21), 4 (20:1-3), 5 (20:4-10), 6 (20:11-15), and 7 (21:1-8). These visions are bound together by a web of motifs that can be tabulated as seen in Table 5.2.

---

[55] That this is the highest level marker in this sequence is supported by the fact that the only other occurrences of Ἰδού (21:3, 5) are emphasis markers in imbedded speech, not discourse markers in John's vision report.

[56] 19:17, 19; 20:1, 4, 11, 12; 21:1. There is a broken καὶ ... εἶδον at 21:2.

[57] So Yarbro Collins, *Combat Myth*, pp. 39-40, following Farrer, *Rebirth of Images*, p. 45. Müller, *Microstructural Analysis*, pp. 671-76, is not tempted by seven visions, but still analyzes on the basis of the occurrences of εἶδον. Wendland, "7 X 7," pp. 384-85, has seven sections headed by εἶδον, up to the end of chapter 20. Then why not another similar section in 21:1-8? Erring in the opposite direction is Ed Christian, "A Chiasm of Seven Chiasms: The Structure of the Millennial Vision, Rev 19:1–21:8," *AUSS* 37 (1999): 209-225, who finds a chiasmus of seven chiasmi by including 19:1-10, overriding the very clear markers at the end of the angelic revelation of Babylon in 19:9-10.

Table 5.2 – Motifs in common among the seven proposed visions in 19:11–21:8

Motif	Vision 1	2	3	4	5	6	7
heaven	19:11	19:17?		20:1	20:9	20:11	21:1, 2
rider on white horse	19:11		19:19, 21				
Faithful and True	19:11						21:5
judgment	19:11				20:4	20:11ff.	?
war	19:11		19:19				
Word of God	19:13				20:4		
armies	19:14		19:19				
sword in his mouth	19:15		19:21				
nations	19:15			20:3	20:8		
God	19:15				20:6		21:2f.
kings	19:16	19:18	19:19		20:4, 6		
angel		19:17		20:1			
birds		19:17	19:21				
flesh		19:18	19:21				
great and small		19:18				20:12	
beast			19:19f.		20:4, 10		
earth			19:19		20:8	20:11	21:1
false prophet			19:20		20:10		
deceive			19:20	20:3	20:8, 10		
mark of beast and its image			19:20		20:4		
thrown into lake of fire			19:20		20:10	20:14f.	21:8
devil				20:2	20:10		
Satan				20:2	20:7		
1000 years				20:2f.	20:4, 6-7		
loosed				20:3	20:7		
throne(s)					20:4	20:11	21:3, 5
the dead					20:5	20:12f.	
holy					20:6		21:2
second death					20:6	20:14	21:8
city					20:9		21:2
one seated on throne						20:11	21:5
place appointed						20:11	21:8
sea						20:13	21:1
death						20:13f.	21:4

This table leads to some very interesting results in terms of discourse structure and the optimization of relevance. Most of the visions have some unique character that is not apparent in this table, except by its absence. But consider first the similarities. Visions 2 and 4 are relatively brief (19:17-18 and 20:1-3) and are related to the others in a somewhat peculiar way. They both involve a vision of an angel and are both closely related to the following vision. Further, the motifs they share with the following vision are, for the most part, not shared with any other vision.[58] This strongly suggests that visions 2 and 3 form a unit, as do visions 4 and 5. But when we now examine the table we find the same phenomenon in the relationship between vision 1 and the composite vision 2+3. The rider on the white horse, war, armies and the sword coming out of the rider's mouth, all these are common to visions 1 and 2+3 and to no other. Grouping visions 1-3 together, leaves four self-coherent vision sequences.[59] It might appear that visions 6 and 7 should be similarly grouped, since they share the one seated on the throne, the idea of a place appointed, the sea and the personification of death, motifs not present in any of the other sequences. But other motifs common to visions 6 and 7 are also linked to previous sequences—heaven, earth, and especially the throwing into the lake of fire which now comes as the final act in each of the four vision sequences. If we relabel these visions A (19:11-21), B (20:1-10), C (20:11-15), D (21:1-8), the table will look something like this:

---

[58] Visions 2 and 3 share kings of the earth (which has only an implicit link to vision 1, and the reference to ruling in vision 5 is not really parallel) and birds eating flesh. Visions 4 and 5 share the deception of the nations, the devil, Satan, the 1000 years, and the loosing of Satan.

[59] Hellholm, "Problem," pp. 51-52, has the same four divisions as ninth-grade sequences, although because he does not follow the angelic revelation structure, they are part of two different eighth-grade sequences. Aune, *Revelation 17–22*, pp. 1045-48, 1076-81, presents a very similar analysis to mine, but without the detailed justification I have given. Giblin, *Revelation*, pp. 16-17, combines the third and fourth to produce 3 sections, but this is less likely, as I will proceed to show.

Table 5.3 – Motifs in common among four proposed vision sequences in 19:11–21:8

Motif	Vision	A	B	C	D
heaven		19:11	20:1, 9	20:11	21:1, 2
Faithful and True		19:11			21:5
judgment		19:11	20:4	20:11ff.	?
Word of God		19:13	20:4		
nations		19:15	20:3, 8		
God		19:15	20:5		21:2f.
angel		19:17	20:1		
great and small		19:18		20:12	
beast		19:19f.	20:4, 10		
earth		19:19	20:8	20:11	21:1
false prophet		19:20	20:10		
deceive		19:20	20:3, 8, 10		
mark of beast and its image		19:20	20:4		
thrown into lake of fire		19:20	20:10	20:14f.	21:8
throne(s)			20:4	20:11	21:3, 5
the dead			20:5	20:12f.	
holy			20:6		21:2
second death			20:6	20:14	21:8
city			20:9		21:2
one seated on throne				20:11	21:5
place appointed				20:11	21:8
sea				20:13	21:1
death				20:13f.	21:4

This is a very compact set of relationships. Every vision is related by one or more motifs to every other vision. Every vision has some *unique* relationship to every other vision.[60] The visions are also linked by common motifs into groups of three: ABC, ABD, BCD, but **not** ACD.[61] And a

---

[60] The motifs shared by each pair which are not in the other visions are: AB (Word of God, nations, angel, beast and its mark, false prophet, and deception); AC (great and small); AD (Faithful and True); BC (dead); BD (holy, city); CD (one seated on throne, place appointed, sea, death).

[61] ABC (judgment); ABD (God); BCD (lake of fire, thrones, second death).

few motifs link all four visions—heaven, earth, being thrown into the lake of fire, and perhaps judgment (although it is only implicit in sequence D).

On the other hand, each vision has unique features, namely:

A: Rider on the white horse and his armies, war with the kings, birds eating the flesh.
B: 1000 years, devil, Satan deceiving the nations, bound and loosed.[62]
C: Books of judgment and of life, judgment by works
D: New heaven, new earth, New Jerusalem, bride, dwelling of God, words of God.

In many ways the fourth vision is the most distinctive, although it picks up concepts from each of the earlier ones. It has very strong semantic links with the subsequent section, 21:9–22:9, which leads many commentators to group it with the latter, though this distorts the obvious parallelism of the two angel-guided journeys. Notice also that there is a sense of progression through the series. Visions A and B depict struggle and conflict on both terrestrial and cosmic planes. Vision C depicts the resolution of the conflict, and in vision D there is no more conflict and the vanquished are only present in one reference to their fate. Interestingly, this movement is also reflected through the four major subdivisions of 15:1–22:9. In 15:1–16:21 and 17:1–19:10, although the final outcome of the cosmic conflict is anticipated, there remains considerable tension over the course of the struggle. Then 19:11–21:8 is pivotal in the resolution of that tension, occupying a similar place as the penultimate vision C does within 19:11–21:8. Finally, 21:9–22:9, like vision D, depicts the eternal state of affairs, with no hint of ongoing conflict and only marginal

---

[62] See William H. Shea, "The Parallel Literary Structure of Revelation 12 and 20," *AUSS* 23 (1985): 37-54 (especially pp. 49, 53), for a comparison of the structure of the whole of chapter 20 with that of 11:19–12:17. It must be said, however, that the surface structures of the two chapters bear little resemblance to each other, while in terms of narrative sequence there is little that is surprising (or significant) in the similarity, as most conflict stories consist of a beginning, a middle and an end, with possible transitions between the stages. Ekkehardt Müller, "Microstructural Analysis of Revelation 20," *AUSS* 37 (1999): 227-55, presents an analysis of the structure of chapter 20 which is essentially similar to mine, and which is much more interested in semantics than his earlier work.

reference to the now vanquished opposition. Thus 19:22–21:8 is a microcosm of 15:1–22:9. This supports the assertion made earlier that the description of the plagues in 15:1–16:1 as πληγὰς ἑπτὰ τὰς ἐσχάτας, ὅτι ἐν αὐταῖς ἐτελέσθη ὁ θυμὸς τοῦ θεοῦ is programmatic for the whole of 15:1–22:9.[63]

5.7.2 Discourse Structure Diagram 9

Discourse Structure Diagram 9 (Rev 19:11–21:8)

This diagram shows the detailed structure of the unnumbered visions between the Jerusalem and Babylon visions. Each section number is preceded by **2.3.2.2.2.2.3**. The whole diagram is a seventh-grade sequence.

19:11–21:8 Visions of the opened heaven
Delimiters: Καὶ εἶδον τὸν οὐρανὸν ἠνεῳγμένον; [Καὶ ἦλθεν εἷς ἐκ τῶν ἑπτὰ ἀγγέλων]
Dramatis personae: John
   (.1) 19:11-21 Vision A – The victory of the rider on the white horse
   Delimiters: καὶ ἰδού; εἰς τὴν λίμνην τοῦ πυρὸς [Καὶ εἶδον]
      (.1.1) 19:11-16 The rider on the white horse and his army
      Delimiters: καὶ ἰδού; [Καὶ εἶδον]
      Personal reference: the nations, God the Almighty
      Dramatis personae: rider on the white horse, armies of heaven
      Temporal signals: present verb, perfect participles and brief future prediction

---

[63] See pp. 121, 157-58. Schüssler Fiorenza, "Composition," p. 364, by taking 19:11–22:9 as a single section, has ignored the role of the angelic revelation in 21:9–22:9. Nevertheless, she makes some interesting observations on the relationship between 19:11-16 and the inaugural vision, 1:12–3:22, suggesting they are related as promise and fulfillment. It must be said, though, that while many of the promises to the conquerors in chapters 2–3 find echoes in this final part of the book, several have no apparent counterpart (e.g., hidden manna and white stones in 2:17; pillars in the temple in 3:12) and some have clearer fulfillment earlier in the book (e.g., the white robes in 3:5; cf. 6:11; 7:9, 13; a name written on them in 3:12; cf. 14:1). The additional step to propose a chiastic structure based on this is less convincing when the plague angel sequence is perceived as a separate section.

(.1.2) 19:17-18 The angel summons the birds
Delimiters: Καὶ εἶδον; [Καὶ εἶδον]
Personal reference: God, kings, captains, horse riders
Dramatis personae: an angel, birds of midheaven (implicit)
(.1.3) 19:19-21 The result of the battle
Delimiters: Καὶ εἶδον; εἰς τὴν λίμνην τοῦ πυρὸς . . . [Καὶ εἶδον]
Dramatis personae: beast, kings of the earth, their armies, rider and his army, false prophet, those who received the mark of the beast, birds
Spatial signals: lake of fire that burns with sulfur
Temporal signals: mostly aorist indicatives
(.2) 20:1-10 Vision B – The 1000 years and the defeat of Satan
Delimiters: Καὶ εἶδον; εἰς τὴν λίμνην τοῦ πυρὸς . . . [Καὶ εἶδον]
Temporal signals: 1000 years
(.2.1) 20:1-3 Satan bound for 1000 years
Delimiters: Καὶ εἶδον ἄγγελον; [Καὶ εἶδον θρόνους]
Personal reference: the nations
Dramatis personae: angel, Satan (= Devil = serpent)
Spatial signals: from heaven, into the bottomless pit
Temporal signals: aorist main verbs until last clause
(.2.2) 20:4-5a Martyrs reign for 1000 years
Delimiters: Καὶ εἶδον θρόνους; [asyndeton]
Personal reference: Jesus, God
Dramatis personae: souls of the beheaded, rest of the dead
Temporal signals: aorist verbs
(.2.3) 20:5b-6 Explanation of double resurrection
Delimiters: asyndeton; . . . χίλια ἔτη [Καὶ ὅταν]
Communication axis: John => audience
Personal reference: those who share the first resurrection, God, Christ
Temporal signals: present and future verbs
(.2.4) 20:7-10 Battle at the end of 1000 years
Delimiters: Καὶ ὅταν τελεσθῇ τὰ χίλια ἔτη; εἰς τὴν λίμνην τοῦ πυρὸς . . . [Καὶ εἶδον]
Personal reference: saints, beast, false prophet
Dramatis personae: Satan, the nations
Spatial signals: earth, camp of the saints, beloved city, lake of fire and sulfur
Temporal signals: anomalous shift future => aorist

(.3) 20:11-15 Vision C – The judgment
Delimiters: Καὶ εἶδον; εἰς τὴν λίμνην τοῦ πυρὸς [Καὶ εἶδον]
Dramatis personae: throne-sitter, the dead, (heaven, earth, Death, and Hades personified)
Spatial signals: earth and heaven, sea, Hades, lake of fire
Temporal signals: aorists

(.4) 21:1-8 Vision D – New heaven and new earth
Delimiters: Καὶ εἶδον; ἐν τῇ λίμνῃ τῇ καιομένῃ πυρὶ [Καὶ ἦλθεν εἰς ...]

(.4.1) 21:1-2 Vision
Delimiters: Καὶ εἶδον; [καὶ ἤκουσα]
Personal reference: God
Dramatis personae: holy city = New Jerusalem
Spatial signals: new heaven and earth, coming down out of heaven
Temporal signals: first heaven and earth passed away

(.4.2) 21:3-4 Audition – voice from the throne
Delimiters: καὶ ἤκουσα; [Καὶ εἶπεν]
Communication axis: voice => John (=> whoever!)
Personal reference: God, mortals
Dramatis personae: voice from the throne
Temporal signals: present and future tenses, "first things have passed away"

(.4.3) 21:5-8 Audition – 3 messages from the throne-sitter[64]
Delimiters: Καὶ εἶπεν ὁ καθήμενος; [Καὶ ἦλθεν]
Dramatis personae: throne-sitter

(.4.3.1) 21:5a First message
Delimiters: Καὶ εἶπεν ....
Communication axis: throne-sitter (embedded) => whoever

(.4.3.2) 21:5b Second message
Delimiters: καὶ λέγει ....
Communication axis: throne-sitter (embedded) => John (implied)

(.4.3.3) 21:6-8 Third message
Delimiters: καὶ εἶπέν μοι ...; ἐν τῇ λίμνῃ τῇ καιομένῃ πυρὶ ... [Καὶ ἦλθεν]

---

[64] Although this is only one paragraph, and I have not normally analyzed below paragraph level, I have included a further breakdown here because of the central role of this passage in Hellholm's analysis.

Communication axis: throne-sitter (embedded) => John (explicit)

Personal reference: the thirsty, the conquerors, the cowardly, etc.

Spatial signals: lake of fire

Temporal signals: present and future verbs

5.7.3 The people of God in 19:11–21:8

It is possible that the people of God are, or are part of, the armies of heaven in vision A (19:14). The battle depicted here is most likely a heavenly combat, but the relationship between God's people and angelic armies is one that must be investigated further.[65] But God's people are much more prominently focused in vision B in a number of significant ways. Sharing Christ's millennial rule are the souls of those beheaded for their faith, last seen crying out for vindication from under the altar in 6:9-11.[66] Here they are further described in terms of their response to the beast (chapter 13), which the earlier reference does not anticipate. Worshiping the beast or its image and receiving its mark has, since chapter 13, become the primary discriminator between humanity as a whole and the people of God. In what is probably another direct aside to his audience, John in 20:5b-6, both addresses the "real" people of God and also forges a strong link with what is happening in the vision. Further, in this scene the armies of the nations surround "the camp of the saints and the beloved city." The embattled people of God are thus, at least, closely associated with Jerusalem, if not identified with it.[67] In vision C the people of God are implicitly part of the company of dead who are judged, although the focus is on those whose names are **not** found in the book of life. Finally, in vision D God's people are again strongly focused on several levels. They are represented symbolically by the heavenly Jerusalem, the

---

[65] See Aune, *Revelation 17–22*, p. 1059 for the widely accepted argument that the armies of heaven in 19:14 are angelic. This is discussed in more detail in Pattemore, "The People of God," pp. 311-12.

[66] They are possibly implicit also at 17:6. The phrase here in 20:4, τὰς ψυχὰς τῶν πεπελεκισμένων διὰ τὴν μαρτυρίαν Ἰησοῦ καὶ διὰ τὸν λόγον τοῦ θεοῦ, is slightly different from that at 6:9, τὰς ψυχὰς τῶν ἐσφαγμένων διὰ τὸν λόγον τοῦ θεοῦ καὶ διὰ τὴν μαρτυρίαν ἣν εἶχον. But the rare use of "souls" and the combination of phrases is clearly intended to recall the same group.

[67] Depending on whether the καὶ is treated as epexegetic or not.

bride of the Lamb. This association is tentatively made at this stage, against the background of 19:7-8 and 20:9, and supported by the explanation of 21:3, but its confirmation awaits the full depiction of the New Jerusalem in 21:9–22:9. The words from the throne directly and explicitly concern the final outcome for the people of God and can be understood to operate both within the vision itself and breaking through into the real communication situation in which the audience of the Apocalypse finds itself.[68]

5.8 Second vision sequence with angel-guided journey (21:9–22:9)

5.8.1 Structural features

The very obvious relationship that Rev 21:9–22:9 has with 21:1-8 has led many to analyze the combination as a single section.[69] However, this is to ignore a number of significant features. First, the concept of the "bride of the Lamb" links back more particularly to 19:7 than to 21:2, where there is only the simile of "a bride adorned for her husband." Second, while the association of the bride and the New Jerusalem is certainly a feature shared between these two juxtaposed sections, the angel's invitation in 21:9, and its surprising fulfillment in 21:10, read awkwardly if regarded as part of the same sequence as 21:1-2. Why should John be invited to be shown something he has already seen? This

---

[68] My analysis does not support Hellholm's contention ("Problem," pp. 44-46) that this speech from the throne is what he calls the "highest grade" text sequence in the book and also the most embedded in terms of communication situations. Such a conclusion is entirely dependent on identifying the whole of 8:1–22:5 as *scriptura interior*, and subsequent decisions on textual hierarchy. I have shown reasons why I accept some but not all of these decisions. Nevertheless, this does not detract from the importance of this passage for the communication of John's intended message to his audience. See also Pattemore, "The People of God," pp. 316-32.

[69] For example, Wendland, "7 X 7," pp. 385-86, who finds seven revelations here; Lambrecht, "Structuration," p. 86; Müller, *Microstructural Analysis*, pp. 677-86; Hellholm, "Problem," p. 52. For James H. Sims, *A Comparative Literary Study of Daniel and Revelation: Shaping the End* (Lewiston, N.Y.: Mellen Biblical Press, 1995), pp. 75-79, 21:1–22:5 comprises the second major subdivision of the visionary part of the book.

is a failure of relevance. Too much processing is required to yield a few extra implicatures (at least at this stage, though the fuller description of the city certainly adds these). Third, the series of four unnumbered visions in 19:11–21:8 each finished with a reference to the lake of fire. In the case of the last vision, 21:1-8, it is somewhat anachronistic and appears to have been deliberately added as part of a speech to form the closure. The lake of fire does not appear again. Fourth, the outline of the angel-guided tour, with its formal, lexical and semantic associations back to the plague angel visions, is too strong and deliberate a feature to be overridden by the connections between 21:1-2 and 21:9-10.[70] The former should instead be treated as an anticipatory mention of the theme of the subsequent text sequence, a form that has become very familiar throughout the book. Finally, we can note that the description of the New Jerusalem is a single unified whole. Although it begins and ends almost identically to 17:1–19:10, in the earlier passage the action passes to John at 17:3b with καὶ εἶδον. There is no such shift here and John takes no obvious part in the scene.[71] The description is largely by means of present and future tense verbs.

I have already discussed the termination of this sequence at 22:9 (rather than 22:5 or 22:11) and the disruption of the communication situations which takes place toward the end of the Apocalypse.[72]

Despite its own internal coherence and integrity, this section is securely anchored front and back. We have already noted the formal parallels with 17:1–20:10, coming mostly at either end of the two sections. But the beginning of this last main section is linked back to the last of the four visions in 19:11–21:8 by the holy city coming down from God out of heaven, by the concept of the bride (which also links to the last scene of the first angelic tour), by the water of life, and by the list of people who cannot enter. It is linked with the final scene of the book in the complex ways we have investigated previously.[73]

---

[70] See again Aune's analysis, note 29, pp. 158-59 above.

[71] The only active verb associated with John before the closing interaction is the negative Καὶ ναὸν οὐκ εἶδον (21:22). This is an additional formal distinction from the sequence of Καὶ εἶδονs in the previous section.

[72] Aune, *Revelation 17–22*, pp. 1141-43, presents a structure essentially the same as mine. Giblin, *Revelation*, pp. 17-18, despite having pointed out the role of the plague angels, includes the whole of 22:6-11 with the Heavenly Jerusalem sequence.

[73] See pp. 95-99.

5.8.2 Discourse Structure Diagram 10

Discourse Structure Diagram 10 (Rev 21:9–22:9)

This diagram shows the detailed structure of the second angel-guided journey, to the New Jerusalem. Each section number is preceded by **2.3.2.2.2.2.4**. The whole diagram is a seventh-grade sequence.

21:9–22:9 Second vision sequence with angel-guided journey – New Jerusalem
Delimiters: Καὶ ἦλθεν εἷς ἐκ τῶν ἑπτὰ ἀγγέλων; καὶ λέγει μοι . . . [καὶ λέγει μοι]
Dramatis personae: angel, John

(.1) 21:9-10a Initial interaction of John and angel – John raptured to high mountain
Delimiters: Καὶ ἦλθεν εἷς . . . ;[καὶ ἔδειξεν μοι]
Personal reference: bride, wife of the Lamb
Spatial signals: to a great high mountain
Temporal signals: aorist verbs

(.2) 21:10b–22:5 What John is shown
Delimiters: καὶ ἔδειξεν μοι; [Καὶ εἶπεν μοι]

(.2.1) 21:10b-14 First description of New Jerusalem
Delimiters: καὶ ἔδειξεν μοι; [Καὶ ὁ λαλῶν μετ᾽ ἐμοῦ]
Personal reference: God, twelve angels, twelve tribes of Israel, twelve apostles of the Lamb
Spatial signals: coming down out of heaven
Temporal signals: aorist main verb, present participles in description

(.2.2) 21:15-21 Angel measures the city – further description
Delimiters: Καὶ ὁ λαλῶν μετ᾽ ἐμοῦ; [Καὶ ναὸν οὐκ εἶδον]

(.2.2.1) 21:15-17 Measurement and its results
Delimiters: Καὶ . . . εἶχεν . . . .
Dramatis personae: angel
Spatial signals: length, breadth and height of city, width of walls
Temporal signals: aorist main verbs, mostly present tense description

(.2.2.2) 21:18-21 Second description of the city
Delimiters: καὶ ἡ ἐνδώμησις . . . .
Spatial signals: physical features of the city

(.2.3) 21:22-27 Third description of the city
Delimiters: Καὶ ναὸν οὐκ εἶδον; [Καὶ ἔδειξέν μοι]
Dramatis personae: John

(.2.3.1) 21:22-23 Two unusual features – no temple, no sun or moon
Delimiters: (see *Temporal signals*)
Personal reference: God, Lamb
Dramatis personae: John, glory of God
Spatial signals: in the city
Temporal signals: aorist main verbs, present description

(.2.3.2) 21:24-27 People and the city – going in
Delimiters: καὶ and future tense
Dramatis personae: the nations, kings of the earth, people, those who are written in the book of life
Spatial signals: into the city
Temporal signals: future tense

(.2.4) 22:1-5 Angel shows some more features
Delimiters: Καὶ ἔδειξέν μοι; [Καὶ εἶπέν μοι]
Dramatis personae: angel

(2.4.1) 22:1-2 Angel shows John the river and its environs
Delimiters: (see *Temporal signals*)
Personal reference: God, Lamb, the nations
Dramatis personae: angel
Spatial signals: from the throne, through the middle of the street, on either side of the river
Temporal signals: aorist main verb, present

(2.4.2) 22:3-5 Further description – who is in
Delimiters: (see *Temporal signals*)
Personal reference: God, Lamb
Dramatis personae: God's slaves, Lord God
Spatial signals: in the city
Temporal signals: future tense, "forever and ever"

(.3) 22:6-9 Concluding interaction between John and the angel
Delimiters: Καὶ εἶπέν μοι; [καὶ λέγει μοι]
Dramatis personae: John, angel, Jesus

(.3.1) 22:6 Final angelic message
Delimiters: Καὶ εἶπέν μοι; [καὶ ἰδοὺ (change of person?)]
Personal reference: Lord, prophets, his angel, his slaves
Dramatis personae: John, angel
Temporal signals: ἐν τάχει

(.3.2) 22:7 Jesus breaks in
Delimiters: καὶ ἰδοὺ; [Κἀγὼ ᾽Ιωάννης]
Communication axis: Jesus => (John) => audience
Personal reference: those who keep the words of prophecy
Dramatis personae: (Jesus)
Temporal signals: ἔρχομαι ταχύ, stative macarism

(.3.3) 22:8-9 John's response and angel's refusal of worship
Delimiters: Κἀγὼ ᾽Ιωάννης
Communication axis: John => audience (moving out of vision narration)
Personal reference: prophets and those who keep the words of this book, God
Dramatis personae: John, angel
Temporal signals: "when I heard and saw," aorist verbs

5.8.3 The people of God in 21:9–22:9

The people of God are a central component of the vision in this section, on a number of levels, and this section is the climax of the message of the book for the real people of God to whom it is addressed. First, on a symbolic level, the city itself is the bride of the Lamb and represents God's people in their completeness, as exemplified by its foundations bearing the names of the twelve tribes and twelve apostles.[74] But in a shift of imagery, the inhabitants of the city are "those who are written in the Lamb's book of life" (21:27) and God's servants are to be found there worshiping him and enjoying his blessings (22:3-5). Finally, on the outermost communication levels (found in 22:10-21), God's servants are also the recipients of the whole revelation, represented by the entire book. They are the ones urged to keep the words of the book, the ones whom Jesus directly addresses in promising his imminent coming. We have noted numerous such crossovers from the inner to the outer communication levels in the course of the analysis, but this is perhaps the most dramatic of all, coming as it does at the end where the "tidiness" of the communication situations is being shattered. The real audience is strongly identified with its visionary representations, and the words of Jesus, and of God, break through the cocoon of the narrative and address it directly.

---

[74] See Robert H. Gundry, "The New Jerusalem: People as Place, not Place for People," *NovT* 29 (1987): 254-64; Jan Fekkes, " 'His Bride Has Prepared Herself': Revelation 19–21 and Isaian Nuptial Imagery," *JBL* 109 (1990): 269-87.

Chapter 6

Conclusions

To conclude this study we will summarize and reflect on the results of the discourse analysis with respect to three questions, the first methodological, the second structural, and the third focusing on the role of the people of God. What contribution has Relevance Theory made to the elucidation of the discourse structure of the Apocalypse? What are some of the significant features of the structure which have emerged (and, as a consequence, do these have any implications for translation)? And where do we find the people of God in the discourse and narrative structures of the book?

6.1 The impact of Relevance Theory on the elucidation of discourse structure

Schüssler Fiorenza attempts to defend her analysis of the structure of Revelation against the accusation that it is "just one more subjectivist enterprise," and Lambrecht, responding, claims that his (quite different) analysis is not so.[1] The constraints inherent in a relevance-theoretic approach do not allow me to make any such claims. The recognition that the cognitive environments which we can reproduce from this distance in time and space may fail accurately to represent aspects of the original communication situation, and especially that we do not know what may be missing from our reconstruction of the context, requires that the structure offered be considered as a tentative model, and a framework for further study, rather than as a definitive result. Nevertheless, some such

---

[1] Schüssler Fiorenza, "Composition," p. 365; Lambrecht, "Structuration," p. 103.

189

CONCLUSIONS

model is a necessary preliminary to studying any given passage with regard to its relevance relations, providing as it does a prioritizing of co-textual environments within which the passage is heard. Furthermore, this analysis has itself been performed with regard to the optimization of relevance over textual units. This has two obvious advantages. First, in the process of exploring cognitive environments that impact the structuring of the text (in particular, but not exclusively, environments created by prior texts), it becomes clear that many of the same environments will have significance when it comes to the reception of the message of the text. Second, an RT approach to the book of Revelation gives priority to auditory linkages (over orthographical ones) and to preceding subtexts (over subsequent ones) in much the same way as the original situation would have done. Thus we can, with some confidence, use this structural outline in any subsequent exegetical process.

An RT approach to discourse analysis has much in common with other approaches such as those reviewed previously.[2] Yet it has a number of distinctive features. First, the RT definition of a unit of text as a unit over which relevance is optimized has given a sharper discriminatory edge to the structural scalpel. This has been applied in a top-down manner, resulting in considerable confidence in the delineation of large-scale textual units.[3] But it has also applied on the smaller scale, functioning both to link units of text and to divide them.[4]

Second, the RT definition of the context of a communication as the "mutual cognitive environment," including situational and intertextual as well as co-textual elements, has led to the identification of structures not apparent if the text is considered in isolation.[5] Further, focusing on the physical and sociological context in which the communication was taking

---

[2] See the discussion in chapter 1, pp. 3-16, 45-58, and chapter 2, pp. 59-88.

[3] A "top-down" approach begins with the whole text and analyzes it into progressively smaller text sequences.

[4] Linking is seen, for example, in establishing the unity of 12:1–22:9, in joining the subunits comprising 19:11-21, and in associating 14:13-20 with the preceding sequence. Examples of division include the separation of 21:1-8 from 21:9–22:9, and the disjuncture between 11:19 and 12:1.

[5] These include the structural role of the phrase ἃ δεῖ γενέσθαι from Dan 2, the place of Dan 7 as a background structure to Rev 7 and 13–14, the role of the ark of the covenant in 11:19, and the relationship of Rev 7 to the Synoptic Apocalypse.

place, has helped to make sense of the apparently disjointed voices at the end of chapter 22, and the earlier embedded shifts in the communication axis.

Third, the necessity under the principle of relevance to prioritize potential contexts, and the limits placed on how far a text is processed, have led to the elimination of certain proposed "background" texts, such as the suggestion of Isa 66 behind 11:19–12:5, or the suggestion that Babylonian or Canaanite mythology has real interpretive significance for John's audience hearing Rev 12.

It may be argued that these same results could have been obtained without recourse to the terminology or rationale of RT. This is certainly true with respect to the terminology. Indeed some, though not all, of these results have been previously proposed by scholars without conscious recourse to RT. Yet I would contend that, precisely because RT is a description of the process of all human communication, in each case it is the search for optimal relevance which has led to the result, and in each case the theoretical framework of RT gives the argument a sound basis which is more than merely subjective.

6.2 The discourse structure of the Apocalypse

It is difficult to summarize concisely the detailed results of the analysis presented in this study. The Apocalypse is structured by means of an intricately woven web of overt discourse markers and semantic motifs, shot through with changes in the communication situation, such that no linear or hierarchical scheme can adequately account for it. Some general comments, however, are possible.

The outer layer of the structure, comprising the title and epistolary envelope, is relatively uncontroversial although some have given insufficient weight to the epistolary form. This study has emphasized this structure and, with the aid of Relevance Theory, gone some way toward precision with regard to the shape of the ending in particular.

The division of the visionary section into two main parts, with the break between 3:22 and 4:1, is likewise almost universally perceived. But it is within the section 4:1–22:9 that most structural debate occurs. One of the main questions has to do with the relationship of the three numbered septets: the seals, trumpets, and bowls. Are they intended to be sequential to each other, and if so, do they recapitulate each other, or are they all part of a single structure with the trumpets part of the seventh seal and the bowls part of the seventh trumpet? I have shown that 8:1 and 11:19 are the crucial hinges in this debate and have concluded that while the trumpets are part of the seventh seal, there is not such a close relationship between the bowls and the trumpets, at least in the text as it has reached us.[6]

The integrity of 12:1–22:9 as a textual unit is supported by the observation that it is only in this, the second half of the vision description 4:1–22:9, that the communication axis shifts on a number of occasions, as the author appears to communicate directly to his audience, rather than via his narration of the vision. Such shifts occur at 13:9-10, 18; 14:12; 16:15; 17:9a; 19:8b; 20:5b-6; 22:7. The breaking of the unitary communication mode prepares the way for and leads into the finale, where the variation of voices may appear confusing. In fact, that variation is seen to be a deliberate structural device, used to bring the voice of God with immediate force to the audience who itself is far removed in time and space from the visionary experience.

The later chapters (15–22) are bound together by the cohesive device of the plague-bearing angels. We have demonstrated overt structuring in the sequence of pouring the bowls, and the two angel-guided journeys to see Babylon and the New Jerusalem. The sequence that intervenes between these two journeys has been shown to have a more subtle semantically based structure, in four (rather than seven) subsequences.

RT leads me to be somewhat suspicious of supposed large-scale chiastic structures. However, there does appear to be a degree of this in the overall structure of the outer layers of the book, and more particularly in chapter 18.

The display of the discourse structure of a large text is always problematical, and, given the intricacy of the textual web that John has woven, this is especially true of Revelation. The displays provided throughout chapters 3–5 do not overcome all problems and cannot hope to show structural relationships that extend over long sequences of text. Appendix A (pp. 197-203) provides a simplified outline of the structure of the entire book and highlights a feature that was not obvious previously. There are a number of places at which there are "empty text shells," junctures at which sequences embedded by two or more levels all begin at

---

[6] If chapters 12–14 form an insertion either by the author or by an editor, then the earlier relationship of the bowls to the trumpets may have been much closer. But I have also demonstrated strong continuities among chapters 12–14 and what precedes them.

the same place. The obvious ones are 1:12; 4:1; 8:2; 12:1 (the most pronounced of all, with five different levels of text beginning at the same point); 13:1; 14:1; 15:1; 17:1; 17:3b; 19:11. With the exception of 17:3b, these have all been determined on other grounds to be important disjunctures in the text.

Finally, we must conclude that Hellholm's claim, that 21:5-8 is the highest grade text sequence and the most embedded in terms of the communication situation and therefore the central message of the book, is not supported by the evidence. This claim is dependent on the assumption that everything from 8:1 onward is what he calls the *scriptura exterior*, a claim that I dispute. But even if it were, there are text sequences in the near vicinity of chapter 21 (notably 18:4-20) which are even more embedded.[7]

6.3 Implications for translation

Although our theories of translation rightly emphasize the priority of function and meaning over surface form, it is nevertheless true that function and thus meaning are communicated through the form and structure of a text. This is nowhere more apparent than in the book of Revelation where function is so intimately tied up with form that we risk losing the function altogether if we change the form. I have elsewhere discussed in some detail the role of repetition in Revelation, especially its contribution to the semantic structure of the text.[8] The conclusion reached there about the implications for translation is:

> Repetition which creates textual structure on both large and small scales must be recognized for what it is. Then the target language text can be structured using suitable natural structuring terms and devices to ensure that the same connections are made. The repetition which carries major themes through the book, which links or identifies or contrasts characters and

---

[7] In fact, the most embedded texts turn out to be the command to measure the temple and the story of the two witnesses in 11:1b-13. Whether this is at all significant has not been determined by this study, though the importance of the passage is not in doubt.

[8] Stephen W. Pattemore, "Repetition in Revelation: Implications for Translation," *BT* 53 (2002): 425-41.

events, must be very carefully rendered by consistent translation of words and phrases.

This conclusion is equally true of other structural features. Only by an appreciation of the structure, from the largest to the smallest scales, can the translator know whether particular syntactic or semantic features may be ignored or downplayed in the translation process, or whether their function must be adequately conveyed in the new language in order to faithfully render the meaning of the whole text.[9]

6.4 The people of God in the structure of the Apocalypse

As might be expected, every major section of the Apocalypse has some reference to the people of God. However, there are long stretches in which they are present only by implication, or as a contrastive image to those actually in focus. As a result of the discourse analysis presented above, it is now possible to identify three different ways in which the people of God are represented in the Apocalypse: as addressees, as audience, and as actors. The third can be further analyzed into three categories.

(1) Addressees: In the outermost layer of the Apocalypse, 1:1-11 and 22:10-21 (which includes slightly more than what is traditionally referred to as the "epistolary envelope"), real Christians in a particular social and religious environment are directly addressed by the author. While it is true that the whole book is a communication from the author to this audience, for the majority of the book he is narrating his visions, and other modes of reference are superimposed on the direct address to the readers/hearers. In this outer layer, by use of the conventions of letter writing supplemented by prophetic words, the author is in the most direct, unmediated communication with his addressees.[10]

(2) Audience: Within the first vision narrative, 1:12–3:22, while formally recounting his own experience, and indeed *by means of* recounting that experience, John is in fact communicating messages of encouragement, rebuke, challenge and hope to the particular congregations to whom the letter is addressed. It is by means of references in this layer of

---

[9] Pattemore, "Repetition in Revelation," p. 441.

[10] These addressees potentially include not only the members of the seven churches to whom the letter is addressed, but also the wider group envisaged as the audience by the title and some elements in the ending.

vision narration, rather than the outer one, that we find out most about the congregations, both those who receive approval and those who are rebuked. The real audience is very much in view. This is rarely the case in the second vision narrative, 4:1–22:9, but the exceptions prove to be important. These occur exclusively in the second half, 12:1–22:9, and take the form of short asides to the audience, sometimes only a few words long. They are text sequences that do not have any obvious source or target within the vision narrative itself and make most sense as direct words from the author to his audience, although some are prophetic words and have a similar communication axis to the messages of Jesus to the churches. They occur, as already mentioned, at 13:9-10, 18; 14:12; 16:15; 17:9a; 19:8b; 20:5b-6; 22:7.[11] Further, the significance of these is enhanced when we note that all seven macarisms of the Apocalypse (1:3; 14:13; 16:15; 19:9; 20:6; 22:7, 14) are either part of the outer envelope of direct address to the audience, or are closely linked with one of these embedded situations of direct address. Taken together, the macarisms and the asides to the audience appear to be highly significant places where the content of the vision is integrated with John's relationship to the churches and is given ethical and hortatory impact.

(3) Actors: With the exception of the direct asides mentioned above, the people of God feature in the second vision narrative (4:1–22:9) as actors in the drama that is being presented, in three distinct ways. First, and most commonly, they are referred to in speeches by other actors, though they themselves are *offstage* in these particular scenes.[12] They are part of creation (4:11), and more particularly the focus of the redemption effected by the death of the Lamb (5:9-10); they are secured against disaster (7:1-8; cf. 9:4); their prayers are offered to God as incense (5:8; 8:3). God's victory is theirs too and is their vindication and reward (11:18; 12:10-11; 17:14). The condemnation of the whore, Babylon, is based, at least in part, on her treatment of the people of God (17:6; 18:24), and they

---

[11] Vanni, "Liturgical Dialogue," pp. 365-70, suggests that at these points we have a "tendency towards dialogue." The liturgical nature of these asides must be questioned on the principle of relevance—by means of what assumptions would the audience infer that a liturgical process is inserted into the vision narration? Nevertheless, Vanni clearly emphasizes the change in communication situation which they demand.

[12] These are passages in which the people of God, in one guise or another, occupy the *Personal reference* slot in the discourse structure diagrams in chapters 3–5.

are called on to celebrate her downfall (18:4-7, 20). In none of these passages does John report seeing the saints, prophets, or witnesses to Jesus. They are offstage, but very much part of the drama.

The second mode of appearance of the people of God as actors is as members of a larger group on the heavenly stage. Frequently this group is involved in the worship of God (and so could be described as *in the chorus*), but there are a number of other occasions when they are present. In these places the people of God are not directly in focus, but nevertheless they are located within the cosmic scheme and, more particularly, in relationship to God. Thus they are implicitly part of the heavenly worship of all creation (5:13) and of the great crowd (19:1, 6), but are also presumably among those ("on earth") who are not found worthy to open the seals (5:3) and among those judged at the great white throne (20:11-15). We may also include here the references to the twenty-four elders, who are also a part of the chorus of heavenly worship (4:4, 10-11; 5:8-9; 11:16-18; 19:4), and who probably stand in some relationship to the old and new people of God.[13]

Finally, we should note the relatively few occasions in which the people of God, in one form or another, take *center stage* as the focus of John's vision. Here we are shown the souls of those beheaded, under the altar (6:9-11 and perhaps 16:7), the great crowd of those who have come through the tribulation worshiping the Lamb (7:9-17), and the two witnesses and prophets in the suffering and victory contingent on their ministry (11:3-13). The people of God are attacked by the dragon and the beasts (chapters 12–13, though it is the dragon and the beasts who are more clearly in focus through these chapters); the 144,000 followers of the Lamb stand with him on Mount Zion (14:1-5); the conquerors of the beast worship God in heaven (15:2-4); and the martyrs rule with Christ for 1000 years, before again becoming the target of enemy attacks (20:4-10). In the New Jerusalem passages, we have to deal with a complex image of the people of God, both as place and as inhabitants of that place (21:1–22:5). It is the city itself that is explicitly described, but the inhabitants are referred to as well, and the controlling image is of God dwelling in and with his people.

---

[13] In this and the following category, the symbolic representatives of the people of God occupy the *Dramatis personae* slot in the discourse structure diagrams in chapters 3–5.

Appendix A

Abbreviated Discourse Outline of Revelation

This display of discourse structure summarizes for easier reference the displays presented in detail in chapters 3–5. Text sequences are indented according to their grade (or level of embedding) and the scales at the top and bottom of the page show the position of indentation of each grade. Significant disjunctures in the text can be recognized by large movements outward to lower grades, and by rapid entry to successively higher grades (e.g., at 4:1; 7:9; 12:1; 15:1; 17:1; 21:9; 22:10). Italicized text represents embedded text sequences that are on a different communication level from surrounding text.

Grade of text sequence
0   1   2   3   4   5   6   7   8   9   10 11 12 13 14

1:1–22:21 APOCALYPSE
   1:1-3 Introduction
      1:1-2 Title
      1:3 Macarism
   1:4–22:21 Letter
      1:4-6 Formal letter opening
      1:7-8 Prophetic messages and response
      1:9–22:11 Letter body
         1:9-11 Prologue to vision reports – audition of command to write
         1:12–22:9 Vision reports
            1:12–3:22 John's vision of Jesus on Patmos
            1:12-16 John sees Jesus
            1:17ab Reaction and response
               1:17a John falls down
               1:17b Jesus places his hand on John

0   1   2   3   4   5   6   7   8   9   10 11 12 13 14

0 1 2 3 4 5 6 7 8 9 10 11 12 13 14

1:17c–3:22 The words of Jesus

  1:17c-20 The words of Jesus to John

  2:1–3:22 The words of Jesus to the churches through John

    2:1-7 Message to Ephesus

    2:8-11 Message to Smyrna

    2:12-17 Message to Pergamum

    2:18-29 Message to Thyatira

    3:1-6 Message to Sardis

    3:7-13 Message to Philadelphia

    3:14-22 Message to Laodicea

4:1–22:9 John's vision of "things which must happen after this" in heaven

  4:1–11:19 Vision of throne room, leading on to the 7 seals and 7 trumpets

    4:1–7:8 Heavenly worship and the first six seals

    4:1-2a Vision of door in heaven and John's journey

    4:2b-11 God on his throne is worshiped in heaven

    5:1-14 The scroll and the Lamb

    6:1–7:8 Opening the first six seals

      6:1-2 Seal 1

      6:3-4 Seal 2

      6:5-6 Seal 3

      6:7-8 Seal 4

      6:9-11 Seal 5

      6:12–7:8 Seal 6

        6:12-17 First part of sixth seal

        7:1-8 Second part of sixth seal

    7:9–11:19 Heavenly worship and the seventh seal

    7:9-17 Vision of a great crowd worshiping God and the Lamb

    8:1–11:19 Opening the seventh seal

    8:1 Auditory part: silence

    8:2–11:19 Visual part: seven trumpets

      8:2-6 Preparation for blowing the trumpets

      8:2 Seven angels given trumpets

      8:3-5 Another angel offers the prayers of the saints and throws fire to earth

0 1 2 3 4 5 6 7 8 9 10 11 12 13 14

0   1   2   3   4   5   6   7   8   9   10 11 12 13 14
        8:6 Preparation to blow trumpets
        8:7-12 First four trumpets
        8:7 First trumpet
        8:8-9 Second trumpet
        8:10-11 Third trumpet
        8:12 Fourth trumpet
        8:13–11:19 The last three trumpets
        8:13 The woe-crying eagle
        9:1-11 Fifth trumpet
        9:12 Woe cry
        9:13–11:13 Sixth trumpet
          9:13-21 Sixth angel blows trumpet
          10:1–11:13 Major interlude
            10:1-11 The strong angel and the
                little scroll
            11:1-13 The temple and the witnesses
            11:1a John given rod
            11:1b-13 Command to measure
                and story of the two
                witnesses
              11:1b-2 Measure the temple
              11:3-13 Story of the witnesses
          11:14 Woe cry
          11:15-19 Seventh trumpet
            11:15 Seventh trumpet blown
            11:16-18 Worship of the 24 elders
            11:19 Opening of the temple
      12:1–22:9 Signs and visions in heaven
      12:1–14:20 Signs and visions of conflict
       12:1–13:18 Visions of the dragon and the beasts
        12:1-18 The woman and the dragon
         12:1-2 The woman – opening situation
         12:3-4 The dragon – opening situation
         12:5-9 Action on two planes
         12:5-6 Pursuit on earth
         12:7-9 War in heaven
         12:10-12 Interlude – audition of a voice in
            heaven – triumph song

0   1   2   3   4   5   6   7   8   9   10 11 12 13 14

0 1 2 3 4 5 6 7 8 9 10 11 12 13 14
    12:13-17 Action resumes
    12:18 Final state – dragon on seashore
    13:1-18 The two beasts
       13:1-8 The beast from the sea
         13:1-3a Emergence of beast
         13:3b-4 Response of earth to beast
         13:5-8 Empowering of beast and its results
       13:9-10 Direct address to audience
         13:9-10a Prophetic word
         13:10b Challenge to endurance
       13:11-17 The beast from the earth
         13:11 Physical description
         13:12-17 Actions of the earth beast
       13:18 Direct address to audience
    14:1-13 Visions of the Lamb and his followers
       14:1-5 The Lamb and his followers
         14:1 Vision of the Lamb and the 144,000
         14:2-3 Audition of a voice
         14:4-5 Comment on the 144,000
       14:6-11 Vision of three angels
         14:6-7 First angel – with gospel proclamation
         14:8 Second angel – with message of fall of
            Babylon
         14:9-11 Third angel – with description of fate
            of beast-worshipers
       14:12 Direct address to audience
       14:13 Audition of a voice from heaven
       14:14-20 Vision of the Son of Man bringing final
         judgment
         14:14 Description of scene
         14:15-20 Two descriptions of harvest involving
            the cloud-sitter and three angels
           14:15-16 First description
           14:17-20 Second description
    15:1–22:9 Signs and visions of judgment and victory,
         involving plague angels
       15:1–16:21 Seven plague angels pour out their bowls
         15:1-8 Seven angels given seven bowls
0 1 2 3 4 5 6 7 8 9 10 11 12 13 14

0 1 2 3 4 5 6 7 8 9 10 11 12 13 14

15:1 Introduction to seven plague angels scene

15:2-4 Hymn interlude (vision + audition)

15:5-8 Seven angels given seven bowls

16:1-21 Seven angels pour out their bowls

16:1 Angels commanded to pour

16:2-21 Angels fulfill the command

16:2 Angel 1 pours

16:3 Angel 2 pours

16:4-7 Angel 3 pours

16:4 Pouring of bowl turns water to blood

16:5-6 Audition of angel of waters

16:7 Audition of altar

16:8-9 Angel 4 pours

16:10-11 Angel 5 pours

16:12-16 Angel 6 pours

16:12 Pouring of bowl prepares a path for the kings

16:13-14 Assembling of kings by the demons

16:15 Prophetic word and macarism

16:16 Assembly of kings of the earth at Harmagedon

16:17-21 Angel 7 pours

17:1–19:10 First vision sequence with angel-guided journey – Babylon

17:1-3a Initial interaction between John and angel – John raptured to desert

17:3b–19:8 Content of the revelation

17:3b-18 The woman on the beast and the angel's explanation

17:3b-6a John's vision – the woman on the beast

17:6b John's response – amazement

17:7-18 Angel's explanation of the vision

17:7 Angel offers to explain the vision

17:8-14 First part of explanation – the beast and its horns

0 1 2 3 4 5 6 7 8 9 10 11 12 13 14

0 1 2 3 4 5 6 7 8 9 10 11 12 13 14

17:15-18 Second part of explanation –
the waters and the woman
18:1-24 Woe songs over Babylon
18:1-3 Another angel descends from heaven
with a message
18:4-20 Another voice speaks from heaven
18:4-8 Commands to God's people and
prediction of Babylon's fate
18:9-19 Mourning by kings, merchants,
and seafarers
18:9-10 The kings will mourn
18:11-17a The merchants will mourn
18:17b-19 The seafarers mourned
18:20 Call to God's people to rejoice for
the judgment against Babylon
18:21-24 Strong angel throws millstone,
and his message
19:1-8 Worship in heaven
19:1-4 Audition (and vision) of worship of
the multitude
19:5 Voice from the throne
19:6-8 Further audition of worship of the
multitude
19:9-10 Concluding interaction between John and
angel – John forbidden to worship
19:11–21:8 Visions of the opened heaven
19:11-21 Vision A – The victory of the rider on the
white horse
19:11-16 The rider on the white horse and his
army
19:17-18 The angel summons the birds
19:19-21 The result of the battle
20:1-10 Vision B – The 1000 years and the defeat
of Satan
20:1-3 Satan bound for 1000 years
20:4-5a Martyrs reign for 1000 years
20:5b-6 Explanation of double resurrection
20:7-10 Battle at the end of 1000 years

0 1 2 3 4 5 6 7 8 9 10 11 12 13 14

0 1 2 3 4 5 6 7 8 9 10 11 12 13 14
20:11-15 Vision C – The judgment
21:1-8 Vision D – New heaven and new earth
21:1-2 Vision
21:3-4 Audition – voice from the throne
21:5-8 Audition – 3 messages from the throne-
sitter
21:5a First message
21:5b Second message
21:6-8 Third message
21:9–22:9 Second vision sequence with angel-guided
journey – New Jerusalem
21:9-10a Initial interaction of John and angel –
John raptured to high mountain
21:10b–22:5 What John is shown
21:10b-14 First description of New Jerusalem
21:15-21 Angel measures the city – further
description
21:15-17 Measurement and its results
21:18-21 Second description of the city
21:22-27 Third description of the city
21:22-23 Two unusual features – no temple,
no sun or moon
21:24-27 People and the city - going in
22:1-5 Angel shows some more features
22:1-2 Angel shows John the river and its
environs
22:3-5 Further description – who is in
22:6-9 Concluding interaction between John and
the angel
22:6 Final angelic message
22:7 Jesus breaks in
22:7-9 John's response and angel's refusal to
worship
22:10-11 Epilogue to vision reports – audition of command not to
seal
22:12-20 Prophetic messages and response
22:21 Formal letter closing

0 1 2 3 4 5 6 7 8 9 10 11 12 13 14

Appendix B

Narrative Influence of Daniel 7 on Revelation

The display on the next two pages shows the relationship of Dan 7 to Revelation. The first page lists elements in the narrative structure of Dan 7 which are alluded to in Revelation. The second page lists the allusions in Revelation. Indentations are used in the element column on each page to indicate subelements. Italicized references in Revelation are weak allusions, which may not echo all the important features. Most of the references to books in Revelation are italicized since they cover the two scrolls. References to the Lamb's book of life are closer to Daniel. Allusions to the dominion or reign of the Son of Man are only indirect in Rev 4–22 since they actually refer to the Lamb.

Narrative Structure of Daniel 7

Element	Narrations		Explanations	
	1st	2nd	1st	2nd
1. Wind on sea	2			
2. Emergence of beasts	3		17	
3. Nature of beasts	4-7			
3.1. 1st beast	4			
3.2. 2nd beast	5			
3.3. 3rd beast	6			
3.4. 4th beast	7	19		23
3.4.1. Its ten horns	7c	20a		24a
4. Little horn	8, 11	20-21		24-25
4.1. Arrogant words	8c, 11a	20c		25a
4.2. War on saints		21		25
4.3. 3½ times				25c
5. Ancient One enthroned	9-10ab	22		
5.1. Throne attendants	10b			
6. Court in judgment	10c-12	22		26
6.1. Books opened	10c			
6.2. Beast burned	11			
7. Arrival of Son of Man	13			
8. Son of Man given dominion	14			
8.1. Peoples, nations, etc.	14b			
9. Holy ones gain kingdom		22	18	27

Allusions in Revelation

Element	1–3	4–6	7	10–11	12	13–14	17	19–22
1.			7:1					
2.				11:7		13:1	17:8	
3.						13:2		
3.1.								
3.2.								
3.3.								
3.4.						13:1		
3.4.1.					12:3	13:1	17:3, 12; 17:16	
4.				11:7	12:17	13:5, 7	17:12	
4.1.						13:5		
4.2.					12:7, 17	13:7	17:14	20:9
4.3.				11:3	12:14	13:5		
5.	1:14-16	4:1-4						20:4, 11-12
5.1.		5:11	7:9					19:1
6.								20:4, 12
6.1.	3:5	5; 6		10:2, 8		13:8	17:8	20:12, 15; 21:27
6.2.						14:9-11		19:20; 20:10, 15
7.	1:7, 13	5:6-7				14:14		
8.	1:6; 2:28; 3:21	5:12-13	7:17	11:15				19:16; 20:4; 20:6; 22:1-3
8.1.		5:9	7:9	10:11; 11:9		13:7; 14:6	17:15	
9.	1:6; 2:28; 3:21	5:10						20:4, 6; 22:5

Selected Bibliography

Aland, Barbara, Kurt Aland, Johannes Karavidopoulos, Carlo M. Martini, and Bruce M. Metzger, eds. *The Greek New Testament.* 4th rev. edn. Stuttgart: Deutsche Bibelgesellschaft and UBS, 1993.

Aune, David E. "The Apocalypse of John and the Problem of Genre," *Semeia* 36 (1986): 65-96.

————. *Revelation 1–5.* WBC 52A. Dallas: Word, 1997.

————. *Revelation 6–16.* WBC 52B. Dallas: Word, 1998.

————. *Revelation 17–22.* WBC 52C. Dallas: Word, 1998.

Austin, J. L. *How to Do Things With Words.* Oxford: Clarendon, 1962.

Baldinger, Kurt *Semantic Theory: Towards a Modern Semantics.* Edited by Roger Wright. Translated by William C. Brown. Oxford: Basil Blackwell, 1980.

Bartsch, C. "The SSA Approach to Understanding Discourse." *NOT* 3 (1989): 55-58.

Bauckham, Richard. *The Climax of Prophecy: Studies on the Book of Revelation.* Edinburgh: T. & T. Clark, 1993.

Baumgarten, Joseph M. "The Duodecimal Courts of Qumran, Revelation, and the Sanhedrin." *JBL* 95 (1976): 59-78.

Beale, G. K. *The Book of Revelation.* NIGTC. Grand Rapids: Eerdmans, 1999.

————. "The Influence of Daniel upon the Structure and Theology of John's Apocalypse." *JETS* 27 (1984): 413-23.

————. "The Interpretive Problem of Rev. 1:19." *NovT* 34 (1992): 360-87.

———. "Revelation." Pages 318-36 in *It is Written: Scripture Citing Scripture: Essays in Honour of Barnabas Lindars, SSF*. Edited by D. A. Carson and H. G. M. Williamson. Cambridge: Cambridge University Press, 1988.

———. "The Use of Daniel in the Synoptic Eschatological Discourse and in the Book of Revelation." Pages 129-53 in *The Jesus Tradition Outside the Gospels*. Edited by David Wenham. Gospel Perspectives 5. Sheffield: JSOT Press, 1984.

Beasley-Murray, G. R. *The Book of Revelation*. NCB. London: Marshall, Morgan & Scott, 1974.

Beaugrande, Robert-Alain de, and Wolfgang U. Dressler. *Introduction to Text Linguistics*. London: Longman, 1981.

Beckwith, Isbon T. *The Apocalypse of John*. 1919. Repr., Grand Rapids: Baker Book House, 1967.

Beekman, John, and John Callow. *Translating the Word of God*. Grand Rapids: Zondervan, 1974.

Berthiaume, Scott C. "Participant Tracking in Revelation 4–7: Toward a Theory of Markedness." *JOTT* 7 (1996): 87-108.

Biguzzi, Giancarlo. *I settenari nella struttura dell'Apocalisse: Analisi, storia della ricerca, interpretazione*. RivBSup 31. Bologna: Edizione Dehoniane, 1996.

Black, David A., ed. *Linguistics and New Testament Interpretation: Essays on Discourse Analysis*. Nashville: Broadman, 1992.

Blakemore, Diane. "Organisation of Discourse." Pages 229-50 in *Language: The Socio-Cultural Context*. Vol. 4 of *Linguistics: The Cambridge Survey*. Edited by Frederick J. Newmeyer. Cambridge: Cambridge University Press, 1988.

———. *Semantic Constraints on Relevance*. Oxford: Basil Blackwell, 1987.

———. " 'So' as a constraint on relevance." Pages 183-95 in *Mental Representations: The interface between language and reality*. Edited by Ruth M. Kempson. Cambridge: Cambridge University Press, 1988.

Blass, Regina. *Relevance relations in discourse: A study with special reference to Sissala*. Cambridge: Cambridge University Press, 1990.

Boers, Hendrikus. *The Justification of the Gentiles: Paul's Letters to the Galatians and Romans*. Peabody, Mass.: Hendrickson, 1994.

Boismard, M.-E. "<<L'Apocalypse>>, ou <<Les Apocalypses>> de S. Jean." *RB* 56 (1949): 507-541.

Boring, M. Eugene. *Revelation*. Interpretation. Louisville: John Knox Press, 1989.

————. "The Voice of Jesus in the Apocalypse of John." *NovT* 34 (1992): 334-59.

Bornkamm, Günther. *Early Christian Experience*. New York: Harper & Row, 1969.

Bowman, John W. "The Revelation to John: Its Dramatic Structure and Message." *Int* 9 (1955): 436-53.

Brown, Gillian, and George Yule. *Discourse Analysis*. Cambridge: Cambridge University Press, 1983.

Caird, G. B. *New Testament Theology*. Edited by L. D. Hurst. Oxford: Clarendon, 1994.

Callow, Kathleen. *Discourse Considerations in Translating the Word of God*. Grand Rapids: Zondervan, 1974.

Carston, Robyn, and Seiji Uchida, eds. *Relevance Theory: Applications and Implications*. PBNS 37. Amsterdam: John Benjamins, 1997.

Carter, Warren. *Matthew: Storyteller, Interpreter, Evangelist*. Peabody, Mass.: Hendrickson, 1996.

Charles, R. H. *The Revelation of St. John*. 2 vols. ICC. Edinburgh: T. & T. Clark, 1920.

Christian, Ed. "A Chiasm of Seven Chiasms: The Structure of the Millennial Vision, Rev 19:1–21:8." *AUSS* 37 (1999): 209-225.

Clark, David J., and Jan de Waard. "Discourse Structure in Matthew's Gospel." *Scriptura* S1 (1982): 1-97.

Cohn, Norman. *The Pursuit of the Millennium*. New York: Oxford University Press, 1961.

Collingwood, R. G. *The Idea of History*. Oxford: Clarendon, 1946.

Collins, John J. "Introduction: Towards the Morphology of a Genre." *Semeia* 14 (1979): 1-20.

Comblin, J. "La liturgie de la nouvelle Jérusalem (Apoc., XXI, 1–XXII, 5)." *ETL* 29 (1953): 5-40.

Corsini, Eugenio. *The Apocalypse: The Perennial Revelation of Jesus Christ*. Edited and translated by Francis J. Moloney. GNS 5. Dublin: Veritas, 1983.

Cotterell, Peter, and Max Turner. *Linguistics and Biblical Interpretation*. Downers Grove, Ill.: InterVarsity Press, 1989.

Coulthard, Malcolm. *An Introduction to Discourse Analysis*. London: Longman, 1977.

Coulthard, Malcolm, and Martin Montgomery, eds. *Studies in Discourse Analysis*. London: Routledge & Kegan Paul, 1981.

Court, John M. *Revelation*. NT Guides. Sheffield: JSOT Press, 1994.

Crisp, Simon. "Discourse Analysis and the Study of Biblical Greek: Part I." *TIC Talk* 37 (1997): 1-3.

———. "Discourse Analysis and the Study of Biblical Greek: Part II." *TIC Talk* 38 (1997): 1-4.

Davies, W. D., and Dale C. Allison, Jr. *A Critical and Exegetical Commentary on the Gospel according to Saint Matthew*. 3 vols. Edinburgh: T. & T. Clark, 1988.

Davis, R. Dean. *The Heavenly Court Judgment of Revelation 4–5*. Lanham: University Press of America, 1992.

Dawson, David A. *Text-Linguistics and Biblical Hebrew*. JSOTSup 177. Sheffield: Sheffield Academic Press, 1994.

Deibler, Ellis W. *A Semantic and Structural Analysis of Romans*. Dallas: SIL, 1998.

Dijk, Teun A van. *Text and Context: Explorations in the Semantics and Pragmatics of Discourse*. London: Longman, 1977.

Dijk, Teun A. van, ed. *Handbook of Discourse Analysis*. 4 vols. London: Academic Press, 1985.

Dressler, Wolfgang U. "Marked and Unmarked Text Strategies within Semiotically Based NATURAL Textlinguistics." Pages 5-18 in *Language in Context: Essays for Robert E. Longacre*. Edited by Shin Ja J. Hwang and William R. Merrifield. Dallas: SIL and University of Texas at Arlington, 1992.

Duff, Paul B. " 'I Will Give to Each of You as Your Works Deserve': Witchcraft Accusations and the Fiery-Eyed Son of God in Rev 2.18-23." *NTS* 43 (1997): 116-33.

Enroth, Anne-Marit. "The Hearing Formula in the Book of Revelation." *NTS* 36 (1990): 598-608.

Farrell, Tim, and Richard Hoyle. "The Application of Relevance Theory: A Response." *NOT* 11 (1997): 19-26.

———. "Translating Implicit Information in the Light of Saussurean, Relevance, and Cognitive Theories." *NOT* 9 (1995): 1-15.

Farrer, Austin. *A Rebirth of Images: The Making of St. John's Apocalypse*. Westminster: Dacre Press, 1949.

———. *The Revelation of St. John the Divine*. Oxford: Clarendon, 1964.

Fee, Gordon D. *New Testament Exegesis: A Handbook for Students and Pastors*. Philadelphia: Westminster Press, 1983.

Fekkes, Jan. " 'His Bride Has Prepared Herself': Revelation 19–21 and Isaian Nuptial Imagery." *JBL* 109 (1990): 269-87.

Fernández, Dagoberto R. "The Judgment of God on the Multinationals: Revelation 18." Pages 75-100 in *Subversive Scriptures: Revolutionary Readings of the Christian Bible in Latin America*. Edited by Leif E. Vaage. Valley Forge, Pa.: Trinity Press International, 1997.

Feuillet, A. "La moisson et la vendange de l'Apocalypse (14, 14-20): La signification chrétienne de la révélation johannique." *NRTh* 94 (1972): 113-32, 225-50.

Ford, J. Massyngberde. *Revelation*. AB 38. Garden City, N.Y.: Doubleday, 1975.

Fornberg, Tord, and David Hellholm, eds. *Texts and Contexts: Biblical Texts in Their Textual and Situational Contexts, Essays in Honor of Lars Hartman*. Oslo: Scandinavian University Press, 1995.

France, R. T. "The Formula-Quotations of Matthew 2 and the Problem of Communication." *NTS* 27 (1981): 233-51.

―――. *Matthew, Evangelist and Teacher*. Exeter: Paternoster, 1989.

Furlong, Anne. "Relevance Theory and Literary Interpretation." Ph.D. thesis, University College London, 1996.

Gager, John G. *Kingdom and Community: The Social World of Early Christianity*. Englewood Cliffs, N.J.: Prentice-Hall, 1975.

Garrow, A. J. P. *Revelation*. New Testament Readings. London: Routledge, 1997.

Giblin, Charles H. *The Book of Revelation: The Open Book of Prophecy*. GNS 34. Collegeville, Minn.: Liturgical Press, 1991.

―――. "Recapitulation and the Literary Coherence of John's Apocalypse." *CBQ* 56 (1994): 81-95.

―――. "Structural and Thematic Correlations in the Theology of Revelation 16–22." *Bib* 55 (1974): 487-504.

Giora, Rachel. "Discourse coherence and theory of relevance: Stumbling blocks in search of a unified theory." *JPrag* 27 (1997): 17-34.

Givón, Talmy, ed. *Discourse and Syntax*. Syntax and Semantics 12. New York: Academic Press, 1979.

Goerling, Fritz. "Relevance and Transculturation." *NOT* 10 (1996): 49-57.

Goranson, Stephen. "Essene Polemic in the Apocalypse of John." Pages 453-60 in *Legal Texts and Legal Issues: Proceedings of the Second Meeting of the International Organization for Qumran Studies, Cambridge 1995*. Edited by Moshe Bernstein, Florentino García Martínez, and John Kampen. STDJ 23. Leiden: E. J. Brill, 1997.

Goulder, M. D. "The Phasing of the Future." Pages 391-408 in *Texts and Contexts: The Biblical Texts in Their Textual and Situational Context, Essays in Honor of Lars Hartman*. Edited by Tord Fornberg and David Hellholm. Oslo: Scandinavian University Press, 1995.

―――. "The Apocalypse as an Annual Cycle of Prophecies." *NTS* 27 (1981): 342-67.

Grice, H. Paul. "Logic and Conversation." Pages 41-58 in *Speech Acts*. Vol. 3 of *Syntax and Semantics*. Edited by Peter Cole and Jerry L. Morgan. New York: Academic Press, 1975.

———. *Studies in the Way of Words*. Cambridge, Mass.: Harvard University Press, 1989.

Grimes, Joseph E. *The Thread of Discourse*. JLSMi 207. The Hague: Mouton, 1975.

Grootheest, David van. "Relevance Theory and Bible Translation." Ph.D. thesis, Free University of Amsterdam, 1996.

Gülich, Elisabeth, and Wolfgang Raible. *Linguistische Textmodelle: Grundlagen und Moglichkeiten*. Uni-Taschenbücher 130. Munich: Fink, 1977.

Gundry, Robert H. "The New Jerusalem: People as Place, not Place for People." *NovT* 29 (1987): 254-64.

Guthrie, George H. "Cohesion Shifts and Stitches in Philippians." Pages 36-59 in *Discourse Analysis and Other Topics in Biblical Greek*. Edited by Stanley E. Porter and D. A. Carson. JSNTSup 113. Sheffield: Sheffield Academic Press, 1995.

———. *The Structure of Hebrews: A Text-Linguistic Analysis*. NovTSup 73. Leiden: E. J. Brill, 1994.

Gutt, Ernst-August. "Matthew 9:4-17 in the Light of Relevance Theory." *NOT* (1986): 13-20.

———. "Relevance Theory and Increased Accuracy in Translation." *NOT* (1985): 29-31.

———. *Relevance Theory: A Guide to Successful Communication in Translation*. Dallas: SIL, 1992.

———. *Translation and Relevance: Cognition and Context*. Oxford: Basil Blackwell, 1991.

———. "Unravelling Meaning: An Introduction to Relevance Theory." *NOT* (1986): 10-20.

Hahn, Ferdinand. "Zum Aufbau der Johannesoffenbarung." Pages 145-54 in *Kirche und Bibel: Festgabe für Bischof Eduard Schick*. Edited by O. Böcher et al. Paderborn, Germany: Ferdinand Schöningh, 1979.

Halliday, M. A. K., and Ruqaiya Hasan. *Cohesion in English*. ELS 9. London: Longman, 1976.

————. *Language, context, and text: Aspects of language in a social-semiotic perspective*. Victoria, Australia: Deakin University, 1985.

Hanson, Anthony T. *The Wrath of the Lamb*. London: SPCK, 1957.

Hargreaves, Mark. "Telling Stories: The Concept of Narrative and Biblical Authority." *Anvil* 13 (1996): 127-39.

Harris, Zellig S. "Discourse Analysis." *Lang* 28 (1952): 1-30.

Hartman, Lars. "Form and Message: A Preliminary Discussion of 'Partial Texts' in Rev 1–3 and 22, 6ff." Pages 129-49 in *L'Apocalypse johannique et l'Apocalyptique dans le Nouveau Testament*. Edited by J. Lambrecht. BETL 53. Gembloux, Belgium: J. Duculot, 1980.

————. *Prophecy Interpreted: The Formation of Some Jewish Apocalyptic Texts and of the Eschatological Discourse, Mark 13 Par*. Translated by Neil Tomkinson, with the assistance of Jean Gray. ConBNT 1. Lund, Sweden: CWK Gleerup, 1966.

Hays, Richard B. *Echoes of Scripture in the Letters of Paul*. New Haven: Yale University Press, 1989.

Hellholm, David. "Amplificatio in the Macro-Structure of Romans." Pages 123-51 in *Rhetoric and the New Testament: Essays from the 1992 Heidelberg Conference*. Edited by Stanley E. Porter and Thomas H. Olbricht. JSNTSup 90. Sheffield: JSOT Press, 1993.

————. *Das Visionenbuch des Hermas als Apokalypse: Formesgeschichtliche und texttheoretische Studien zu einer literarischen Gattung*. Vol. 1 of *Methodologische Vorüberlegungen und makrostrukurelle Textanalyse*. ConBNT 13:1. Lund, Sweden: CWK Gleerup, 1980.

————. "The Problem of Apocalyptic Genre and the Apocalypse of John." *Semeia* 36 (1986): 13-64.

————. "The Visions He Saw or: To Encode the Future in Writing. An Analysis of the Prologue of John's Apocalyptic Letter." Pages 109-146 in *Text and Logos: The Humanistic Interpretation of the New Testament. Essays in Honor of Hendrikus W. Boers*. Edited by Theodore W. Jennings. Atlanta: Scholars Press, 1990.

Higashimori, I., and D. Wilson. "Questions on Relevance." *UCLWPL* 8 (1996): 111-24.

Hill, David. *New Testament Prophecy*. London: Marshall, Morgan & Scott, 1979.

Hollander, John. *The Figure of an Echo: A Mode of Allusion in Milton and After*. Berkeley: University of California Press, 1981.

The Holy Bible: New Revised Standard Version. New York: Division of Christian Education of the National Council of Churches of Christ in the United States of America, 1989.

Humphrey, Edith M. "The Sweet and the Sour: Epics of Wrath and Return in the Apocalypse." *SBLSP* 30 (1991): 451-60.

Hurtgen, John E. *Anti-Language in the Apocalypse of John*. Lewiston, N.Y.: Mellen Biblical Press, 1993.

Hwang, Shin Ja J., and William R. Merrifield, eds. *Language in Context: Essays for Robert E. Longacre*. Dallas: SIL and University of Texas at Arlington, 1992.

Jauss, Hans R. *Toward an Aesthetic of Reception*. Translated by Timothy Bahti. Theory and History of Literature 2. Brighton: Harvester Press, 1982.

Johanson, Bruce C. *To All the Brethren. A Text-Linguistic and Rhetorical Approach to 1 Thessalonians*. ConBNT 16. Stockholm: Almqvist & Wiksell, 1987.

Kaiser, Walter C. *Toward an Exegetical Theology: Biblical Exegesis for Preaching and Teaching*. Grand Rapids: Baker Book House, 1981.

Kang, Sa-Moon. *Divine War in the Old Testament and in the Ancient Near East*. BZAW 177. Berlin: Walter de Gruyter, 1989.

Keck, Leander E. "What Makes Romans Tick?" Pages 3-29 in *Romans*. Edited by David M. Hay and E. Elizabeth Johnson. Vol. 3 in *Pauline Theology*. Edited by Jouette M. Bassler, David M. Hay, and E. Elizabeth Johnson. Minneapolis: Fortress Press, 1995.

Kempson, Ruth M., ed. *Mental Representations: The interface between language and reality*. Cambridge: Cambridge University Press, 1988.

SELECTED BIBLIOGRAPHY

Kinneavy, James L. *A Theory of Discourse: The Aims of Discourse*. New York: W. W. Norton, 1971.

Korner, Ralph J. " 'And I Saw . . .' An Apocalyptic Literary Convention for Structural Identification in the Apocalypse." *NovT* 42 (2000): 160-83.

Lambrecht, Jan. "The Opening of the Seals (Rev 6,1–8,6)." *Bib* 79 (1998): 198-220.

———. "A Structuration of Revelation 4, 1–22, 5." Pages 77-104 in *L'Apocalypse johannique et l'Apocalyptique dans le Nouveau Testament*. Edited by J. Lambrecht. BETL 53. Gembloux, Belgium: J. Duculot, 1980.

Lambrecht, J., ed. *L'Apocalypse johannique et l'Apocalyptique dans le Nouveau Testament*. BETL 53. Gembloux, Belgium: J. Duculot, 1980.

Lee, Michelle V. "A Call to Martyrdom: Function as Method and Message in Revelation." *NovT* 40 (1998): 165-94.

Levinsohn, Stephen H. *Discourse Features of New Testament Greek*. Dallas: SIL, 1992.

———. "A Discourse Study of Constituent Order and the Article in Philippians." Pages 60-74 in *Discourse Analysis and Other Topics in Biblical Greek*. Edited by Stanley E. Porter and D. A. Carson. JSNTSup 113. Sheffield: Sheffield Academic Press, 1995.

Levinson, Stephen C. *Pragmatics*. Cambridge: Cambridge University Press, 1983.

Lilje, Hanns. *Das letzte Buch der Bibel: Eine Einführung in die Offenbarung Johannes*. Hamburg: Furche-Verlag, 1955.

Lohmeyer, Ernst. *Die Offenbarung des Johannes*. HNT 16. Tübingen: J. C. B. Mohr, 1953.

Longacre, Robert E. *The Grammar of Discourse*. New York: Plenum Press, 1983.

———. "A Spectrum and Profile Approach to Discourse Analysis." *Text* 1 (1981): 337-59.

Louw, Johannes P. "Discourse Analysis and the Greek New Testament." *BT* 24 (1973): 101-118.

―――. "The Function of Discourse in a Sociosemiotic Theory of Translation." *BT* 39 (1988): 329-35.

―――. "A Semiotic Approach to Discourse Analysis with Reference to Translation Theory." *BT* 36 (1985): 101-107.

Lund, Nils W. *Chiasmus in the New Testament: A Study in the Form and Function of Chiastic Structures.* Chapel Hill: University of North Carolina Press, 1942. Repr., Peabody, Mass.: Hendrickson, 1992.

Maartens, P. J. "The Relevance of 'Context' and 'Interpretation' to the Semiotic Relations of Romans 5:1-11." *Neot* 29 (1995): 75-108.

Mays, James L. *Amos.* OTL. London: SCM Press, 1969.

Mazzaferri, Frederick D. *The Genre of the Book of Revelation from a Source-critical Perspective.* BZNW 54. Berlin: Walter de Gruyter, 1989.

McKnight, Edgar V. *Post-Modern Use of the Bible: The Emergence of Reader-Oriented Criticism.* Nashville: Abingdon, 1988.

McKnight, Scot. "New Testament Greek Grammatical Analysis." Pages 75-95 in *Introducing New Testament Interpretation.* Edited by Scot McKnight. Grand Rapids: Baker Book House, 1989.

Meadowcroft, Tim J. *Aramaic Daniel and Greek Daniel: A Literary Comparison.* JSOTSup 198. Sheffield: Sheffield Academic Press, 1995.

Metzger, Bruce M. *A Textual Commentary on the Greek New Testament.* 2nd edn. Stuttgart: Deutsche Bibelgesellschaft and UBS, 1994.

Michaels, J. Ramsey. *Interpreting the Book of Revelation.* GNTE 7. Grand Rapids: Baker Book House, 1992.

―――. "Revelation 1.19 and the Narrative Voices of the Apocalypse." *NTS* 37 (1991): 604-620.

Miller, Kevin E. "The Nuptial Eschatology of Revelation 19–22." *CBQ* 60 (1998): 301-318.

Müller, Ekkehardt. *Microstructural Analysis of Revelation 4–11.* AUSDDS 21. Berrien Springs, Mich.: Andrews University Press, 1996.

―――. "Microstructural Analysis of Revelation 20." *AUSS* 37 (1999): 227-55.

Nida, Eugene A. "Basic Elements of Discourse Structure." Pages 47-50 in *Language in Context: Essays for Robert E. Longacre*. Edited by Shin Ja J. Hwang and William R. Merrifield. Dallas: SIL and University of Texas at Arlington, 1992.

Olsson, Birger. "A Decade of Text-Linguistic Analyses of Biblical Texts at Uppsala." *ST* 39 (1985): 107-126.

Patte, Daniel. *Ethics of Biblical Interpretation: A Reevaluation*. Louisville: Westminster John Knox, 1995.

Pattemore, Stephen W. "The People of God in the Apocalypse: A Relevance-Theoretic Study." Ph.D. thesis, University of Otago, 2000.

———. "Relevance Theory, Intertextuality, and the Book of Revelation." Pages 43-60 in *Current Trends in Scripture Translation*. Edited by Philip Noss. UBS Bulletin 194/195. Reading, England: UBS, 2003.

———. "Repetition in Revelation: Implications for Translation." *BT* 53 (2002): 425-41.

Petersen, Rodney L. *Preaching in the Last Days: The Theme of 'Two Witnesses' in the Sixteenth and Seventeenth Centuries*. New York: Oxford University Press, 1993.

Pike, Kenneth L. *Language in Relation to a Unified Theory of the Structure of Human Behavior*. 2nd edn. JLSMa 24. The Hague: Mouton, 1967.

Pike, Kenneth L., and Evelyn G. Pike. *Grammatical Analysis*. Rev. edn. Dallas: SIL and University of Texas at Arlington, 1982.

Pilkington, Adrian. "Poetic Thoughts and Poetic Effects: A Relevance Theory Account of the Literary Use of Rhetorical Tropes." Ph.D. thesis, University College London, 1994.

Porter, Stanley E. "Discourse Analysis and New Testament Studies: An Introductory Survey." Pages 14-35 in *Discourse Analysis and Other Topics in Biblical Greek*. Edited by Stanley E. Porter and D. A. Carson. JSNTSup 113. Sheffield: Sheffield Academic Press, 1995.

———. "How Can Biblical Discourse be Analyzed?: A Response to Several Attempts." Pages 107-116 in *Discourse Analysis and Other Topics in Biblical Greek*. Edited by Stanley E. Porter and D. A. Carson. JSNTSup 113. Sheffield: Sheffield Academic Press, 1995.

Porter, Stanley E., ed. *The Language of the New Testament: Classic Essays*. JSNTSup 60. Sheffield: JSOT Press, 1991.

Porter, Stanley E., and D. A. Carson, eds. *Discourse Analysis and Other Topics in Biblical Greek*. JSNTSup 113. Sheffield: Sheffield Academic Press, 1995.

———. *Biblical Greek Language and Linguistics: Open Questions in Current Research*. JSNTSup 80. Sheffield: JSOT Press, 1993.

Porter, Stanley E., and Jeffrey T. Reed, eds. *Discourse Analysis and the New Testament: Approaches and Results*. JSNTSup 170. Studies in New Testament Greek 4. Sheffield: Sheffield Academic Press, 1999.

Prigent, P. "L'Apocalypse: exégèse historique et analyse structurale." *NTS* 26 (1979): 127-37.

Rand, Jan A. du. "A 'Basso Ostinato' in the Structuring of the Apocalypse of John?" *Neot* 27 (1993): 299-311.

Reed, Jeffrey T. "Discourse Analysis as New Testament Hermeneutic: A Retrospective and Prospective Appraisal." *JETS* 39 (1996): 223-40.

———. "Identifying Theme in the New Testament: Insights from Discourse Analysis." Pages 75-101 in *Discourse Analysis and Other Topics in Biblical Greek*. Edited by Stanley E. Porter and D. A. Carson. JSNTSup 113. Sheffield: Sheffield Academic Press, 1995.

———. "Modern Linguistics and the New Testament: A Basic Guide to Theory, Terminology, and Literature." Pages 222-65 in *Approaches to New Testament Study*. Edited by Stanley E. Porter and David Tombs. JSNTSup 120. Sheffield: Sheffield Academic Press, 1995.

———. "To Timothy or Not? A Discourse Analysis of 1 Timothy." Pages 90-118 in *Biblical Greek Language and Linguistics: Open Questions in Current Research*. Edited by Stanley E. Porter and D. A. Carson. JSNTSup 80. Sheffield: JSOT Press, 1993.

Resseguie, James L. *Revelation Unsealed: A Narrative Critical Approach to John's Apocalypse*. Biblical Interpretation Series 32. Leiden: E. J. Brill, 1998.

Ricoeur, Paul. *Essays on Biblical Interpretation*. Edited by Lewis S. Mudge. Philadelphia: Fortress Press, 1980.

——. *Hermeneutics and Human Sciences: Essays on Language, Action, and Interpretation.* Edited and translated by John B. Thompson. Cambridge: Cambridge University Press, 1981.

——. *Interpretation Theory: Discourse and the Surplus of Meaning.* Fort Worth: Texas Christian University Press, 1976.

Robertson, A. T. *A Grammar of the Greek New Testament in the Light of Historical Research.* 3rd edn. London: Hodder & Stoughton, 1919.

Rogers, Elinor M. *A Semantic Structure Analysis of Galatians.* Dallas: SIL, 1989.

Ross, J. M. "The Ending of the Apocalypse." Pages 338-44 in *Studies in New Testament Language and Text: Essays in Honour of George D. Kilpatrick.* Edited by J. K. Elliott. Leiden: E. J. Brill, 1976.

Schenk, Wolgang "Hebräerbrief 4.14-16. Textlinguistik als Kommentierungsprinzip." *NTS* 26 (1980): 242-52.

——. "Textlinguistische Aspekte der Strukturanalyse, dargestellt am Beispiel von 1 Kor XV.1-11." *NTS* 23 (1977): 469-77.

Schüssler Fiorenza, Elisabeth. *The Book of Revelation: Justice and Judgment.* Philadelphia: Fortress Press, 1985.

——. "Composition and Structure of the Book of Revelation." *CBQ* 39 (1977): 344-66.

——. *Revelation: Vision of a Just World.* Proclamation Commentaries. Minneapolis: Fortress Press, 1991.

Searle, John R. *Speech Acts: An Essay in the Philosophy of Language.* Cambridge: Cambridge University Press, 1969.

Shannon, Claude E., and Warren Weaver. *The Mathematical Theory of Communication.* Urbana: University of Illinois Press, 1949.

Shea, William H. "Chiasm in Theme and by Form in Revelation 18." *AUSS* 20 (1982): 249-56.

——. "The Covenantal Form of the Letters to the Seven Churches." *AUSS* 21 (1983): 71-84.

——. "The Parallel Literary Structure of Revelation 12 and 20." *AUSS* 23 (1985): 37-54.

———. "Revelation 5 and 19 as Literary Reciprocals." *AUSS* 22 (1984): 249-57.

Siegert, Folker. "Die Makrosyntax des Hebräerbriefs." Pages 305-316 in *Texts and Contexts: Biblical Texts in Their Textual and Situational Contexts: Essays in Honor of Lars Hartman*. Edited by Tord Fornberg and David Hellholm. Oslo: Scandinavian University Press, 1995.

Silva, Moisés. *Biblical Words and Their Meaning: An Introduction to Lexical Semantics*. Grand Rapids: Zondervan, 1983.

———. "Discourse Analysis and Philippians." Pages 102-106 in *Discourse Analysis and Other Topics in Biblical Greek*. Edited by Stanley E. Porter and D. A. Carson. JSNTSup 113. Sheffield: Sheffield Academic Press, 1995.

Sims, James H. *A Comparative Literary Study of Daniel and Revelation: Shaping the End*. Lewiston, N.Y.: Mellen Biblical Press, 1995.

Skinner, Quentin. "Meaning and Understanding in the History of Ideas." Pages 29-67 in *Meaning and Context: Quentin Skinner and His Critics*. Edited by James Tully. Cambridge: Polity Press, 1988.

Smalley, Stephen S. *Thunder and Love: John's Revelation and John's Community*. Milton Keynes, England: Word, 1994.

Smith, Christopher R. "Reclaiming the Social Justice Message of Revelation: Materialism, Imperialism and Divine Judgement in Revelation 18." *Transformation* 7 (1990): 28-33.

———. "The Structure of the Book of Revelation in Light of Apocalyptic Literary Conventions." *NovT* 36 (1994): 373-93.

Snyder, Barbara W. "Triple-Form and Space/Time Transitions: Literary Structuring Devices in the Apocalypse." *SBLSP* 30 (1991): 440-50.

Snyman, A. H. "A Semantic Discourse Analysis of the Letter to Philemon." Pages 83-99 in *Text and Interpretation: New Approaches in the Criticism of the New Testament*. Edited by P. J. Hartin and J. H. Petzer. NTTS 15. Leiden: E. J. Brill, 1991.

Sperber, Dan. *Explaining Culture: A Naturalistic Approach*. Oxford: Basil Blackwell, 1996.

Sperber, Dan, and Deirdre Wilson. *Relevance: Communication and Cognition*. Oxford: Basil Blackwell, 1986.

———. *Relevance: Communication and Cognition.* 2ⁿᵈ edn. Oxford: Basil Blackwell, 1995.

Spinks, L. C. "A Critical Examination of J. W. Bowman's Proposed Structure of the Revelation." *EvQ* 50 (1978): 211-22.

Steinmann, Andrew. "The Tripartite Structure of the Sixth Seal, the Sixth Trumpet, and the Sixth Bowl of John's Apocalypse (Rev 6:12–7:17; 9:13–11:14; 16:12-16)." *JETS* 35 (1992): 69-79.

Sterner, Robert H. *A Semantic and Structural Analysis of 1 Thessalonians.* Dallas: SIL, 1998.

Strand, Kenneth A. "Chiastic Structure and Some Motifs in the Book of Revelation." *AUSS* 16 (1978): 401-408.

———. "The Eight Basic Visions in the Book of Revelation." *AUSS* 25 (1987): 107-121.

———. "Two Aspects of Babylon's Judgment Portrayed in Revelation 18." *AUSS* 20 (1982): 53-60.

———. "The 'Victorious Introduction' Scenes in the Visions in the Book of Revelation." *AUSS* 25 (1987): 267-88.

Stubbs, Michael. *Discourse Analysis: The Sociolinguistic Analysis of Natural Language.* Oxford: Basil Blackwell, 1983.

Surridge, Robert. "Redemption in the Structure of Revelation." *ExpTim* 101 (1990): 231-35.

Sweet, J. P. M. *Revelation.* SCM Pelican Commentaries. London: SCM, 1979.

Swete, Henry B. *The Apocalypse of St John.* London: Macmillan & Co., 1911.

Talbert, Charles H. *The Apocalypse: A Reading of the Revelation of John.* Louisville: Westminster John Knox, 1994.

Tenney, Merrill C. *Interpreting Revelation.* Grand Rapids: Eerdmans, 1957.

Thiselton, Anthony C. *New Horizons in Hermeneutics.* Grand Rapids: Zondervan, 1992.

Unger, Christoph. "The scope of discourse connectives: implications for discourse organization." *JLing* 32 (1996): 403-438.

———. "Types of Implicit Information and Their Roles in Translation." *NOT* 10 (1996): 18-30.

Van Otterloo, Roger. "Towards an Understanding of 'Lo' and 'Behold': Functions of ἰδού and ἴδε in the Greek New Testament." *OPTAT* 2 (1988): 34-64.

Vanhoozer, Kevin J. *Biblical Narrative in the Philosophy of Paul Ricoeur: A Study in Hermeneutics and Theology.* Cambridge: Cambridge University Press, 1990.

———. *Is There a Meaning in This Text?: The Bible, the Reader and the Morality of Literary Knowledge.* Leicester: Apollos, 1998.

Vanni, Ugo. *La struttura letteraria dell' Apocalisse.* 2nd edn. Aloisiana 8a. Brescia, Italy: Morcelliana, 1980.

———. "Liturgical Dialogue as a Literary Form in the Book of Revelation." *NTS* 37 (1991): 348-72.

———. "Un esempio di dialogo liturgico in Ap 1,4-8." *Bib* 57 (1976): 453-67.

Vos, Louis A. *The Synoptic Traditions in the Apocalypse.* Kampen: J. H. Kok, 1965.

Waal, C. van der. "The last book of the Bible and the Jewish Apocalypses." *Neot* 12 (1978): 111-32.

Waldman, Nahum M. *The Recent Study of Hebrew: A Survey of the Literature with Selected Bibliography.* Bibliographica Judaica 10. Cincinnati: Hebrew Union College Press, 1989.

Waltke, Bruce K., and M. O'Connor. *An Introduction to Biblical Hebrew Syntax.* Winona Lake, Ind.: Eisenbrauns, 1990.

Webster, John. "Texts: Scripture, Reading, and the Rhetoric of Theology." *Stimulus* 6 (1998): 10-16.

Wendland, Ernst R. *The Discourse Analysis of Hebrew Poetic Literature: Determining the Larger Textual Units of Hosea and Joel.* Mellen Biblical Press Series 40. Lewiston, N.Y.: Mellen Biblical Press, 1995.

———. "On the Relevance of 'Relevance Theory' for Bible Translation." *BT* 47 (1996): 126-37.

———. "A Review of 'Relevance Theory' in Relation to Bible Translation in South-Central Africa: Part I." *JNSL* 22 (1996): 91-106.

———. "A Review of 'Relevance Theory' in Relation to Bible Translation in South-Central Africa: Part II." *JNSL* 23 (1997): 83-108.

———. "A Tale of Two Debtors: On the Interaction of Text, Cotext, and Context in a New Testament Dramatic Narrative (Luke 7:36-50)." Pages 101-143 in *Linguistics and New Testament Interpretation*. Edited by David A. Black. Nashville: Broadman, 1992.

———. "7 X 7 (X 7): A Structural and Thematic Outline of John's Apocalypse." *OPTAT* 4 (1990): 371-87.

Wilcox, Max. " 'Silence in Heaven' (Rev 8:1) and Early Jewish Thought." Pages 241-44 in *Mogilany 1989: Papers on the Dead Sea Scrolls offered in memory of Jean Carmignac. Part II: The Teacher of Righteousness / Literary Studies*. Edited by Zdzislaw J. Kapera. Qumranica Mogilanensia 3. Kraków: Enigma Press, 1991.

Wilson, Deirdre. "Discourse, coherence and relevance: A reply to Rachel Giora." *JPrag* 29 (1998): 57-74.

Wilson, Deirdre, and Dan Sperber. "Representation and relevance." Pages 133-54 in *Mental Representations: The interface between language and reality*. Edited by Ruth M. Kempson. Cambridge: Cambridge University Press, 1988.

Winedt, Marlon. "The Narrative and Communicative Function of ἀλλὰ in the Gospel of Luke: A Relevance-Theoretic Perspective." Paper presented at the UBS Triennial Translation Workshop. Malaga, Spain, June 2000.

———. "A Relevance-Theoretic Approach to Translation and Discourse Markers: With Special Reference to the Greek Text of the Gospel of Luke." Ph.D. thesis, Free University of Amsterdam, 1999.

Winer, Georg B. *A Grammar of New Testament Diction Intended as an Introduction to the Critical Study of the Greek New Testament*. 4th edn. Edinburgh: T. & T. Clark, 1863.

Wolterstorff, Nicholas. *Divine Discourse: Philosophical reflections on the claim that God speaks*. Cambridge: Cambridge University Press, 1995.

Yarbro Collins, Adela. *The Apocalypse*. NTM 22. Wilmington, Del.: Michael Glazier, 1979.

———. *The Combat Myth in the Book of Revelation*. HDR 9. Missoula, Mont.: Scholars Press, 1976.

———. "Introduction: Early Christian Apocalypticism." *Semeia* 36 (1986): 1-12.

———. "Revelation 18: Taunt-Song or Dirge?" Pages 185-204 in *L'Apocalypse johannique et l'Apocalyptique dans le Nouveau Testament*. Edited by J. Lambrecht. BETL 53. Gembloux, Belgium: J. Duculot, 1980.

———. "Source Criticism of the Book of Revelation." *BR* 43 (1998): 50-53.

———. "Vilification and Self-Definition in the Book of Revelation." *HTR* 79 (1986): 308-320.

Glossary

For a fuller glossary, refer to Robyn Carston and Seiji Uchida, eds., *Relevance Theory: Applications and Implications* (PBNS 37; Amsterdam: John Benjamins, 1997), pp. 295-99, from which this is abbreviated and adapted.

ACCESSIBILITY is the ease with which an assumption can be recalled from memory or constructed on the basis of new information being processed.

CODING versus **INFERENCE** is the distinction between those aspects of an utterance which are inherent in the linguistic form of the utterance (i.e., encoded) and those which must be derived (inferred) by the interaction of the encoded meaning with a person's existing cognitive environment, in the attempt to achieve **OPTIMAL RELEVANCE**.

COGNITIVE ENVIRONMENT is the set of assumptions that are manifest to a person at a given moment.

COMMUNICATIVE INTENTION is an intention to make **MUTUALLY MANIFEST** to the audience and communicator that the communicator has an informative intention.

CONTEXT is the subset of a person's mentally represented assumptions which interacts with new information received so as to give rise to **CONTEXTUAL EFFECTS**.

CONTEXTUAL EFFECTS are the results that new information must bring about when it interacts with a person's existing assumptions, if it is to have **RELEVANCE**. There are three types of contextual effects it may have: it may support (and so strengthen) existing assumptions, it may contradict (and so eliminate) existing assumptions, or it may combine with them to produce new conclusions. See also **CONTEXTUAL IMPLICATION**.

CONTEXTUAL IMPLICATION is a conclusion inferred by people on the basis of *both* their existing assumptions *and* the new information they receive. A contextual implication cannot be derived from either of these two sources alone.

EXPLICATURE is an assumption derived from the logical form of an utterance only (i.e., from the information encoded in the linguistic form). It is distinct from an **IMPLICATURE**.

IMPLICATURE is an assumption derived from an utterance by a process of inference, involving the interaction of the encoded information with the context of interpretation.

MANIFEST describes an assumption that people can form a mental representation of and hold it to be true or probably true.

MUTUAL COGNITIVE ENVIRONMENT is the set of assumptions that are **MUTUALLY MANIFEST** to two or more people.

MUTUALLY MANIFEST describes something that is **MANIFEST** to two or more people and the fact of its manifestness is also manifest to them.

OPTIMAL RELEVANCE is the property of an utterance when it is interpreted such that (a) it has enough **CONTEXTUAL EFFECTS** to be worth the hearer's attention and (b) it requires no unnecessary **PROCESSING EFFORT** in achieving those effects.

OSTENSIVE COMMUNICATION is the transmission of information by means of a stimulus that comes with a **COMMUNICATIVE INTENTION**. It is communication that also communicates its intention to communicate; that is, it excludes accidental or purely mechanical transmission of information.

PRINCIPLES OF RELEVANCE:
    1. **FIRST (COGNITIVE) PRINCIPLE OF RELEVANCE:** human cognition is geared toward the maximization of relevance (that is, achieving as many **CONTEXTUAL EFFECTS** as possible for as little processing effort as possible).
    2. **SECOND (COMMUNICATIVE) PRINCIPLE OF RELEVANCE:** every ostensive stimulus communicates a presumption of its own optimal relevance.

PROCESSING EFFORT is the mental effort that a person must expend in order to arrive at a satisfactory interpretation of incoming information. This includes the accessing of an appropriate **CONTEXT** in which to interpret the information, and the inferential work of integrating the new information with existing assumptions.

RELEVANCE describes an assumption that is pertinent in a particular context to the extent that its **CONTEXTUAL EFFECTS** in that context are large, and to the extent that the effort required to process it in that context is small.

WEAK COMMUNICATION is the communication of assumptions (usually **IMPLICATURES**) where there is a degree of uncertainty about which particular assumptions are part of the speaker's informative intention and which are not. This sort of communication is typical of poetic language.

General Index

This index includes all authors and only terms for which the book contains a discussion that is helpful.

Allison, D. C. 14
analogy 48-49
apocalypse 64
appropriated discourse 41
appropriateness 50-51
Aune, D. E 39, 64-65, 70, 85-87,
  89-91, 96, 107-108, 114-15,
  118-19, 126-28, 131, 133-37,
  145-46, 149-50, 159, 161-62,
  165-68, 171, 176, 182, 184
Austin, J. L 11
Baldinger, K. 65-66
Bartsch, C. 75
Bauckham, R. 61, 118-19, 150,
  160, 168
Baumgarten, J. M. 142
Beale, G. K. 61, 64, 86-87, 91,
  104, 107, 127-29, 160
Beasley-Murray, G. R. 160
Beaugrande, R.-A. de 8, 46,
  50-51, 60
Beckwith, I. T. 40
Beekman, J. 68, 75
Berthiaume, S. C. 131
Biguzzi, G. 82, 127, 131
Black, D. A. 8
Blakemore, D. 23, 52
Blass, R. 23, 52-57, 89

Boers, H 9, 15
Boismard, M.-E. 90
Boring, M. E. 64, 83-85, 87,
  96-97, 160
Bornkamm, G. 98
bottom-up approach 7
Bowman, J. W. 61
Brown, G. 5, 8, 46-49, 51, 53-55
Caird, G. B. 27
Callow, J. 68, 75
Callow, K. 8
Carson, D. A. 3
Carston, R. 229
Carter, W. 14
Charles, R. H. 90
Christian, E. 174
Clark, D. J. 9, 14
code model 16
cognitive environment 17-18, 59,
  75
  mutual cognitive environment
  18, 190
cognitive principle 21
coherence 52
cohesion 7, 52
Cohn, N. 40
Collingwood, R. G. 28
Collins, J. J. 64

colon analysis 15, 76-77, 85
combinatorial explosion 51
Comblin, J. 158
communication 18
communication axis 100-101
communicative intention 19
communicative principle 21
context 7, 33-34, 45-58
contextual effects 18-21, 36
contextual implications 18
cooperation, principle of 17
Corsini, E. 129, 159
Cosgrove, C. H. 15
co-text 7, 47
Cotterell, P. 4, 13, 29
Coulthard, M. 8
Court, J. M. 65
Crisp, S. 6, 12-13
Davies, W. D. 14
Davis, R. D. 104, 129
Dawson, D. A. 8
deep structure 15
Deibler, E. W. 12, 75
deixis 26-27
delimitation 66
 markers 66-67
delimiter 100
deputized discourse 41
diachronic 26, 38-39
Dijk, T. A. van 8
directly addressed 44
discourse 4-5
discourse analysis 5, 7, 11-12,
 45, 54-55
 schools of 7-9
discourse segmentation 59
dramatis personae 101
Dressler, W. U. 8, 46, 50-51, 60
Duff, P. B. 108
echo 149

effectiveness 50-51
efficiency 50-51
empty text shell 192-93
Enroth, A.-M. 107-108
eisegetical interpretation 27
evolution 44-45
explicature 21
Fanning, B. 3
Farrell, T. 29-30
Farrer, A. 61, 82, 85, 103, 147,
 151, 159, 174
Fee, G. D. 76
Fekkes, J. 187
Fernández, D. R. 167
Feuillet, A. 150
Ford, J. M. 90
France, R. T. 14, 31-32
Furlong, A. 27, 32, 34. 36, 38
Gager, J. G. 62-63
Garrow, A. J. P. 30
Giblin, C. H. 61, 70, 85, 96, 121,
 128, 159, 176, 184
Giora, R. 57
Givón, T. 8
Goerling, F. 30
Goranson, S. 108
Goulder, M. D. 61, 129
Grice, P. 17
Grimes, J. E. 7, 14, 55
Grootheest, D. van 30, 33
Gülich, E. 66, 81
Gundry, R. H. 187
Guthrie, G. H. 9-10, 59
Gutt, E.-A. 16, 29-33, 38
Hahn, F. 130, 135, 159
Halliday, M. A. K. 8, 14
Hanson, A. T. 150
Hargreaves, M. 43
Harris, Z. S. 4

Hartman, L. 61, 64, 69, 81-82, 84, 87, 129
Hasan, R. 8, 14
Hays, R. B. 42, 149
Hellholm, D. 8-9, 59-61, 64-74, 77-82, 84, 87, 90, 94-96, 104, 110-11, 114-15, 118, 130-31, 133, 135, 137, 158-59, 176, 181, 183, 193
Higashimori, I. 36
Hoyle, R. 30
Hill, D. 97
Hollander, J. 149
Humphrey, E. M. 134
Hurtgen, J. E. 151
implicature 21-22
incarnate discourse 44
indirectly addressed 44
informative intention 19
inspiration 38-40
intercalation 62-63, 122
interpretive resemblance 31
Jauss, H. R. 37
Johanson, B. C. 10
Kaiser, W. C. 76
Kang, S.-M. 120
Keck, L. E. 15
Kempson, W. R. 106, 121
Kinneavy, J. L. 8
Korner, R. J. 61, 117
Lambrecht, J. 61, 63, 74, 80, 91, 94-96, 104, 115, 118, 126, 131, 135, 137, 145-46, 159, 161, 183, 189
Lee, M. V. 61-64
Levinsohn, S. H. 8, 10, 12
Levinson, S. C. 26-27
Lilje, H. 150
local interpretation 47-48
Lohmeyer, E. 96, 150

Longacre, R. E. 8, 14
Louw, J. P. 8, 85
Lund, N. W. 63, 151, 158
Maartens, P. J. 30
macrostructure 7
manifestness 17-18
mutually manifest 18
Mays, J. L. 134
Mazzaferri, F. D. 91, 96, 106, 121, 130, 133, 135, 137, 160, 165
McKnight, E. V. 76
McKnight, S. 76
Meadowcroft, T. J. 116
metalepsis 149
meta-level 66-67
meta-reference 92
Metzger, B. M. 91
Michaels, J. R. 76, 92, 96
microstructure 7
Miller, K. E. 159
Montgomery, M. 8
Moo, D. J. 15
Müller, E. 61, 64, 73-81, 85, 87, 104, 118, 125, 127-28, 130-32, 134, 136-39, 145, 159, 166, 174, 178, 183
Nida, E. A. 8
O'Connor, M. 3-4
Olsson, B. 7, 9
onomasiology 65-66
optimal relevance 20-21
ostensive communication 19
ostensive-inferential communication 19
participant 60
Patte, D. 43
Pattemore, S. W. 1, 23, 26, 34, 36, 39, 64, 87, 90, 136, 149,

151, 157, 159, 165, 173, 182-83, 193-94
personal reference 101
Petersen, R. L. 40
Pike, K. L. 7-8
Pike, E. G. 7-8
Pilkington, A. 36
Porter, S. E. 3-4, 6-13, 45-46
Prigent, P. 63
processing effort 19-21
pro-form 60
prominence 7
Raible, W. 66, 81
Rand, J. A. du 117-18
recapitulation 86
Reed, J. T. 6, 9-13, 15, 46, 60
relevance 18-20
Relevance Theory 2, 16-21, 24, 38
Resseguie, J. L. 62
Ricoeur, P. 26, 41-43
Robertson, A. T. 4
Rogers, E. M. 12, 75
Ross, J. M. 91
Schenk, W. 10
Schüssler Fiorenza, E. 5, 62-64, 80, 95, 103-104, 108, 115, 118, 122, 134-37, 159, 179, 189
Searle, J. R. 11
semasiology 65-66
sentence flow 76-77
Shannon, C. E. 16
Shea, W. H. 107, 168-69, 178
Siegert, F. 10
Silva, M. 3-4, 10, 15
Sims, J. H. 183
Skinner, Q. 19, 25, 27-28
Smalley, S. S. 90

Smith, C. R. 62, 107, 168, 171, 173
Snyder, B. W. 94, 96, 106-107, 166
Snyman, A. H. 9
spatial signal 101
Speech-Act Theory 11
Sperber, D. 16-25, 31, 35-36, 39, 48, 51-53
Spinks, L. C. 62, 80
staging 55
Steinmann, A. 131
Sterner, R. H. 12
Strand, K. A. 62-63, 117-18, 168
Stubbs, M. 5, 8
surface-level structure 15, 75
Surridge, R. 62
Sweet, J. P. M. 103, 137
Swete, H. B. 40, 117
synchronic 26, 38-39
Synoptic Apocalypse 129
Talbert, C. H. 82, 96
temporal signal 101
Tenney, M. C. 106
text 4-5
text sequence 58, 190
textlinguistics 5
Thiselton, A. C. 11, 35, 37
top-down approach 7, 190
topic 48-49
transumption 149
Turner, M. 4, 13, 29
Uchida , S. 229
Unger, C. 30, 57
Van Otterloo, R. 116
Vanhoozer, K. J. 41-43, 93
Vanni, U. 62, 84, 91-92, 96, 104, 107, 115, 118, 126, 131, 137, 161, 195
Vos, L. A. 129

Waal, C. van der 134
Waard, J. de 9, 14
Waldman, N. M. 4
Waltke, B. K. 3-4
Weaver, W. 16
Webster, J. 40, 42
Wendland, E. 9, 29, 30, 33-38,
   62, 64, 82-83, 87, 94, 96,
   104, 107, 115, 151, 169, 174,
   183
Wilcox, M. 126

Wilson, D. 16-25, 31, 35-36, 39,
   48, 51-53, 57
Winedt, M. 30
Winer, G. B. 4
Wolterstorff, N. 41, 44, 98
Yarbro Collins, A. 62-63, 65, 80
   82-83, 85, 90, 94, 96, 98,
   108, 117, 127, 130, 134-36,
   145-46, 151, 159, 168, 174
Yule, G. 5, 8, 46-49, 51, 53-55

Index of Scripture References

This index includes only Scripture references outside of Revelation.

Exo 19:16	126	Jer 1:1-2	94
Exo 25–26	119	Jer 1:4	94
Exo 31	119	Jer 1:4-10	134
Exo 37–40	119		
Exo 40:21	120	Ezek 1:1–3:11	134
Exo 40:34-35	119	Ezek 2–3	134
		Ezek 2:10	135
Deut 28–29	93		
Deut 28:58	93	Dan 1:5	115
Deut 28:61	93	Dan 2	87, 92, 104, 190
Deut 29:20-21	93	Dan 2:28	92
		Dan 2:28-29	86, 91
1 Kgs 19:11-12	126	Dan 2:29	115
		Dan 2:45	86, 91, 115
1 Chr 16	120	Dan 3:92	116
1 Chr 16:6	120	Dan 7	3, 87, 116, 149-50, 157-58, 190, 205-206
Psa 2:9	145		
		Dan 7:1-7	149
Isa 1:1	94	Dan 7:1	94
Isa 6:1	94	Dan 7:2	94
Isa 6:1-13	134	Dan 7:3	149
Isa 6:8-9	45	Dan 7:4-7	149
Isa 34:4	128	Dan 7:6	115, 150
Isa 66	191	Dan 7:7	149
Isa 66:6	119	Dan 7:8	150
Isa 66:6-7	119	Dan 7:21	150
Isa 66:7	119	Dan 7:25	150
		Dan 8:19	116

239

Dan 11:2	116	Luke 16:6-7	92
		Luke 17	129
Hos 1:1-8	94	Luke 21	129
Hos 3:1	94		
		Rom 15:4	43
Amos 7:14-17	134		
		1 Cor 5:3-5	98
Micah 1:1	94	1 Cor 7:10	98
Micah 1:8	94	1 Cor 9:10	43
		1 Cor 10:11	43
Hab 1:1	94	1 Cor 16:20-24	98
Hab 1:2	94		
		Heb 1:1-2	43
Zech 1:7	94	Heb 9:4	119
Zech 1:8	94		
		2 Macc 2:4-8	120
Matt 2	31		
Matt 13:14	45	*1 Enoch 1:1*	94
Matt 18:20	97	*1 Enoch 1:2*	94
Matt 24	14, 129	*1 Enoch 12:1*	94
Matt 24:29-32	129	*1 Enoch 12:3*	94
		1 Enoch 13:1	94
Mark 13	129	*1 Enoch 13:3*	94
		1 Enoch 37:1	94
Luke 7:36-50	34	*1 Enoch 37:2*	94

Index of Greek Words

This index includes only Greek words for which there is a helpful discussion in the book.

ἃ δεῖ γενέσθαι ἐν τάχει 86, 91,
  96, 190
ἀρνίον 144
βιβλίον 103
γῆ
  ἀπὸ τῆς γῆς 114
  εἰς τὴν γῆν 114
  ἐκ τῆς γῆς 114
  ἐπὶ τῆς γῆς 114
γράφειν 92
γράψον 92
Διάβολος 144
δράκων 144
εἶδον 104, 113, 116-17, 133
εἶδον, καὶ ἰδού 78, 104, 116
ἐν πνεύματι 105, 106-107, 118,
  167
ἤκουσα 113, 116-17, 133
θηρίον 143-44
θυσιαστήριον 119-20
ἰδού 116, 174
καὶ 116-17, 125-26
καὶ εἶδον 85, 117, 121, 125-27,
  145, 173-74, 184

καὶ ἤκουσα 117, 125-26
καὶ ἰδού 117, 121, 173
κιβωτὸς τῆς διαθήκης 119
μετὰ ταῦτα 58, 67, 78, 104-105,
  115-17, 167
μετὰ ταῦτα εἶδον, καὶ ἰδού
  115-17, 130
μετὰ τοῦτο εἶδον 115-17
ναός 119, 159-60
ὁ ἔχων οὖς ἀκουσάτω τί τὸ
  πνεῦμα λέγει ταῖς
  ἐκκλησίαις 107
οὐρανός 105, 113-14
  εἰς τὸν οὐρανὸν 113
  ἐκ τοῦ οὐρανοῦ 113, 124-25
  ἐν τῷ οὐρανῷ 105, 113, 118,
    124-25
ὄφις 143-44
πόλις 144
Σατανᾶς 144
σημεῖον μέγα . . . ἐν τῷ οὐρανῷ
  117, 121
Ὧδε . . . ἐστιν 147-48, 157